GETTING THE MOST
OUT OF LIFE

Getting the Most Out of Life

A *selection of personally helpful articles from past issues of* THE READER'S DIGEST

THE READER'S DIGEST ASSOCIATION
Pleasantville, N.Y.

PRINTED IN THE UNITED STATES OF AMERICA

Contents

The Perfect Blueprint
for
HAPPINESS

By T. E. Murphy   Condensed from The Rotarian

FOR THREE MONTHS I have been asking friends and acquaintances how familiar they were with the greatest blueprint for a happy life that was ever drawn. Of course they had all heard of this famous code of human relations. But not one of 70 persons questioned — most of them churchgoers — could quote a line of it.

The document they failed to remember was the Sermon on the Mount — the Magna Carta of Christian faith. Three months ago, I should have assumed that most persons knew something of what Jesus said in his most notable utterance. Now I am sure comparatively few people have any clear memory of either the words or their meaning. Yet, as recorded in St. Matthew, Chapter V to VII, the Sermon teaches not only the deepest spiritual truths but also practical techniques by which anyone may find health, success and tranquillity; peace of mind and peace of soul.

Now these are keys most sought after. The best-seller books have largely to do with man and his frustrations. Increasing armies of neurotic, discouraged people attest a spreading emptiness in modern life.

Yet the anxieties of average people are generally out of proportion to their problems. Most of our difficulties are fairly simple: the job, the people we work with, the children; our need to be loved, to feel important, to be a part of things.

Why, then, are so many people leading lives of what Thoreau called "quiet desperation"? May it not be because they have wandered from some great foundation of faith, which should be to us as rivers of water in a dry place, as the shadow of a great rock in a weary land?

The remedy for the desperate life, the prescription for heartache and all the thousand shocks that flesh is heir to, lies ready at hand, simple and sure, in one great, neglected utterance — the Sermon's unsurpassed Golden Rule for human relations:

> Therefore all things whatsoever ye would that men should do to you, do ye even so to them.

The Sermon is studded throughout with sound advice on personal conduct in everyday affairs. The human tendency to criticize others, with no blame to ourselves, is thus denounced:

> Judge not, that ye be not judged. For with what judgment ye judge, ye shall be judged: and with what measure ye mete, it shall be measured to you again.

That rule worked for Abraham Lincoln, bringing him strength and faith to hold the Union together and keeping him free of bitterness. No other historical figure quoted so often from the Sermon on the Mount.

Not only must we refrain from condemning; we must forgive. For many of us that is the hardest teaching of all. But physicians and psychologists today agree that it is also, by far, the most necessary:

> Ye have heard that it hath been said, Thou shalt love thy neighbor, and hate thine enemy. But I say unto you, Love your enemies, bless them that curse you, do good to them that hate you, and pray for them which despitefully use you.

You may think that the teaching is unworkable, asking too much of human nature. Yet every mother, every father, must constantly turn the other cheek; forgiving while correcting children — forgiving and going right on loving, trying to help. In the same spirit of love and helpfulness, the Sermon urges us to try to understand, try to forgive, try to love everybody. In the struggle of self-conquest, the Sermon gives us a solemn compact — that the Father is to forgive us our trespasses only as we forgive those who trespass against us.

Once this apparently unrealistic doctrine of love is tried, its practicality appears. Mrs. Jones moved into a tightly knit New England town. Soon she learned that her neighbor Mrs. Smith, noted for a sharp tongue, had been making unkind remarks about her. She restrained an impulse to rush next door and demand a showdown. A few days later she met a close friend of her detractor. She introduced herself. The other woman shrank back as though well briefed in Mrs. Jones's defects. "I live next door to Mrs. Smith," Mrs. Jones said brightly, "and I just can't resist telling you what a fine neighbor she is. I feel lucky to be near her." A few days later Mrs. Smith appeared at Mrs. Jones's door and said rather shamefacedly, "I really would like to be a good neighbor. Maybe I haven't been as good as you think I've been." No mention of the gossip was ever made and they became fast friends.

If we are at odds with our fellows we are blocked in other relations. Nowhere is that more evident than in the problem of drunkenness. Psychiatrists are able to help only about two percent of alcoholic patients, but Alcoholics Anonymous reports success with 80 percent. What is the difference? Alcoholics Anonymous makes a direct attack on all resentments:

"We can't do a thing for you until you get all resentments and hatreds out of your heart."

Forgiveness, release from grudges, as taught in the Sermon, is important also in physical health. In the past 20 years physicians have come to a realization that worry, fear, anger and hatred are poisons that can cripple and destroy the body as well as the mind; grudges can bring arthritis, rage can bring about the need for surgery. A man's thoughts are the theater of his soul.

An eminent doctor, Charles T. Bingham, once said: "Worry, fear and anger are the greatest disease causers. If we had perfect faith we wouldn't worry. Faith is the great healer."

A New York businessman, vice-president of his firm, expected to be chosen president when the founder died. But the directors chose an outsider. The resentment of the vice-president became a secret but all-powerful obsession; he could not sleep or concentrate. One day he was shocked to overhear two office boys talking about him; people were saying he was going to pieces. In despair he asked a wise friend what to do. "Love the man you resent," was the answer. "Help him!"

Next morning he tried it; forced himself to make a suggestion. The new president heartily thanked him. "I'm scared of this new job," he said. "You know more about it than I do. Please help me." Life changed then and there for them both.

To those who spend their lives piling up moneybags for selfish ends, there comes this warning:

> Therefore take no thought, saying, What shall we eat? or, What shall we drink? or, Wherewithal shall we be clothed? . . . But seek ye first the kingdom of God, and his righteousness; and all these things shall be added unto you.

From childhood I have watched this promise being fulfilled before my eyes. My mother believed in it completely, her faith never shaken even at grim times when we were down, literally, to a last crust of bread. But, as Mother expected, things would invariably change for the better, and in ample time.

True, the instructions in the Sermon are not easy to follow. If I really worked at them I should become generous and openhanded, forgiving, loving, free from greed and malice. I should possess superb confidence that things would eventually come out all right and so I should not waste my strength, or ruin my digestion, through worry.

Those who follow these teachings and trust in these promises, so the Sermon declares, are "the light of the world." And the Sermon reminds us to set a decent example in the world:

> Let your light so shine before men, that they may see your good works.

There is also a security we discover, that comes to one only from living the good life:

> Therefore whosoever heareth these sayings of mine, and doeth them, I will liken him unto a wise man, which built his house upon a rock: and the rain descended, and the floods came, and the winds blew, and beat upon that house; and it fell not: for it was founded upon a rock. And every one that heareth these sayings of mine, and doeth them not, shall be likened unto a foolish man, which built his house upon the sand: and the rain descended, and the floods came, and the winds blew, and beat upon that house; and it fell: and great was the fall of it.

Perhaps it is not remarkable that so many have forgotten the profoundest sermon of all time, because its richness is expressed in such simplicity: it is natural, no doubt, for the smart and sophisticated to recoil from such homely faith. But the less faith a man has in his God, the less he has in himself; the more insecure, fearful and purposeless life becomes.

A man may read these forgotten words a thousand times and find within them fresh beauty and wisdom. In the ancient day when Christ first spoke the words, Matthew recorded: "The people were astonished." You will be astonished, too, to discover how pertinent the Sermon on the Mount is when applied to your daily life.

STOP WORRYING

By *A. J. Cronin*   Author of "The Citadel," "Beyond This Place," etc.

MILLIONS of people are beset by a secret enemy responsible for more casualties and greater suffering than almost any other scourge. Its name is Worry. As medical men know, worry can actually induce organic disease. And even when it does not, it can, by devouring our energy in unproductive ways, undermine health, render life intolerably miserable and shorten it by years.

Yet worry, against which the wonder drugs are useless, is quite curable *by the individual himself*. Worry lies in our minds, more often than not the result of simple misdirection of our imagination. By learning to control our processes of thought we can put worry in its proper place and make the world we live in cheerful instead of gloomy.

In setting out to achieve this control, the first popular fallacy of which we must rid ourselves is that worry is a peculiarity of the weak, the failures. On the contrary, worry may be a sign of potential strength, proof that a man cares about life and wants to make something worthwhile of his career. Men who have achieved the greatest heights, whose names are immortal, have been instinctive worriers. Yet they have nearly always had to contend, at some stage of their lives, with mental strain, and have taught themselves to overcome it.

Charles Spurgeon, celebrated 19th-century English preacher, confessed that when he was first obliged to speak in public he

14

worried for weeks beforehand, even to the extent of hoping he would break a leg before the fateful occasion. The result was that when he entered the pulpit he was so exhausted by worry and tension that he made a poor showing.

Then one day Spurgeon faced up to the situation. "What is the worst thing that can happen to me during my sermon?" he asked himself. Whatever it might be, he decided, the heavens would not fall. He had been magnifying a personal problem into a world-shaking disaster. When he saw his worry in proper perspective, he found that he spoke much better, simply because he had not distracted his mind with empty fears. He eventually became the outstanding preacher of his time.

We should look on worry as a manifestation of nervous intensity, and therefore a potential source of good. Only when this latent force exhausts itself fruitlessly on unreal problems does it harm us. The remedy is to accept worries as part of our life and learn to handle them by redirecting the energy we are misusing into productive channels.

This is easier if we make a list of the tangible things that worry us. When they are down on paper we realize how many of them are vague, indefinite and futile. An estimate of what most people worry about runs as follows: Things that never happen: 40 percent. Things over and past that can't be changed by all the worry in the world: 30 percent. Needless health worries: 12 percent. Petty miscellaneous worries: ten percent. Real, legitimate worries: eight percent.

If we study our worries, keeping our sense of proportion, at least some of them should be eliminated. What we imagine most easily, for example, what we dread, in reality rarely comes to pass.

One evening at La Guardia airport I found myself next to a young man who was meeting his fiancée. Presently it was announced that the plane we were awaiting had been held up by bad weather. It was half an hour, then an hour overdue. The young man's agitation increased. It was not difficult to see that he was picturing some horrible disaster.

Finally I felt compelled to speak to him. I knew it was useless simply to tell him to stop worrying. Instead, I set up other pictures, asking whom he was expecting, what the girl was like, what she would be wearing. Soon he was telling me all about his fiancée, how they had met, and so on. In a few minutes his mind was so full of other things that he had crowded worry out — indeed, the plane came in before he realized it.

Financial worries, on the other hand, are real enough and constitute a considerable part of all human anxieties. I believe there is only one way to solve them — provided we are already using our resources to the best advantage. That is to apply Thoreau's famous exhortation: "Simplify, simplify." Thoreau found that by cutting down his needs to the minimum he was able to savor life to the full, undistracted by cares consequent upon trying to satisfy superfluous desires. With Socrates, who had applied the same remedy 2000 years earlier, Thoreau could exult: "How many things I can do without!" Yet few men have led fuller, richer lives.

One of the most contented men I know is an old Maine fisherman whose sole possessions are a battered scow and his little shack on the clam flats. Completely at the mercy of wind and weather, indifferent to money, cherishing only his independence and his freedom, he manifests always a serene, sublime tranquillity — a perfect example for those of us who worry ourselves to death seeking material possessions, striving desperately to insulate ourselves against the hardships and misfortunes that may lie ahead. For worry never robs tomorrow of its sorrow; it only saps today of its strength.

Self-pity is the root of many of our worries. When I was practicing medicine in London one of my patients, a young married woman, was stricken with infantile paralysis. She was sent to a good hospital, where it soon became apparent that she was responding to treatment and would eventually recover. Some weeks later I received a visit from her husband. In a state of intense nervous upset, he complained of sleeplessness and inability to concentrate. After a checkup I found nothing whatever the matter with him. But when I suggested that he get back to his job he turned on me furiously. "My wife is seriously ill. And you expect me to go on as though nothing had happened. Haven't you any feeling *for me?*" The basic cause of his worry was self-pity, masquerading as concern for his wife.

For self-commiseration there is only one answer. We must

effect a revolution in our lives by which, instead of seeing ourselves as the center of existence, we turn our thoughts toward
others and come thus to realize our true place, as members of
a family, community and nation. There are many ways by
which we can come to see our difficulties in true perspective.
André Gide played the piano: he found that his worries became insignificant in the harmony of great music. Tolstoy,
contemplating the sunsets on the steppes, felt ashamed to concentrate on his own obsessions when there was so much beauty
in the world. Winston Churchill, burdened with the cares of
the free world, took time off from war to paint a landscape for
a Christmas card!

But the finest antidote to worry is work. Lawrence of Arabia
was one of the most brilliant men of action this century has
produced. His mother has described how, after his failure at
the Peace Conference to fulfill his promises to the Arabs, he
would sit entire mornings in the same position, without moving and with the same blank expression on his face. Worry over
his defeat transformed him from a man of action into a brood-
ing, lifeless shadow. His eventual self-cure was achieved by
translating this wasting energy into creative effort. He set out
to write *The Seven Pillars of Wisdom,* a masterpiece that
changed the course of history.

"It is not work that kills men," wrote Henry Ward Beecher.
"It is worry. Work is healthy; you can hardly put more upon a
man than he can bear. Worry is rust upon the blade."

Lionel Barrymore, the distinguished actor, when past 70,
gave as his prescription for a long and happy life: Keep busy.
He said: "I go along getting the most out of life on a day-to-
day basis. I don't worry about tomorrow, and I don't care what
happened yesterday. Once you start thinking about life and
its problems, and begin worrying over the future or regretting
the past, you're likely to become confused. I figure if a person
does his work well and extracts all he can from the present
he'll have as happy a life as he's supposed to have." By idling
away the hours or wasting them on unproductive time-fillers
which do not fully occupy our attention or energies, we leave
the door open for worry.

When troubles presented themselves, my old Scottish grandmother would remark with a shake of her head: "What cannot be cured must be endured." Then she would smile and add: "It's the Lord's will."

Worry, in the final analysis, is a form of atheism, a denial of the human need of God. It is like saying: "I shall never get the better of this, for there is no God to help me." The good Lord in His daily conversations was always warning His listeners against this particular lack of faith. After an enumeration of the various worries about the future with which men and women harass their minds, He said: "Take therefore no thought for the morrow."

No wiser philosophy could be evolved for a self-tormented humanity. If we follow it trustfully in all its prayerful implications, we shall raise ourselves beyond the reach of Private Enemy Number One and know true peace of mind.

Progress Notes

REPLACING the old-time small-town hotel near the depot, where the trains kept you awake all night, with the modern highway motel where the big trucks do the same is, we guess, progress of a sort.   — Detroit *News*

THE NEWEST dream kitchen has a lounge with TV, bookcase and fireplace, but most women would chuck the whole thing for a good old-fashioned hired girl.   — *Changing Times, The Kiplinger Magazine*

WE'RE NOT going to consider any of these models the real dream car of tomorrow until one of them includes a disposal unit built into the ledge behind the back seat to chew up all the comic books, graham cracker boxes, youngsters' mittens and road maps.

— Bill Vaughan, NANA

GRACIOUS LIVING is when you have the house air conditioned, and then load the yard with chairs, lounges and an outdoor oven so you can spend all your time in the hot sun.   — Detroit *News*

TYPICAL of man's genius is the way he develops a bomb designed to drive us into the cellar about the time he starts building homes without any cellars.   — Homer King in Hemet, Calif., *News*

Even though you do the right thing,
do you do it in the right way?

Have You
an Educated Heart?

By Gelett Burgess

Condensed from "The Bromide and Other Theories"

LAST OCTOBER I sent Crystabel a book. She acknowledged it, and promptly. But two months afterward she actually wrote me another letter, telling me what she thought of that book; and she proved, moreover, that she had read it. Now, I ask you, isn't that a strange and beautiful experience in this careless world? Crystabel had the educated heart. To such as possess the educated heart thanks are something like mortgages, to be paid in installments. Why, after five years Crystabel often refers to a gift that has pleased her. It is the motive for a gift she cares for, not its value; and hence her gratefulness.

Everything can be done beautifully by the educated heart, from the lacing of a shoe so that it won't come loose to passing the salt before it is asked for. If you say only "Good morning," it can be done pleasingly. Observe how the polished actor says it, with that cheerful rising inflection. But the ordinary American growls it out with surly downward emphasis. Merely to speak distinctly is a great kindness, I consider. You never have to ask, "What did you say?" of the educated heart. On the other hand, very few people ever really listen with kindly attention. They are usually merely waiting for a chance to pounce upon you with their own narrative. Or if they do listen, is your story heard with real sympathy? Does the face really glow?

Consider the usual birthday gift or Christmas present. By universal practice it is carefully wrapped in a pretty paper and tied with ribbon. That package is symbolical of what all friendly acts should be — kindness performed with style. Then what is style in giving? Ah, the educated heart makes it a business to know what his friend really wants. One friend I have to whom I can't express a taste that isn't treasured up against need. I said once that I loved watercress, and lightly wished that I might have it for every meal. Never a meal had I at his table since, without finding watercress bought specially for me.

Do you think it's easy, this business of giving? Verily, giving is as much an art as portrait painting or the making of glass flowers. And imagination can surely be brought to bear. Are you sailing for Brazil? It isn't the basket of fine fruits that brings the tears to your eyes, nor the flowers with trailing yards of red ribbon — all that's ordinary everyday kindness. It's that little purse full of Brazilian currency, bills and small change all ready for you when you go ashore at Rio.

There was old Wentrose — he understood the Fourth Dimension of kindness, all right. Never a friend of his wife's did he puffingly put aboard a streetcar, but he'd tuck apologetically into her hand the nickel to save her rummaging in her bag. Real elegance, the gesture of inherent nobility, I call that.

Is it sufficient simply to offer your seat in a streetcar to a woman? The merely kind person does that. But he does it rather sheepishly. Isn't your graciousness more cultured if you give it up with a bow, with a smile of willingness? Besides the quarter you give the beggar, can't you give a few cents' worth of yourself too? The behavior of the educated heart becomes automatic: you set it in the direction of true kindness and courtesy and after a while it will function without deliberate thought. Such thoughtfulness, such consideration is *not* merely decorative. It is the very essence and evidence of sincerity. Without it all so-called kindness is merely titular and perfunctory.

Suppose I submit your name for membership in a club. Have I done you (or my club) any real service unless I also do my

best to see that you are elected? And so if I go to every member of the committee, if I urge all my friends to endorse you, that is merely the completion of my regard for you. It is like salt —
"It's what makes potatoes taste bad, if you don't put it on."

Must you dance with all the wallflowers, then? I don't go so far as that, although it would prove that you had imagination enough to put yourself in another's place. All I ask is that when you try to do a favor you do it to the full length of the rope. Don't send your telegram in just ten carefully selected words. Economize elsewhere, but add those few extra phrases that make the reader perceive that you cared more for him than you did for the expense.

No one with the educated heart ever approached a clergyman, or a celebrity, or a long-absent visitor with the shocking greeting: "You don't remember me, do you?" No, he gives his name first. No one with the educated heart ever said, "Now do come and see me, sometime!" The educated heart's way of putting it is apt to be, "How about coming next Wednesday?" And strongly I doubt if the educated heart is ever tardy at an appointment. It knows that if only two minutes late a person has brought just that much less of himself.

You call once or twice at the hospital. Do you ever call again? Not unless you have the educated heart. Yet the patient is still perhaps quite ill. One there was who used to bring a scrapbook every morning, pasted in with funny items from the day's news.

Truly nothing is so rare as the educated heart. And if you wonder why, just show a kodak group picture — a banquet or a class photograph. What does every one of us first look at, talk about? Ourself. And that's the reason why most hearts are so unlearned in kindness.

If you want to enlarge that mystic organ whence flows true human kindness, you must cultivate your imagination. You must learn to put yourself in another's place, think his thoughts. The educated heart, remember, does kindness *with style*.

WE'RE ALL PECULIAR

Condensed from "The Human Frontier"

Roger J. Williams

Director of the Biochemical Institute, University of Texas

I N OUR APPROACH to various human problems we tend to think of society as made up of average individuals, all more or less alike. But society is composed mostly of abnormal people. For each of us may be regarded as abnormal in one or several respects. And we will come much closer to understanding problems of human relationship if we are aware of the many deep-seated physiological differences that make each of us act, think and feel differently from everyone else.

Take the matter of taste, for example. A large group of scientists tasted phenyl thiocarbimide. It was bitter to some while many insisted that it was really tasteless. Each group suspected the other either of untruth or of some gross physical abnormality. One man to whom it was tasteless tried to get his wife (to whom it was very bitter) to taste it again and again to convince her of her error. Since such differences are common, and occur in *all* our senses, the incident showed how easily human conflict may arise from physical differences we cannot help.

I know of three people who have a normal sense of smell in most respects but are not able to detect the odor of skunk. And variations in the reaction to color are very wide. Red may accelerate the pulse rate and raise blood pressure while blue may have the opposite effect. Some individuals are unusually sensitive to these stimuli and others relatively indifferent. Thus one man may be thrilled with delight at a colorful sunset while another may not give it a second's thought.

The variations in our eyes give rise to many differences in

vision besides the common ones the ordinary oculist observes. The person with poor peripheral vision cannot see anything unless he is looking almost directly at it. If two persons, one with good peripheral vision, one with poor, are looking for an item in the newspaper, the former will be able to find it in a fraction of the time that the other takes. But if they play golf together, the one who has excellent peripheral vision may see *too much* and be distracted. Poor peripheral vision on the part of either pedestrians or drivers is probably an important factor in accidents.

People vary widely in their reactions to drugs. Morphine puts most individuals to sleep, but an occasional individual is stimulated in such a manner that thoughts race through his mind pell-mell, causing great distress. Reactions to caffeine vary so widely that some can sleep soundly after having drunk several cups of strong coffee while others may be kept awake for hours by a portion of a cup. Similarly with nicotine: some people can smoke all day long without becoming ill while others, pharmacologists say, can never get adapted to the free use of tobacco.

For each of us the nervous system functions differently with respect to waking and sleeping rhythms. When we have probed more deeply into the nature of sleep we shall probably find reasonably satisfying answers to the problem which will enable us to make more efficient use of our waking and sleeping hours. But meantime we can cease regarding people who need a great deal of sleep or seem to need almost none as freakish or abnormal.

Sexual patterns also show a wide range of variance. One man in his 30's suffers exhaustion for several days as a result of sexual indulgence. At the other extreme, a man past 70 consults his doctor in fear of impotence because of his inability to perform the sexual act more than twice daily. The many factors involved in a successful marriage and the wide differences already known to exist between individuals make it rather surprising that so many marriages work out as well as they do! But recognition of natural variability and its physiological basis should tend to make members of the partnership more tolerant.

Just as we have tended to judge men and women as "normal" or "subnormal" in physical respects instead of recognizing how variable physical characteristics are, so we have been wide of the mark in judging their relative intelligence. To classify members of the human family as either intelligent or dumb may be convenient for some purposes, but it is not justified by the scientific facts.

Men we rate as brilliant are not necessarily brilliant in every respect. There is no reason for thinking that Albert Einstein's mind is in *every* respect phenomenal. There are plenty of good mathematicians who are relatively poor in mental arithmetic and from stories told of Einstein's boyhood it would appear that he belongs in this group. In fact, as a child he was so slow in learning to talk, his parents feared he might be abnormal.

We can rate individuals on their mental ability at certain specific tasks — their ability as spellers, their ability to memorize, the facility with which they handle numbers. But when it comes to total intelligence we human beings cannot be rated 1, 2, 3, etc., any more than we could rate in the same classification Shetland ponies, race horses and draft horses.

If we wish to be intelligent on the subject of intelligence we must face the fact that each human mind is a mixture of many (perhaps as many as 300) distinct mental abilities, tendencies and traits, any of which we may have in either high or low degree.

Consider the "idiot-savants" — individuals who according to ordinary tests and educational standards are feeble-minded or even idiots. Some of them have remarkable mental powers.

One man of 21 was found by intelligence test to be a low-grade moron. In some phases of intelligence, particularly those which are indispensable for book-learning, he had the mental age of a small child. It was observed, however, that he could repair door locks, bicycle bells, almost any mechanical contrivance. He was given the Stenquist Mechanical Aptitude Test; it showed that in mechanical aptitude he was a superior adult. There are records of a considerable number of such people; some of them have developed into highly skilled wood carvers.

A school principal took a feeble-minded youth to a special clinic for examination. Among the tests applied was a structural visualization test involving fitting together irregularly cut segments of a block. It took the principal "18 minutes of unhappy fumbling." The feeble-minded boy did it in one minute.

The "feeble-minded" often have outstanding memories. A feeble-minded boy in an Ohio town memorized the telephone directory and the automobile license numbers of many of the citizens and would call them off on request. A Texas imbecile would ask any man he met the date of his birth, his father's and mother's dates, his wife's maiden name, and so on. Years later he could recite the complete details. His memory was so perfect that he was consulted when the county records were found not to be clear.

These instances demonstrate the independence of the different kinds of mental abilities. Idiot-savants are simply extreme caricatures of you and me and our neighbors and friends — strong in some traits and weak in others. As psychological testing is usually carried out these ups and downs are overlooked. Too much is lumped together and called general intelligence. For purposes of predicting school behavior conventional tests are generally successful. But they still overlook the significant fact that *individuals possess different mental abilities in highly variable degrees.*

Our failure to pay more attention to individual children in schools has been due in part to the idea of carrying out education on a mass-production basis and attempting to reduce everything to statistics. There are articles and books galore dealing with educating "the child," but the importance of recognizing each child as an individual with widely different aptitudes has rarely been stressed.

One of the functions of education is to help the student find his place in the world. We could start on this problem much earlier than we do. Students go all the way through college without learning what their aptitudes are or what they might be fitted for. I know of one who found out his aptitudes for the first time after college graduation, in an Army examination. If he had been tested in grade school, he could have been saved four years of misdirected study and a good deal of unhappiness.

The need for better understanding of individual differences is great in all activities directed toward improvement of our physical and mental health. But the need is even greater in our management of public affairs.

One of the inevitable results of an increasing knowledge of human beings, I believe, will be an appreciation of the fact that no man is by nature equipped to be *the* leader in every avenue of life.

Society needs leaders badly; leaders in industry, in science, education, government, every other line of human activity. But it doesn't need universal leaders — those who lead, or rather dominate, in every field. No one is able to qualify for such leadership.

Actually dictatorships and unwarranted dominance by individuals arise partly because of our general ignorance of individual limitations. When a human being shows unusual prowess or ability along one line, and thus possibly qualifies for leadership in that field, we can often be led to imagine that these abilities carry over into other fields.

The abuse of power has often come about in this fashion — the individual demonstrates some special ability, often as a maker of speeches, whereupon other virtues and abilities are attributed to him and gradually he becomes an authority and finally *the* authority on all subjects. A better knowledge of human abilities and human frailties would make this impossible. It is difficult to imagine a dictatorship arising in a country well informed about the attributes of individual human beings.

Food for Thought

A DOCTOR in Berkeley, Calif., is making a name for himself by his success in reducing overweight women. Asked his secret, he replied, "I get a head start on a case, that's all. On the patient's first call I spend only a few minutes with her, just long enough to weigh her and instruct her to keep a complete written record of every bite she eats during the two weeks until her second appointment. And," he smiled, "by the end of those two weeks most patients have already lost about ten pounds!"

— Contributed by John C. Sergeant

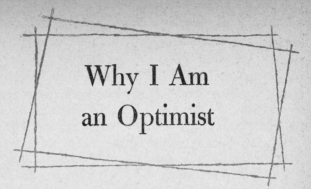

Why I Am
an Optimist

By André Maurois

My wife, my children, my friends tell me that I am an optimist. "Too much of an optimist" is what they say. "If you fell off a cliff," one of them told me, "you'd be thinking that the bottom was cushioned, and until you landed you'd be quite serene."

I am, I admit, an optimist; but I do not believe, like Voltair's Pangloss, that all is for the best in this best of all possible worlds. I know the horrors and difficulties of life: I have had my share of them. But I refuse to regard humanity's condition as terrible. True, we are spinning on a lump of dirt in illimitable space, without being too sure why; true, we will surely die. To me this is a set of facts, a situation to be accepted courageously. The only problem is: What can we do, and what ought we to do, while we are here?

I am optimistic in the sense that I believe it is possible to better our own lives and, in a general way, humanity's life. I believe that tremendous progress has been made in this direction. Man has, to a large extent, overcome nature. His command of things is far greater than it used to be. The Pessimist replies: "Yes, but these marvelous inventions are used only for war, and humanity is on the road to self-destruction."

I do not believe that this is necessarily so. It depends upon ourselves, and my optimism is largely a product of my faith in human nature. I know that human nature also has its greatnesses.

My natural reaction to a circumstance is to seek what good there may be in it rather than what evil it may bring. I believe that it has its origin in a happy childhood. I had the finest parents a boy could have; they always treated me with love and justice; and that gave me, in those first formative years, a robust confidence in human nature. School might have marred my innocent faith, because children are only too willing to give one another a foretaste of harshness. But it was there, in my philosophy class, that I had the good fortune of meeting Alain, the greatest of my teachers. He too was reproached by some, as I am, for his "blind confidence."

Alain and I after him pledged ourselves to be optimists because if one does not adopt invincible optimism as a standard, pessimism will be justified. For despair engenders misfortune and failure. If I believe that I am going to fall, I will fall. If I believe that there is nothing I can do about my country's affairs, then there is nothing I can do. In the human tribe I make the fair weather and the tempest, primarily within myself. Pessimism is contagious. If I believe my neighbor to be dishonest and show my distrust, I make him distrustful and dishonest.

"Look here," says the Pessimist. "Do you really believe that this confidence in mankind, in life, is wisdom? Hasn't it brought you some frightful disappointments?" Yes, I confess that I have had some great disappointments. The long war years — particularly with the horrors of Nazism, with exile, my family arrested, my home pillaged, with the dangerous defection of certain friends — have given me strong reason for doubting the perfection of this universe and the people in it.

But after all, I have always known that wicked people existed; I have always known that in times of disaster crowds can become stupid and bestial. My optimism consisted, and still consists, solely in this: We can have a certain influence upon events, and even if we must suffer misfortune we can overcome it by our manner of enduring it.

To love the fine people about me, to avoid the wicked, to rejoice in good, endure evil — and to remember to forget: this is my optimism. It has helped me to live.

Do What You Want— and Live Longer

Condensed from
The American Magazine

Thurman B. Rice, M.D.
Professor of public health, Indiana University

"No matter how I coax and threaten," a worried mother told me, "my Tommy simply will not eat his spinach. Whatever am I going to do?"

I suggested that she give him strawberries and cream instead. "You're not serious!" she gasped. I told her I never was more serious. Strawberries and cream happen to be packed with vitamins and minerals, and Tommy *liked* strawberries and cream while he detested spinach.

I am a strong believer in doing what you like. The very fact that you enjoy a thing is reason enough for doing it. This does not mean that I favor selfish indulgence or unbridled dissipation. It does mean that I'm in favor of getting more fun out of life.

Down through the centuries men have searched for some formula that would prolong the span of human existence — an elixir to endow men and women with eternal youth. The famous Pasteur Institute of Paris recently announced that it, too, is working on a "youth serum." The project is still in an experimental stage; but even if it were to succeed, how much better off would humanity be? What point is there in extending the span of one's existence if it simply means increasing the number of years in which to be old and futile?

Wouldn't it be more to the point to study ways and means of packing more living into the span of life already allotted to us?

A doctor friend has told me of a patient whom he inherited from his father. The patient is nearing 90 and apparently is in the best of health; yet my friend has never known him to draw an uncomplaining breath, or to be other than a burden to himself and a pain in the neck to those around him. For all his years, such a man can scarcely be said to have "lived" at all.

You're not truly living unless you get a kick out of life; you're simply existing. Yet I know plenty of people who actually go out of their way to deny themselves fun and enjoyment.

One man never does anything because it would be pleasant or enjoyable but always because it is his bounden obligation. He is one of those fellows of whom it is aptly said that they were "born old." His oppressive sense of duty makes him a bore to his acquaintances and a trial to his family. An overly conscientious woman considers it a sin to laugh since her husband died. Hugging her grief, she denies not only herself but her children the right to a happy, normal existence.

Many people make themselves miserable by adhering to a disagreeable "health" regimen under the mistaken notion that such practices are somehow good for them. They persist in sleeping beside open windows in cold weather though nose and throat specialists condemn the practice. Millions of American males start the day in fear and trembling with a cold shower that shocks the nervous system, leaves them chilled and under par and causes them to become drowsy by midmorning. They do it on the theory that it "hardens" them, whereas in a majority of cases it actually makes them more susceptible to colds.

One of my friends knocks himself out every morning doing setting-up exercises to keep himself fit. U. S. Army tests prove that recruits subjected to intensive calisthenics probably do not possess more physical endurance under combat conditions than soldiers who have had little or no "toughening."

I know a woman who feeds her family quantities of raw carrots, cracked wheat and brown sugar. Her meals are scientifically apportioned blends of proteins, carbohydrates, fats, minerals, vitamins and roughage; nevertheless, they are so unappetizing that her family fails to get much benefit.

Then are people who ruin their lives by being overparticular about their physical surroundings. A woman in our town is a perfectionist and a fuss-budget. She makes both her family and visitors uncomfortable by her prissy insistence on having everything arranged just so — from chairs and ash trays in the living room to umbrellas and overshoes in the coat closet. Basically a well-intentioned wife and mother, this woman would be all right if only she could learn to relax and take things as they come.

And I know couples who are so determinedly conventional that they don't get fun even out of their amusements. They play bridge or golf not because they enjoy it but because it's "the thing to do."

Then there are those who have fallen into the habit of putting off the things that make for real living. One woman is forever buying a new suit or gown. But she rarely wears any of her smart clothes. She is saving them for some indefinite future occasion that never seems to arrive. Another young woman, a schoolteacher, went without her summer vacations for years in order to take more and more college courses. Last summer, having at last received her doctorate, she visited a summer resort for the first time. But she was so miserable there that she cut short her stay. It was too late — she had forgotten how to play. She isn't as good a teacher with a degree and a grouch as she was with no degree and a cheery outlook on life.

It's possible to wreck your life by trying to play things too safe. No man can be happy if he's excessively anxious about his home, his bank roll, his job or his health. When you get right down to it, *all* living involves risk. The people who try always to play it safe not infrequently find themselves more vulnerable to trouble than those who are willing to take some chances.

Many who entertain the notion that because a thing is unpleasant it must be good for them also believe that whatever is pleasant is bad. This is equally absurd. The world is full of good and pleasant things put there for our enjoyment: sun and rain and food and sleep and love and play and laughter. If we turn our backs on them, are we not guilty of ingratitude to their Creator?

Living, as I see it, is an art, the most important art there is. Yet few people learn to practice it successfully. Mrs. Anne Mary ("Grandma") Moses probably offers the perfect example of the fun you can enjoy once you relax and start doing what you really want to do. Grandma Moses always wanted to paint, but never got around to it till she was 78. Even in her 90's, unflustered by fame and wealth, she painted for the sheer joy of it.

Nobody needs to go on living in the squirrel cage of a dull existence. Anybody who really wants to can emancipate himself and start enjoying life. The owner of a filling station far off the usual tourist routes in the Rocky Mountains was a man of obvious education and refinement. It eventually came out that he had been for a time a partner in a Manhattan law firm; but he hated the work and hated the life, in spite of all the money he was making. "So I quit and came out here," he says. "It may not be for everybody, but this part of the world suits me. My ulcers have disappeared; my nerves are steady again. I'm my own boss. Any time I feel like it I go fishing for a week. I don't make much money, but I'm having more fun than I ever had in my life."

The really successful man is the fellow who gets paid for doing the thing he likes to do. He'll not only be happier but the chances are he'll live longer, too. In the *Book of Proverbs* it is written: "A merry heart doeth good like a medicine." There's no other medicine to be compared with it.

Request Performance

THE master of ceremonies on a Los Angeles radio program was interviewing engaged couples, asking for the details of their romances. When one couple came to the microphone, the bride-to-be explained that it was a second romance for both of them. They had both been married before — to each other — but extreme youth and the separation of war had broken their marriage.

"Just what made you two decide that you were meant for each other after all?" asked the M.C.

"Well," explained the lady, "our young daughter wrote a composition in school entitled, 'I wish my father would marry my mother.'"

— Contributed by Mrs. Martin Gordon

Three tested rules anyone
can use to advantage

How to Sell an Idea

Condensed from Your Life

Elmer Wheeler

 Have you ever approached your boss with a red-hot idea for increasing efficiency — only to have him become resentful instead of enthusiastic? Have you ever offered your wife or the neighbors "good advice"? If you have, you know what I mean when I say that people resent having other people's ideas forced on them.

When someone approaches us with a new idea, our instinctive reaction is to put up a defense against it. We feel that we must protect our individuality; and most of us are egotistical enough to think that our ideas are better than anyone else's.

There are three tested rules for putting your ideas across to other people so as to arouse their enthusiasm. Here they are:

Rule One: Use a fly rod — not a feeding tube. Others won't accept *your* idea until they can accept it as *their* idea.

It was said during World War I that Colonel House was the most powerful man in the world because he controlled the most powerful man in the world — Woodrow Wilson. "I learned that the best way to convert him to an idea," explained House, "was to plant it in his mind casually, to get him thinking about it on his own account."

When you want to sell someone an idea, take a lesson from the fisherman who casts his fly temptingly near the trout. He could never ram the hook into the trout's mouth. But he can entice the trout to come to the hook.

Don't appear too anxious to have your ideas accepted. Just bring them out where they can be seen.

"Have you considered this?" is better than "This is the way."

"Do you think this would work?" is better than "Here's what we should do."

Let the other fellow sell himself on your idea. Then he'll stay sold.

Rule Two: Let the other fellow argue your case. He instinctively feels called upon to raise some objection to save his face. Give him a chance to disagree with you — by presenting your own objections!

"The way to convince another," said wise old Ben Franklin, "is to state your case moderately and accurately. Then say that of course you may be mistaken about it; which causes your listener to receive what you have to say and, like as not, turn about and convince you of it, since you are in doubt. But if you go at him in a tone of positiveness and arrogance you only make an opponent of him."

Franklin used this technique, against great opposition, in his sale of the idea of adopting the Constitution of the United States.

"I confess," he began, "that I do not entirely approve of this Constitution; but, Sir, I am not sure I shall never approve it; for having lived long, I have experienced many instances of being obliged by better information or fuller consideration to change opinions, even on important subjects, which I first thought right. I cannot help expressing a wish that every member of the convention who may still have objections to it would with me on this occasion doubt a little of his own infallibility, and, to make manifest our unanimity, put his name to this instrument."

Abraham Lincoln used the same technique in selling his ideas to a jury. He argued both sides of the case — but there was always the subtle suggestion that his side was the logical one. An opposing lawyer said of him: "He made a better statement of my case to the jury than I could have made myself."

Another technique is to sell the other fellow the idea as his, not yours. "You gave me an idea the other day that started me thinking," you begin.

Tom Reed, for many years Speaker of the House, was an adroit persuader. At a committee hearing he would remain silent until everyone had had his say, making notes of all objections. Then, when everyone else was argued out, Reed would say, "Gentlemen, it seems to me that what has been said here can be summarized as follows. . . ." Reed would then present *his* ideas — and sell them.

Once Dudley Nichols, the movie director, wasn't satisfied with a scene in one of his pictures. To remedy the situation, he said to Rosalind Russell, the star, "Wonderful, wonderful, but I could see, Miss Russell, when you hesitated that brief instant, that you were thinking about the possibility of playing the scene down just a trifle more. Shall we try it once the way you were thinking?"

Rule Three: Ask — don't tell. Patrick Henry, another famous idea salesman, was a political unknown when first elected to Virginia's House of Burgesses — but every resolution he introduced was passed. Listen to him in his famous "Liberty or Death" speech and see how he uses questions to get his ideas across:

"Our brethren are already in the field — why stand we here idle?"

"Shall we lie supinely on our backs?"

"What is it that gentlemen wish? What would they have? Is life so dear or peace so sweet as to be purchased at the price of chains and slavery?"

Try saying the same thing in positive statements and see how much antagonism it would invoke.

When you put your ideas across with questions, you give the other fellow a share in the idea. You don't tell him — you ask him for the answer. You're giving him a chance to sell himself.

Try these rules the next time you want to put an idea across to your boss, your family or the neighbors.

Copyright 1948 by The Reader's Digest Association, Inc. (December 1948 issue)
Condensed from Your Life, September 1948

Traveler's Lament

A SIX-YEAR-OLD was motoring to the West Coast with his family. The weather had been bad, the traveling rough. After a particularly hard day they stopped in a Texas town, took the only available hotel rooms and sank wearily into their beds. Suddenly the silence was broken by the six-year-old. "Mommy," he wailed, "why don't we just go back home and live happily ever after?"

— Claire MacMurray in Cleveland *Plain Dealer*

In marriage there is security in numbers

Love, Marriage, Children
— and Security

Condensed from
"The Way to Security"

Henry C. Link
Author of "The Return to Religion," etc.

IF YOU had to choose one of the following — an interesting job, an independent income of $100 a week, a happy family and home life — which would you choose? That question was asked recently of a cross section of husbands and wives. Eighty percent answered: a happy family and home life.

A happy family life is probably the principal factor in the security of adults — as it is in the security of children. Much has been written about marital security. Yet most discussions of what makes a happy marriage place little emphasis on the necessity of having children. Wars can come, jobs can go, money can run out, but if father, mother and children stand by each other, hope and happiness may survive.

Recently I was talking with a father who expressed concern about the approaching arrival of a fifth child. "And yet," he remarked, "in spite of the trouble and expense, my wife and I are convinced that a large family is better than a small one. There is a certain security in numbers."

He was right, of course.

In my experience with unhappy couples, the one most apparent cause of unhappiness is their unwillingness to have children, or their prolonged postponement of parenthood. They do not want children until they can afford them, or the wife wants to keep on working until they can buy a home. In their quest for security before having children they risk the chance of not having any security at all.

36

The case of one young husband who was worried about his marriage is not uncommon. "We seem to be drifting apart," he told us, "and for no reason that we can see." He and his wife had agreed before marriage, six years ago, that she would keep her job until his salary was up to $5000 a year. He was still short of the mark by $400. He was now 31 and she 28.

For six years they had defied their natural desire to have children. For six years they had said, in effect: "We can live without the risks of children until we can have children without risk." They did not realize that meanwhile they had probably lost the very security they were working toward.

Man has concocted many theories and notions about marriage, among them the theory that each couple has the right to decide whether to have children. Regardless of theories, the chief purpose of sex and marriage is children. This is a law of human nature which cannot be defied with impunity. A couple who enter marriage without planning to have children soon are courting disaster from the beginning.

Having children is a physical process but the experience is a spiritual one as well. It involves continuous self-sacrifice of many kinds, possibly even the sacrifice of immediate financial security. It is through the choice of spiritual values, where they conflict with material values, that true security is to be found.

Probably the most popular as well as the most dangerous theory about love is that it is something one falls out of as well as into. This ignores the truth that love, no matter how it starts, is something that must be consciously created. Lasting love depends on permanent sex compatibility, and this in turn depends heavily on having children. When the experience of sex is subordinated to the birth and care of children it takes on a new spiritual significance. This is the basis for true and lasting love, a continuous process of creation and self-sacrifice centered around raising a family.

One of the most important studies of marriage is that by the psychologist Lewis M. Terman, at Stanford University. The results have been published in his book *Psychological Factors in Marital Happiness*. Of all the influences that determine a happy marriage probably the four most important are:

Being eager to have children.

Having parents who are happily married.

Having a mature character and effective personality.

Being religious and of religious parents.

Sexual compatibility alone is not regarded by psychologists and sociologists as a major factor. The reason is that such compatibility is something that has to be achieved, and its achievement depends on the four factors just mentioned.

Lack of money has often been given as a principal cause of marital unhappiness and divorce. And yet the higher the income, the higher the divorce rate. Obviously, people without sufficient money to indulge their whims, their impulses, their selfish desires, must of necessity make greater efforts to overcome their difficulties. These difficulties often prove temporary and so the couple remain united and regain their happiness. Thus financial *insecurity* may be a help in achieving marital *security*.

Having a child is the final and strongest pledge of a couple's love for each other. It is an eloquent testimony that their marriage is a complete one. It lifts their marriage from the level of selfish love and physical pleasure to that of devotion centered around a new life. It makes self-sacrifice rather than self-indulgence their guiding principle. It represents the husband's faith in his ability to provide the necessary security, and it demonstrates the wife's confidence in his ability to do so. The net result is a spiritual security which, more than any other power, helps to create material security as well.

Capsule Course in Human Relations

Five most important words: I AM PROUD OF YOU.

Four most important words: WHAT IS YOUR OPINION?

Three most important words: IF YOU PLEASE.

Two most important words: THANK YOU.

Least important word: I.

— *Forbes Magazine*

Seven Reasons Why a Scientist Believes in God

Adapted from the book "Man Does Not Stand Alone"

A. Cressy Morrison

We are still in the dawn of the scientific age and every increase of light reveals more brightly the handiwork of an intelligent Creator. In the 90 years since Darwin we have made stupendous discoveries; with a spirit of scientific humility and of faith grounded in knowledge we are approaching even nearer to an awareness of God.

For myself, I count seven reasons for my faith:

First: *By unwavering mathematical law we can prove that our universe was designed and executed by a great engineering Intelligence.*

Suppose you put ten pennies, marked from one to ten, into your pocket and give them a good shuffle. Now try to take them out in sequence from one to ten, putting back the coin each time and shaking them all again. Mathematically we know that your chance of first drawing number one is one to ten; of drawing one and two in succession, one to 100; of drawing one, two and three in succession, one in a thousand, and so on; your chance of drawing them all, from number one to number ten in succession, would reach the unbelievable figure of one chance in ten billion.

By the same reasoning, so many exacting conditions are necessary for life on the earth that they could not possibly exist in proper relationship by chance. The earth rotates on its axis one thousand miles an hour; if it turned at one hundred miles an hour, our days and night would be ten times as long as now, and the hot sun would then burn up our vegetation each long day while in the long night any surviving sprout would freeze.

Again, the sun, source of our life, has a surface temperature of 12,000 degrees Fahrenheit, and our earth is just far enough away so that this "eternal fire" warms us *just enough and not too much!* If the sun gave off only one half its present radiation, we would freeze and if it gave half as much more, we would roast.

The slant of the earth, tilted at an angle of 23 degrees, gives us our seasons; if it had not been so tilted, vapors from the ocean would move north and south, piling up for us continents of ice. If our moon was, say, only 50 thousand miles away instead of its actual distance, our tides would be so enormous that twice a day all continents would be submerged; even the mountains would soon be eroded away. If the crust of the earth had been only ten feet thicker, there would be no oxygen, without which animal life must die. Had the ocean been a few feet deeper, carbon dioxide and oxygen would have been absorbed and no vegetable life could exist. Or if our atmosphere had been much thinner, some of the meteors, now burned in space by the millions every day, would be striking all parts of the earth, setting fires everywhere.

Because of these and a host of other examples, there is not one chance in millions that life on our planet is an accident.

Second: *The resourcefulness of life to accomplish its purpose is a manifestation of all-pervading Intelligence.*

What life itself is, no man has fathomed. It has neither weight nor dimensions, but it does have force; a growing root will crack a rock. Life has conquered water, land and air, mastering the elements, compelling them to dissolve and reform their combinations.

Life, the sculptor, shapes all living things; an artist, it designs every leaf of every tree, and colors every flower. Life is a musician and has taught each bird to sing its love songs, the insects to call each other in the music of their multitudinous sounds. Life is a sublime chemist, giving taste to fruits and spices, and perfume to the rose, changing water and carbonic acid into sugar and wood, and, in so doing, releasing oxygen that animals may have the breath of life.

Behold an almost invisible drop of protoplasm, transparent, jellylike, capable of motion, drawing energy from the sun. This single cell, this transparent mistlike droplet, holds within itself the germ of life, and has the power to distribute this life to every living thing, great and small. The powers of this droplet are greater than our vegetation and animals and people, for all life came from it. Nature did not create life; fire-blistered rocks and a saltless sea could not meet the necessary requirements.

Who, then, has put it here?

Third: *Animal wisdom speaks irresistibly of a good Creator who infused instinct into otherwise helpless little creatures.*

The young salmon spends years at sea, then comes back to his own river, and travels up the very side of the river into which flows the tributary where he was born. What brings him back so precisely? If you transfer him to another tributary he will know at once that he is off his course and he will fight his way down and back to the main stream and then turn up against the current to finish his destiny accurately.

Even more difficult to solve is the mystery of eels. These amazing creatures migrate at maturity from all ponds and rivers everywhere — those from Europe across thousands of miles of ocean — all bound for the same abysmal deeps near Bermuda. There they breed and die. The little ones, with no apparent means of knowing anything except that they are in a wilderness of water, nevertheless start back and find their way not only to the very shore from which their parents came but thence to the rivers, lakes or little ponds — so that each body of water is always populated with eels. No American eel has ever been caught in Europe, no European eel in American waters. Nature has even delayed the maturity of the European eel by a year or more to make up for its longer journey. Where does the directing impulse originate?

A wasp will overpower a grasshopper, dig a hole in the earth, sting the grasshopper in exactly the right place so that he does not die but becomes unconscious and lives on as a form of preserved meat. Then the wasp will lay her eggs handily so that her children when they hatch can nibble without killing the insect on which they feed; to them dead meat would be fatal. The mother then flies away and dies; she never sees her young. Surely the wasp must have done all this right the first time and every time, else there would be no wasps. Such mysterious techniques cannot be explained by adaptation; they were bestowed.

Fourth: *Man has something more than animal instinct — the power of reason.*

No other animal has ever left a record of its ability to count ten, or even to understand the meaning of ten. Where instinct is like a single note of a flute, beautiful but limited, the human brain contains all the notes of all the instruments in the orchestra. No need to belabor this fourth point; thanks to human reason we can contemplate the possibility that we are what we are only because we have received a spark of Universal Intelligence.

Fifth: *Provision for all living is revealed in phenomena which we know today but which Darwin did not know — such as the wonders of genes.*

So unspeakably tiny are these genes that, if all of them responsible for all living people in the world could be put in one place, there would be less than a thimbleful. Yet these ultramicroscopic genes and their companions, the chromosomes, inhabit every living cell and are the absolute keys to all human, animal and vegetable characteristics. A thimble is a small place in which to put all the individual characteristics of two billions of human beings. However, the facts are beyond question. Well, then — how do genes lock up all the normal heredity of a multitude of ancestors and preserve the psychology of each in such an infinitely small space?

Here evolution really begins — at the cell, the entity which holds and carries the genes. How a few million atoms, locked up as an ultra-microscopic gene, can absolutely rule all life on earth is an example of profound cunning and provision that could emanate only from a Creative Intelligence; no other hypothesis will serve.

Sixth: *By the economy of nature, we are forced to realize that only infinite wisdom could have foreseen and prepared with such astute husbandry.*

Many years ago a species of cactus was planted in Australia

as a protective fence. Having no insect enemies in Australia the cactus soon began a prodigious growth; the alarming abundance persisted until the plants covered an area as long and wide as England, crowding inhabitants out of the towns and villages, and destroying their farms. Seeking a defense, the entomologists scoured the world; finally they turned up an insect which lived exclusively on cactus, and would eat nothing else. It would breed freely, too; and it had no enemies in Australia. So animal soon conquered vegetable and today the cactus pest has retreated, and with it all but a small protective residue of the insects, enough to hold the cactus in check forever.

Such checks and balances have been universally provided. Why have not fast-breeding insects dominated the earth? Because they have no lungs such as man possesses; they breathe through tubes. But when insects grow large, their tubes do not grow in ratio to the increasing size of the body. Hence there never has been an insect of great size; this limitation on growth has held them all in check. If this physical check had not been provided, man could not exist. Imagine meeting a hornet as big as a lion!

Seventh: *The fact that man can conceive the idea of God is in itself a unique proof.*

The conception of God rises from a divine faculty of man, unshared with the rest of our world — the faculty we call imagination. By its power, man and man alone can find the evidence of things unseen. The vista that power opens up is unbounded; indeed, as man's perfected imagination becomes a spiritual reality, he may discern in all the evidences of design and purpose the great truth that heaven is wherever and whatever; that God is everywhere and in everything but nowhere so close as in our hearts.

It is scientifically as well as imaginatively true, as the Psalmist said: *The heavens declare the glory of God and the firmament showeth His handiwork.*

When It's Best to Forget

Condensed from Guideposts

By W. E. Sangster

Minister, The Central Hall, London

I HAPPEN to have a good memory. I can remember pretty well anything I want to. But more important, I have learned the truth that lies in the words of the French philosopher Henri Bergson: "It is the function of the brain to enable us not to remember but to forget."

Plenty of people are forgetful in an absent-minded way. Every article the great missionary Temple Gairdner possessed came back to his office through the post. Shoes, Bible, toothbrush, waistcoat followed one another in an unending stream. On one occasion, visiting in Birmingham, he met a friend on the street and put down his bag to make a note in his diary. Then he went blithely down the street minus the bag.

Perhaps this absent-mindedness isn't as funny as it sounds. Perhaps a wife whose birthday is forgotten by her husband doesn't think it hilarious. But if I were asked what causes more trouble in the world — the things forgotten which should have been remembered or the things remembered which should have been forgotten — I'm sure I should fix on the latter. What most of us need is not so much a good memory as a good forgettery.

Some forgetting is natural, a consequence of the passing of time and not the outcome of conscious effort. There is sense, as well as nonsense, in the old saying that time heals. For time brings new experiences — happy ones — and revives sweet memories to overlay the bitterness of loss.

The fact is that conscious memory has a preference for the pleasant. She is always trying to stuff painful experiences down the hole of oblivion and to preserve only the things we are glad to recall. Yet natural memory alone cannot deal with all unpleasant things. It starts us right but we must find ways of working with it.

One may not always be able to forget a tragic occurrence, but one can learn, in remembering it, not to be emotionally overwhelmed. The real danger in remembering the wrong things is that we remember them not as facts but as convulsive experiences, and we keep resentment, self-pity or embarrassment alive in our souls.

I meet people who think that if someone has played them a dirty trick resentment is justified. Justified or not, resentment and the ache for revenge are poison. It is better to get rid of them, and the way to get rid of them is to learn to forget.

If you say, "I *can't* forget," I will say, "You are wrong. You imply that the will has no power over the memory. But the will can be trained to do the work."

Immanuel Kant lived for years in entire and trustful dependence on his manservant, Lampe. Then, one sad day, he discovered that Lampe had systematically robbed him, and he felt compelled to sack his old servant. But how he missed him! In his journal this pathetic line appears: "Remember to forget Lampe."

Remember to forget! Here is one of the foremost philosophical figures of all time, and he studies to forget.

You forget by reversing the process of remembering. To remember, one must revive the image, hold it in the mind for so long, revive it again — regularly; then it's there for good.

Reverse that process. *Don't* revive the image. When it rises of itself, summoned by some association of ideas, turn your thoughts immediately from it. Have in the antechamber of your mind a few interesting themes always on call: things you find particularly absorbing and which have power to grip your thought and imagination. All of us have such themes — our work, our vacation plans, our sports or hobbies.

None of these substitute themes is of any use unless it has power to grip the mind, and what grips one mind may not grip another. A friend of mine, a shy soul, outwits the recollection of a public gaucherie by instantly remembering an occasion when he was a social success. I know another man who blots out unwanted memories by trying to write a poem, and another who daydreams about a fortune he plans to make. It does not matter what the substitute image is, if it can thrust the other thing from your attention. Prayer will not do if it is prayer *about the thing itself*. That keeps it in the memory. But prayer is excellent if it creates receptivity to love, forgiveness, peace and poise.

Dealt with in this way, the thing you want to forget loses mastery. Remember that the deeper laws of the mind are working with your will to help you forget. Most of the things you want to forget want to be forgotten; you are not working *against* but *with* nature if you learn to forget.

A recollection firmly rejected in a disciplined way recurs less and less frequently. Fewer and fewer will be its associations in your mind. When it does recur it will be as a cold fact only: the emotions will not be overheated by it. Thus you bring science to the aid of sense.

Restitution helps forgetfulness. No man should hope to forget the wrong things he's done till he has done also whatever he can to put them right. A false statement can be corrected, hurt feelings can be healed by honest apologies. To make amends helps your misdeeds into oblivion. A gnawing conscience keeps the memory terribly alert.

I saw the need and the possibility of forgetting years ago, and I've been at it long enough to know that my method works. Indeed, I proved it at Christmas. One of my guests had come a couple of days early and saw me sending off the last of my Christmas cards. He was startled to see a certain name and address on an envelope.

"Surely you are not sending a greeting to *him*," he said.

"Why not?" I asked.

"But you remember," he began, "18 months ago . . ."

I remembered then the thing the man had done to me. But I also remembered resolving at the time that I would remember to forget. And I had forgotten!

I posted the card.

Learn to Live with Your Nerves

By Walter C. Alvarez, M.D.

A condensation from the book

To LIVE easily with your nerves, the first thing is to get acquainted with the ways in which they play tricks on you. Often I must say to a worried patient, "There is nothing seriously wrong with you; your symptoms are all produced by your erratic nerves." And the patient will ask, "But why do they play such tricks?"

Often the most distressing spells follow a trying experience, a sleepless night, a tiring day. For instance, a businessman began to suffer severe heart palpitation the day he had to face the unpleasant task of dismissing an old employe. A woman who woke one night with the feeling that she was strangling had spent the evening arguing angrily with a relative over money. One can easily see why the nerves of these persons were on edge and ready to go on a rampage.

Many times, however, the storm seems to come out of a clear sky. A highly nervous woman tells me that her life is easy — she has a loving husband, a comfortable home, good children, no worries. Why, then, should she have spells in which she is jittery, terribly tired, apprehensive or depressed? Usually in such cases I find marked nervousness in the family. Let us say that you have inherited your father's quick temper or your mother's tendency to worry. You cannot entirely get rid of these tendencies, but you can learn to control them and to live with them better.

When, as a young man, I faced failure and poor health because of my inheritance of my mother's bad nerves, I resolved that I would do the many wise things she did, but I would struggle hard never to do the foolish things she did, such as worrying and fretting and living life the hard way. I decided I would hoard my energies. And when I did, I found I had enough for two jobs: one earning a living and the other doing research, writing, teaching and lecturing. I even had enough left over for hobbies. Someone once said our relatives are given us to show us what we shouldn't do and be!

Learn to keep your nervous system as fit as possible with the help of good mental hygiene. By this I mean living sensibly — getting the proper amount of sleep and rest and recreation. People forget that the brain is a delicate and complicated bit of apparatus, and that it should be given care and consideration. Today many of us work too long hours, then stay up much too late. We would be much healthier if we were always in bed by 10 p.m. Our vacations may be so strenuous that we get no real rest or recreation and do not store up energy. Many people, also, abuse their nerves by smoking and drinking too much.

Many nervous persons wear themselves out on nonessential activities. They put too much energy and thought into doing things that another person does almost automatically. That is why they get so little done and become so terribly tired doing it. Dr. W. J. Mayo, carrying on a huge surgical and consultant practice, administering and building up a huge institution, lecturing and writing and serving on many boards, never seemed hurried or impatient. As he once told me, he tried never to waste energy or emotion on things that did not count.

Years ago a woman gave me the key to nervous breakdowns. I asked her why she, who had wealth and little to do, was so worn out. She said, "I wear *myself* out." She wore herself out with petty worries.

Often I find people wasting energy on needless conflicts — especially with themselves. They are full of resentments, animosities, hates, jealousies, envies. Blessed is the man or woman who goes through life easily — not irritable, touchy, impatient, irascible. It is wonderful how helpful this way of life is to the nervous system; and it is wonderful how much energy it leaves free for useful work.

I admire my sensible daughter who is never ruffled by the ceaseless activity of her two little boys. She says, "I would much rather have them active and into everything than sickly or apathetic." One day when she left a can of paint within reach of the baby, and he spilled it on the floor, her only comment was that she should have had more sense than to leave it where he could reach it. As a result of such serenity, she always has energy to spare to run a house, play tennis, swim and engage in civic affairs.

If we want calm nerves we must not nurse resentments and jealousies or indulge in envy. In every business one can find envious men who spend more time trying to hold back the leaders among their associates than they spend in studying and working to advance themselves. How much energy they waste and how bad it is for their nerves! I have seen envy of this type wreck a man's health.

One of the greatest curses of life today, and one of the greatest breeders of nervousness, is working under tension. The late Stewart Edward White once built himself a cabin in the California Sierras. An old mountaineer used to come and watch him. One day, as White was sawing violently at a log, the mountaineer remarked that White sawed like all city fellows, going as fast as he could to get the log sawed. "Now," said the old man, "when *I* saw, I just saws."

All of us with tense nerves could almost cure ourselves by learning to "just saw." We must learn to tackle just the job in hand and stay with it quietly. I often have said to my secretary, if she could see in one pile all the letters she is going to write in the next ten years, she might want to jump out the window. But by writing them one at a time, the job is bearable.

When Will Rogers was asked what he'd do if he had only five days to live, he said he'd live each day one at a time. All of us would do well to learn to live each day in a sort of compartment, not weeping over the mistakes of the past or holding constant post-mortems over them, and not worrying about the morrow. A man can work efficiently in this way. All he needs then is to do quickly and as well as possible the work that lies right at hand. It is helpful, also, to learn to tackle a difficult job without hesitation and get it done. Many nervous persons break down after putting off work that must be done.

The same goes for indecision. Nervous persons could save themselves worlds of now-wasted energy if they would only learn to make decisions quickly — and make them stick. Mayor

LaGuardia used to call after a man who had just gotten a decision from him about a matter, "And don't bring that back to me!"

A wonderful saver of energy is Sir William Osler's trick which he called "burning one's own smoke." He meant that we should not indulge in the miserable habit of taking out on others our discomforts, griefs and annoyances.

I belong to the Sierra Club of California, which each year takes 200 members into the high mountains. Their most important but unwritten bylaw goes something like this: "Thou shalt never utter the least word of complaint if it rains all day and all night, or if the pack train is late and thy food does not arrive until 10 p.m." Many a night I have seen the party wet, cold, hungry and without shelter, but always there was fun and good humor and never any grousing. Among those people to "crab" is the unpardonable sin.

There is another hint that we can take from the teachings of Osler, and that is to cultivate equanimity and serenity. As he said, we must learn not to be too upset by the pinpricks — and even the big shocks — of life. We must learn to take them in our stride. As one writer said so wisely and well: "O Lord, grant me the serenity to accept the things I cannot change; the courage to change the things I can; and the wisdom to know the difference."

Satchel's Secret ·

In *Collier's,* Satchel Paige, the famous baseball player, gave his six rules for staying young:

1. Avoid fried meats which angry up the blood.

2. If your stomach disputes you, lie down and pacify it with cool thoughts.

3. Keep the juices flowing by jangling around gently as you move.

4. Go very light on the vices, such as carrying on in society. The social ramble ain't restful.

5. Avoid running at all times.

6. Don't look back. Something might be gaining on you.

Making Habits

Work for You

Condensed from "Psychology: Briefer Course"

William James

"Habit a second nature? Habit is ten times nature," the Duke of Wellington exclaimed; and the degree to which this is true no one can appreciate as well as a veteran soldier. Daily drill and years of discipline make a man over in most of his conduct.

Habit is the flywheel of society, its most precious conserving agent. The great thing, then, is to make our nervous system our ally instead of our enemy. We must make automatic and habitual, as early as possible, as many useful actions as we can, and guard against growing into ways that are disadvantageous as we guard against the plague. The more of the details of our daily life we can hand over to the effortless custody of automatism, the more our higher powers of mind will be set free for their proper work. There is no more miserable person than one in whom nothing is habitual but indecision, and for whom the lighting of every cigar, the drinking of every cup, the time of rising and going to bed every day, and the beginning of every bit of work, are subjects of deliberation. Half the time of such a man goes to deciding or regretting matters which ought to be so ingrained in him as practically not to exist for his consciousness at all.

In the acquisition of a new habit, or the leaving off of an old one, there are four great maxims to remember: First, *we must take care to launch ourselves with as strong an initiative as possible*. Accumulate all possible circumstances which reinforce the right motives; make engagements incompatible with the old way; take a public pledge, if the case allows; in short, envelop your resolution with every aid you know. This will give your new beginning such momentum that the temptation to break down will not occur as soon as it otherwise might; and every day a breakdown is postponed adds to the chances of its not occurring at all.

Second, *never suffer an exception to occur till the new habit is securely rooted in your life.* Each lapse is like letting fall a ball of string which one is carefully winding up; a single slip undoes more than a great many turns will wind up again. Continuity of training is the great means of making the nervous system act infallibly right.

Success at the outset is imperative. Failure is apt to dampen the energy of all future attempts, whereas past successes nerve one to future vigor. Goethe said to a man who consulted him about an enterprise but mistrusted his own powers: "Ach! You need only blow on your hands!" And the remark illustrates the effect on Goethe's spirits of his own habitually successful career.

The question of tapering off in abandoning such habits as drink comes under this head, and is a question about which experts differ in individual cases. In the main, however, all expert opinion would agree that abrupt acquisition of the new habit is the best way, *if there be a real possibility of carrying it out.* We must be careful not to give the will so stiff a task as to ensure its defeat at the outset; but *provided one can stand it,* a sharp period of suffering, and then a free time is the best thing to aim at, whether in giving up a habit like drinking, or in simply changing one's hours of rising or of work. It is surprising how soon a desire will die if it be *never* fed.

"One must first learn to proceed firmly before one can begin to make oneself over again," writes Dr. Bahnsen. "He who every day makes a fresh resolve is like one who, arriving at the edge of the ditch he is to leap, forever stops and returns for a fresh run. Without *unbroken* advance there is no such thing as *accumulation* of positive forces."

The third maxim is: *Seize the first possible opportunity to act on every resolution you make.* It is not in the moment of their forming, but in the moment of their producing *motor effects* that resolutions communicate the new "set" to the brain. No matter how full a reservoir of *maxims* one may possess, and no matter how good one's *sentiments* may be, if one has not taken advantage of every concrete opportunity to *act,* one's character may remain entirely unaffected for the better. With mere good intentions hell is proverbially paved. And this is an obvious consequence of the principles we have laid down. A "character," as J. S. Mill says, "is a completely fashioned will"; and a will, in the sense in which he means it, is an aggregate of tendencies to act in a firm, prompt and definite way upon all the principal emergencies of life.

A tendency to act becomes effectively ingrained in us only in proportion to the frequency with which the actions actually occur, and the brain "grows" to their use. When a resolve or a fine glow of feeling is allowed to evaporate without bearing practical fruit it is worse than a chance lost; it works so as positively to hinder the discharge of future resolutions and emotions. There is no more contemptible human character than that of the nerveless sentimentalist and dreamer, who spends his life in a weltering sea of sensibility and emotion, but who never does a manly concrete deed. The weeping of the Russian lady over the fictitious personages in the play, while her coachman is freezing to death outside, is the sort of thing that everywhere happens on a less glaring scale. Never should we suffer ourselves to have an emotion at a play, concert, or upon reading a book, without expressing it afterward in some active way. Let the expression be the least thing in the world — speaking genially to one's grandmother, or giving up one's seat in a car, if nothing more heroic offers — but let it not fail to take place.

If we let our emotions evaporate, they get into a way of evaporating. Similarly, if we often flinch from making an effort, before we know it the effort-making capacity is gone; and if we suffer the wandering of our attention, presently it will wander all the time. As the fourth practical maxim, we may, then, offer something like this: *Keep the faculty of effort alive in you by a little gratuitous exercise every day.* That is, be systematically ascetic or heroic in little unnecessary points, do every day or two something for no other reason than that you would rather not do it, so that when the hour of dire need draws nigh, it may find you nerved and trained to stand the test. Asceticism of this sort is like the insurance a man pays on his house. The tax does him no good at the time and possibly may never bring him a return. But if the fire does come, his having paid it will be his salvation from ruin. So with the man who has daily inured himself to habits of concentrated attention, energetic volition, and self-denial in unnecessary things. He will stand like a tower when everything rocks around him, and when his softer fellow mortals are winnowed like chaff.

The hell to be endured hereafter, of which theology tells, is no worse than the hell we make for ourselves in this world by habitually fashioning our characters in the wrong way. If we realize the extent to which we are mere walking bundles of habits, we would give more heed to their formation. We are spinning our own fates, good or evil, and never to be undone. Every smallest stroke of virtue or of vice leaves its never so little scar. The drunken Rip van Winkle in Jefferson's play excuses himself for every fresh dereliction by saying, "I won't count this time!" Well! he may not count it, and a kind Heaven may not count it: but it is being counted none the less. Down among his nerve cells and fibers the molecules are counting it, registering it and storing it up to be used against him when the next temptation comes. Nothing we ever do is, in strict scientific literalness, wiped out. Of course this has its good side as well as its bad one. As we become permanent drunkards by so many separate drinks, so we become saints in the moral, and experts in the practical and scientific spheres, by so many separate acts and hours of work. Let no one have anxiety about the upshot of his education, whatever its line may be. If he keep faithfully busy each hour of the working day, he may safely leave the final result to itself. He can with perfect certainty count on waking up some fine morning, to find himself one of the competent ones of his generation, in whatever pursuit he may have singled out.

LOVE is not blind — it sees more, not less. But because it sees more, it is willing to see less.

— Rabbi Julius Gordon, *Your Sense of Humor* (Didier)

I Learned to Conquer Grief

Condensed from The Atlanta Journal
and Constitution Magazine   Catherine Marshall

W HEN Peter Marshall was pastor of the West-minster Presbyterian Church in Atlanta, we had a close friend who had known much sorrow. She used to look quizzically at Peter and me — young as we were, very much in love, fresh in the enthusiasm of our faith in the goodness of God.

"Neither of you has ever had any real trouble," she would say. "You're bound to have some sooner or later. I wonder if you will feel then as you do now?"

In the years which followed, we had our share of trouble — much illness, and finally my husband's premature death at 47. But today I still feel as we did then. In fact, I believe in God's love more firmly than ever, because now my faith has stood trial.

Trouble of some kind, especially bereavement, is the common experience of mankind. Since my husband's death, many people have written me to ask: How does one endure it? How does one keep one's faith and deal with it constructively? Let me quote one typical letter which reveals a number of quite human reactions to grief:

"My wife, Marie, died three years ago. I just don't know how I've gotten through the agony of separation since then. People are always saying, 'Time heals,' but in my case each day is worse than the last.

CATHERINE MARSHALL is the widow of Peter Marshall, who was one of the most widely known and popular chaplains of the U. S. Senate. *A Man Called Peter,* Mrs. Marshall's biography of her husband, has sold hundreds of thousands of copies and also has been made into an outstandingly successful moving picture.

"I've tried plunging into work 16 hours a day. But everything seems futile without Marie. I try to pray, but my prayers just hit the ceiling and bounce back. What good purpose could God have had in taking Marie and leaving me here alone?"

First, let me say that I deeply sympathize with all who have suffered thus. Sorrow is a wound in the personality, as real as any physical mutilation. After a time, during busy hours, one can forget the pain. Then tiny things bring it back: opening a drawer and coming across a Christmas card written in a well-known hand; the sight of a distant figure reminiscent of a well-beloved form, wearing the same kind of slouch hat. And suddenly, the old pain is back with stabbing force.

But though I sympathize, I have learned that the first really helpful step is to face up to the fact that your grief is essentially selfish. Most of us grieve not for the interrupted happiness of the one who died but because of our own loneliness and need. Sorrow is usually interlaced with self-pity. Facing up to this squarely for the sin it is, is like opening a window to let a breath of fresh air into a fetid room. We must deal with this selfishness as we deal with all other sins: by confessing it to God and asking His forgiveness and release. Such a confession requires stern action of oneself at a time when the heart is sore, but it is more healing than all the expressions of sympathy from others.

Everyone bereaved goes through a period of sharp questioning and self-reproach: "I wasn't sympathetic and understanding enough. Why didn't I show more love and gratitude while he was alive?" There is one healthy road out of this self-reproach. If your conscience bothers you about any past mistakes or failures, deal with them as you dealt with self-pity. Confess them one by one to God, have them freely forgiven and forget them even as God has promised to do.

Few people avoid this merciless self-reproach. The only healthy road out of it is to face up to life as it is, not as we wish it might have been. For the God I know is a realist, and He expects us to be realists too.

I often wonder how those who during sunny days can't be bothered with God manage to survive sorrow. I have found, in time of trouble, that there is no substitute for Him. For grief is sickness of the spirit, and God alone is physician to the spirit.

But, my typical correspondent asked, "What good purpose could God have had in taking Marie and leaving me here alone?"

The problem of evil — why a good God lets good people suffer — is forever with us. Certainly I have no pat answer. But we must remember that this old earth is enemy-occupied territory. Disease and death are of the enemy — not of a loving Father. Yet I do believe that when Marie was stricken God had some plan by which He could bring real good out of it.

Admittedly, it takes courage and no little faith to take the next constructive step: hunt for the open door, the new creative purpose, rather than stand weeping before the closed door of grief. But God is the Creator. It isn't possible for Him to be negative. If we are to coöperate with His purposes (the only way of getting our prayers answered) we too must be creative and positive. For God's way of binding up our broken hearts will be to give us worthwhile work to do in the world.

At one time I did not think life worth living without my husband. Yet I can testify that today I am truly happy with a deep, satisfying contentment. That happiness by no means dishonors Peter; it is exactly as he would have it.

How did that come about? I took the steps of confession I have mentioned. Then I prayed that this tragedy which I did not understand would nonetheless "work together for good." God has answered that prayer in an astonishing way.

Once during a long illness I wrote in my journal, "One of my deepest dreams is to be a writer. Through my writing I would like to make a contribution to my time and generation." Less than a month after Peter's death, it was as if God put a pencil in my hand and said, "Go ahead and write. Make your contribution. I promise to bless what you write." And He has blessed every attempt, beyond all imagining.

Something else even more wonderful came of this new-found career. Peter and I were drawn closer together than ever before. And through a divine alchemy my writing has become the vehicle for continuing Peter's earthly ministry. Many people who have read what I have written about my husband say that they have been profoundly helped by his words and the example of his deeds. In so-called "death," his ministry has been widened, deepened, "multiplied by infinity."

And, as a final benediction, slowly, imperceptibly there has come into my life the definite feeling of still being loved, cherished and cared-for. This I cannot explain. I only know it is a great reality. It has become the most comforting and sustaining force of my life.

I would not have you think that there is anything unique about my case. The help for which I prayed awaits your prayer. God's answer for you will not be the answer He had for me. It will be made to fit your needs, your own dreams, by a God who loves you personally.

Copyright 1953 by The Reader's Digest Association, Inc. (July 1953 issue)
Condensed from The Atlanta Journal and Constitution Magazine, March 22, 1953

The Understanding Heart

Sir William Osler, visiting one of London's leading children's hospitals, noticed that in a convalescent ward all the children were clustered at one end of the room dressing their dolls, playing games and playing in the sandbox — all except one little girl, who sat forlornly on the edge of her high, narrow bed, hungrily clutching a cheap doll.

The great physician looked at the lonely little figure, then at the ward nurse. "We've tried to get Susan to play," the nurse whispered, "but the other children just won't have anything to do with her. You see, no one comes to see her. Her mother is dead, and her father has been here just once — he brought her that doll. The children have a strange code. Visitors mean so much. If you don't have any visitors, you are ignored."

Sir William walked over to the child's bed and asked, in a voice loud enough for the others to hear, "May I sit down, please?" The little girl's eyes lit up. "I can't stay very long this visit," Osler went on, "but I have wanted to see you so badly." For five minutes he sat talking with her, even inquiring about her doll's health and solemnly pulling out his stethoscope to listen to the doll's chest. And as he left, he turned to the youngster and said in a carrying voice, "You won't forget our secret, will you? And mind, don't tell anyone."

At the door he looked back. His new friend was now the center of a curious and admiring throng.

— Contributed by John P. Eaton

Every Child Has a Gift

By Hughes Mearns

Author of "Creative Youth" and "The Creative Adult"

I⁣T WAS over 50 years ago, and I was not much more than a boy myself when I faced my first class. I went into teaching simply because the job paid enough to keep me until I could find something better. But those boys and girls captured me at the start. What I began to learn from them kept me in teaching for the remainder of my active life.

To relieve their tension at meeting a new teacher, I joked with them about my own ignorance. They laughed, but not too loud. I asked them what I was supposed to teach them, and they named some of the subjects. "Oh, yes, and physiology," one small girl piped up.

"What's that?" I asked.

Laughter, but pleasant and friendly. "It's about the bones," she reported rapidly, "and the blood and the intestines and the stomach."

"Ugh!" I interrupted. That amused them immensely. I pondered, "Physiology? I don't believe I could even spell the word." Then they did laugh, a roar and a scream of laughter.

A teacher looked into the room. "Any trouble?" she asked.

"Why, no," I replied.

"I heard a laugh," she snapped.

Later the children told me about whippings at home whenever they got a low mark in "conduct" — a common practice in the late '90's.

"From now on," I said, "each of you will get the highest

mark in conduct." This had the eventual effect of making that class the best-behaved in the school. To bring out the best in a child, I was discovering, one must be on his side, a defender against adult-imposed customs aimed at suppressing his good natural instincts.

After school those boys and girls gathered around my desk and stayed until the janitor's sweeping drove them home. In those after-school meetings I came upon a treasure of unsuspected gifts. I found a boy who had invented quick ways of adding. He could add up a column of figures as fast as one could call out the numbers. There was a girl who drew continuously in her beloved sketchbook. I am glad that I did not order her to stop that nonsense and attend to me! The famous William Chase later opened to her a career as an artist. Here, too, I came upon the boy with absolute pitch. With his back to the piano he could name any note struck on the instrument.

Though few children are geniuses, all children, I discovered, possess gifts which may become their special distinction. A thousand talents await recognition! In the able ones who decline to push into first place; in the slow worker who eventually does a superior job; in those with special interests beyond school demands, like entomology or stamp collecting; in those with a flair for decoration or design; in the natural housekeeper. The young inventor may be so absorbed in his work that he neglects important studies; the skillful user of tools may need adult appreciation to protect him from the snobbishness of the book learners, including teachers.

I became convinced that someone should stand by in the early years to watch for and foster these natural endowments. It is not enough to discern a native gift; it must be enticed out again and again. Above all it must be protected against the annihilating effect of social condemnation. The fair-minded boy may be called "softie" by his mates; the polite girl be accused of posing for adult favors; the budding scholar may be discouraged by the epithet "bookworm." All too often adults encourage only a limited range of traits, those commonly believed to be essential for success, to the detriment of the whole vast range of gifts which children possess.

Often it is the seemingly unimportant gift which is most useful in life. The ability to communicate confidence may at times serve a doctor better than his medical skill; a passionate love of justice, discouraged as forwardness in a child, may one day contribute more to a lawyer's success than the ability to prepare a brief.

This discovery opened for me a way into the secret hopes and delights of childhood. With like-minded teachers, I helped to found a private school which specialized in discovering and encouraging hidden abilities. We watched the children in their recess periods — not for the bad traits, which we noted, but for the good traits that show up best in free play.

A fifth-grade boy who was uncommunicative in class had been labeled stupid by his teacher. I watched him as the catcher in a sand-lot ball game where his vocabulary was profuse, strident and authoritative. He kept his team together and won the game by continuous invective behind the plate. I asked him to write me an account of that game, but insisted he do it in his own colorful language.

Here was a naturally fluent lad who had been driven into silence by unsympathetic correction. Now I made him feel that his rough way of telling a story had merit. After a year or two his lapses into slang were eliminated. Later that "stupid" boy had no difficulty with college-entrance examinations. Approval is a powerful stimulant to the forces of self-education.

"But how," I am constantly asked, "can parents go about discovering unsuspected gifts in their children?"

By cool observation. Stop trying to make children what they eventually ought to be, and see what they really are now. Set aside the reproving eye and the authoritative command, and substitute impersonal observation as if these were some other person's children.

Once I told a mother that her boy had given me a long, stumbling lecture on insects. He had made a considerable collection of beetles and had read a lot about them. She asked me why I had let him bother me. "Oh," I said, "he *was* boring, but it is most important that someone should share his interest just now in order to keep it alive." I watched that boy on into high school. There he shone as a high-ranking member of the science club.

The author of some distinguished books writes to me that I was an inspiration in his boyhood. All I did that I now remember was to accept from him a daily outpouring of his writings. I never stopped his early effusions with a word of instruction. There would be time enough for that later. What he needed at the moment was encouragement.

The best time for watching children is when they are off guard: on picnics, at sand-lot games, during visits to places of public interest, at young people's parties, in the informal hours of home life. Here the often-overlooked gifts are exposed: wholehearted sharing, grit to contest against odds, natural leadership, care for the younger and the weak, cheerfulness, an interest in planning.

I think that parents should be as interested in having their children become members of the Scouts, the Campfire Girls and the like as in their getting high grades in school. The important thing is to expose children to a multiplicity of activities and interests, so that their inherent gifts will have as many chances as possible to show themselves.

Besides the discovery and encouragement of an aptitude, it goes without saying that opportunities for its exercise should be made convenient. The wise parent will see that the raw materials are at hand. Parents who take a childish interest to heart will go out of their way (and even stop the car) to aid a quest. It may be for rocks or for snakes or for words; it may involve a house-wrecking search for some secret in chemistry. Whatever it is, let it develop.

For some adults, discovering hidden gifts in children will demand a change in personality; for self-effacement in an adult is what draws the child out. Children think about the world, and come to worthy conclusions — their own. They think about themselves and those around them, and come to worthy conclusions — their own. The parent who values these judgments as steppingstones to higher judgments will have the enjoyment of seeing unsuspected gifts appear and grow. It is hard to learn to listen, even to one's own children, but the fascination of the game is worth every effort.

How to Get Along with Older People

Condensed from
Maclean's Magazine

Julietta K. Arthur

Even the most saintly have asked at some time, "Why are so many old people difficult to get along with?" Dr. Erwin Ackerknecht of the University of Wisconsin believes he has the answer: "Two thirds of old persons feel unwanted, and many of them are right."

Psychologically, our society is geared to the young. Movies, sports, advertisements, fashions all stress the importance of youth, and we give the elderly less of a role to play than any other older generation ever had. At the same time the life span is increasing. This extra time can be years of tragedy unless younger people help their elders overcome the frustrations of old age.

The day when some older person's attitudes or actions conflict with your own, stop and ask: What do older people want to get out of life?

Years ago a member of the Society of Friends summed up the basic needs of the aged simply and succinctly: "Somewhere to live, something to do and someone to care."

How can you help your relatives fulfill these basic desires? You can do nothing at all unless you put yourself in an older person's place. To do so you must rid yourself of the misconceptions about age.

63

One misconception is that old age makes people different. Most of us assume that putting on grandmotherhood automatically assures a halo of sweetness and light. Or we take the opposite view: that old age makes people crabbed.

Any elderly person has taken a long time to get the way he is, and he is going to remain that way. The father who was a young autocrat at the breakfast table will remain so. The mother who was frivolous and vain in her younger years is not going to turn automatically into a self-effacing granny. And, of course, the man or woman who has always pulled his own oar is going to try to keep on doing it.

Another major misconception is that the old like to be in a safe and cozy nest. This probably accounts for more unhappy relationships than anything else. No older person likes to have his life planned for him, whether his children tuck him away in an old people's home or put him in a gilded cage.

Dr. Lillien J. Martin, who entered the field of old-age counseling when she herself was 69 and continued in it till she died at 91, used to say many older people are forced into loss of self-assurance by their offspring. "Children," she said, "may coddle aged parents not only out of concern for them but also because they really want their parents to live restricted lives so they will not interfere."

Most older people, Dr. Martin found, are remarkably tough and capable, even if they have physical limitations. In our anxiety to spare them worry and make them comfortable we underestimate their capacities and undermine their initiative. Plan with, not for, old people. To accept direction — very often correction — from those you used to have authority over in the diaper and romper stage is a soul-trying process.

When we say "tolerance must be mutual," we usually mean we expect older people to abandon some cherished activity which interferes with one of ours. Most of us can say of a teenager who has difficulty in adjusting to life: "It is because he is an adolescent. He'll get used to things." People of 70 or 80 are also entitled to have periods of adjustment: they have spent a lifetime accumulating habits and patterns.

If Grandfather refuses to stop smoking in bed, or Grandmother won't change the fashion of her clothes, neither one is doing it to annoy you. They may be biologically too old to change their ways, or they may be making an effort to adjust themselves and haven't yet succeeded. If you force them, the result is likely to be a bitter, dejected individual.

There is no reason to feel guilty if you are apprehensive about sharing your home with your parents or in-laws. There are other ways of honoring your father and mother besides giving them a place at your fireside. Nor need you feel you must do for your older relatives what they did for theirs. Two or three generations had a much better chance, 50 years ago, of living amicably together. When households overflowed with children and space, there was always ample work and ample room for elderly relatives. Machine housekeeping has taken away much of that solace of the old.

If your older relative wants to cling to the living quarters where he's been content for so long, stand up for him. Older people value their own homes first, and privacy at all costs anywhere.

If you are the one on whose shoulders it will fall to make a decision there is only one safe rule to follow. If an aging individual doesn't *want* to live with you or someone else, it is more economical, in terms of the eventual strain that will develop on both sides, to help him stay where he wants to be, even if dollars-and-cents expenditure is greater.

Where an elderly person lives is not the major consideration. Making him know he is valued is all that counts. You can ask advice or confide your troubles to him. You can make such a simple gesture as asking a relative to write down his memories of family history or to preserve family heirlooms for the grand-children. One woman stimulated her whole community when she asked people over 70 to talk before her club about their relics of pioneer days. This exhibition, now held annually, gives young people a chance to hear about local history and to respect their elders who shaped it.

If you want to get along with older people, whether they live in your home or not, discuss all grievances openly, even if there's danger of hurting their feelings. If you treat the elderly as if they are too eccentric or too old-fashioned to know what to do, you will only strengthen their conviction that they are being abused. If you bring pressure to bear through doctors, nurses or family counselors when they are facing a devastating break in long-established routine, they will feel you are persecuting them.

To prevent this, be candid. Older people can stand more shocks than younger ones think they can. What they can't bear is to feel baffled and helpless because relatives too often act as if crises in family life ought not to be discussed with them.

Learning to live in amity with older people is a challenge that is worth more than passing study. For, even if it doesn't face you right now, remember that you are going to be "an older person" yourself someday.

Copyright 1954 by The Reader's Digest Association, Inc. (August 1954 issue)
Condensed from Maclean's Magazine, April 15, 1954
In expanded form this material is included in the book,
"How to Help Older People," published by J. B. Lippincott Co., Philadelphia 5, Pa.

The Vague Specific

WOMEN HAVE a conversational peculiarity which I have named the Vague Specific. For example, I overheard a conversation between my wife and the maid.

"Here," my wife said, "you can put these out there somewhere."

"With the others?"

"No," said my wife, decisively. "Put them with those things behind the others."

The terrifying thing was that each knew exactly what the other meant.

I could make an indefinite list of Vague Specifics my wife pulls on me, such as: "Do you remember that time we were at the shore, and it rained?" (We've been to the shore 14 or 15 times, and it always rains.) Or, "What was the name of that couple we met that night?"

I come home from work and my wife greets me: "The men came today." Once I thought I had a system figured out to beat her at that one. I asked (craftily), "What did you tell them?" But that's where my system backfired, because she answered: "I told them to go ahead." The only satisfaction I got was that, whatever the men had gone ahead and done, it was going to cost me money.

— Richard B. Gehman in *Collier's*

THE ART OF
STAYING AT HOME

By Charles W. Ferguson   *Condensed from Southwest Review*

"STAY-AT-HOME" is a term commonly used for the person who *has* to stay at home. It conjures up untidy visions of the aged and infirm, the shut-ins, the unsociables. Yet there is an art to staying at home. And a good many of us, tired of aimless visiting, too much bridge and strenuous journeys to nowhere in particular, would like to practice it. We should like to stay at home with a greater sense of fitness and fun.

The kind of home you have, its size or its magnificence, is of slight importance. You don't need a vaulted temple for gracious living. Nor are there any hard-and-fast rules. Some find that ceremony helps — customs that lend dignity and importance to routine. I remember once running out of gas in the Connecticut hills and finding a retired broker all alone at table, wearing a dinner coat. It was a habit, and he said it seemed to make things more important. One young couple read aloud to each other. A family I often visit play fine phonograph records after dinner several evenings a week. Another couple find great amusement in reading the dictionary.

Practices of this sort, however, are auxiliaries at best. It is much more essential to understand, first of all, that a man's house is his castle, a refuge where he can do as he pleases. Obviously the first great step in mastering the art of staying home is to build up fortifications which make home a place of privacy and luxurious solitude.

The best thing is to have a schedule of privacy as rigid as your social calendar and stick with it at all costs. It is not stretching the truth too far, when someone calls up and asks if you are doing anything that evening, to say that you *are* — even if you intend only to read that book you've put off six months. And it can be gently suggested to friends that on certain nights you are simply not at home to anyone but yourself. Nights in are just as important as nights out: indeed, the former add endless zest to the latter.

Yet so few of us will pull up the drawbridge at sunset! We are like the woman Arnold Bennett speaks of — alive only in public. Our days and our nights are spent in being in public, or in preparing to be in public, or in recovering from the effects of being in public. Thoreau points out in one of his lightning flashes that "society is commonly too cheap. We meet at very short intervals, not having had time to acquire any new value for each other. We meet at meals three times a day and give each other a new taste of that old musty cheese that we are. We have had to agree on a certain set of rules, called etiquette and politeness, to make this frequent meeting tolerable. We live thick and stumble over one another."

Once you have the idea of the home as a refuge, the change wrought in your activities is automatic. Then comes quite naturally the will to be yourself. You begin to learn the pleasures of voluntary confinement, of taking the veil in the quietness of your own house. There is nothing anti-social about this attitude. "Our first duty to society," the Abbé Dimnet once said, "is to be somebody — that is to say, be ourselves; and we can only be ourselves if we are often enough by ourselves."

The first concrete thing likely to result from staying at home is the discovery that you are doing something you've always wanted to do. One couple have spent the past few months making a private guidebook for a trip they plan one day to take through Europe. Another couple have been spending their evenings classifying the negatives of hundreds of pictures taken in days when they roamed freely. There is something you want to do; but you'll never do it until you learn to stay at home.

You've always wanted to learn French. Or you like geography. Or you think you can write or draw or do something with sculpture, or make furniture.

But to be constantly puttering about the house is still not the kind of solitude of which I am speaking. It would seem to most of us old-fashioned and queer if we set aside a definite period of the day in which to meditate. Yet, while "thinking can be dull, it also can be a glorious and exciting adventure," to quote Justice Holmes, who was a past master of the art of staying at home.

The first experiments in thinking creatively will probably result in disheartening failure. "That brain of yours will be hopping all over the place," Arnold Bennett wrote, "and every time it hops you must bring it back by force to its original position. The mind can be conquered only by never leaving it idle, undirected, masterless, to play at random like a child in the streets after dark."

It might help us to realize that thinking, after all, is only a process of talking to oneself — intelligently. When you learn to talk to yourself coherently, you will, if you persevere, discover a lively pastime. You will be forced to talk to yourself about something important. The reason conversation is at such a low ebb just now is that we do not know how to talk to ourselves.

Seated alone in your room, you begin to talk to yourself. You have innumerable vague notions about war, for instance, but you perhaps have never held a conversation with yourself about it. Try it. You must be exact — marshaling your notions, reconnoitering the subject, pitting contentions against each other. By the end of the evening you will be weary, but you will be better able to talk to others the next day.

Solitude is not always a matter of being grimly edifying. Much has been said in favor of purposive reading — reading with some lofty aim — but there is also reading for fun. It might be well if for a while we allayed our itch for culture and came to realize that there is real sport in the contacts of the mind with new ideas, in the repartee of great authors, in the free play of our minds with books and essays. Reading for fun by no means implies that the reading matter be frothy. I can imagine that some folks would enjoy reading philosophy for fun. Others could take history, others science, but in any case they would not read out of any compulsion of convention.

It is a struggle to learn any art, much more of a struggle to master it. It cannot be done in ten easy lessons. But you must admit this art of staying at home is important enough to be worth trying. Its cultivation would help solidify family life, stabilize our thinking, tone us up generally and develop self-sufficiency and serenity. What is required most of all is the realization that the gadabouts are missing something, that the satisfactions of a flea are greatly exaggerated. He is a happy man who has simplified his tastes to the point where a good book and a fire and a quiet evening are for him not a chore or a sign of increasing age, but a preference and a badge of wisdom and distinction.

Food to Grow On

No one seems to agree about what a well-balanced diet for children is, but here's what my two-year-old Johnnie eats:

Breakfast. Three bites of cereal, a sip of milk, a handful of rice (raw; he got it out of the box when the doorbell rang), a greenish ribbon, origin unknown (I saw it just before it disappeared), a dog biscuit (stolen from the dog) and a peach.

Lunch. A soft-cooked egg, half a glass of milk, two bites of soap (he wanted more, but I caught him), a rubber band (I got that just before it went down the hatch), and some toast (spread liberally with chlorophyll tooth paste when I was concentrating on the washing).

Dinner. A hamburger steak (complete with onions and ketchup because his daddy uses them and he won't eat it unless he gets the same), some peas, one bite of cottage cheese (deposited later on the rug), a glass of milk and a half bottle of hair oil (which he took on while his daddy and I were watching television).

My son is a healthy, red-cheeked boy, heavier and taller than other children of his age in the neighborhood, and the doctor says his diet is responsible.

— Letter from Mrs. D. W. McCarthy, in the Wichita, Kans., *Beacon*

The Delightful Game

of Conversation *Condensed from Your Life*

Gelett Burgess

I N SAN FRANCISCO once I belonged to a small group which met weekly for the purpose of reviving the lost art of conversation. We realized that there is a fundamental principle underlying good talk. This principle — the basis of all good manners — is the avoidance of friction in social contacts, emotional friction caused by irritation, boredom, envy, egotism or ridicule. Here are some of the rules we finally adopted to guide our conversation and make it a delightful game.

1. *Avoid all purely subjective talk.* Don't dilate on your health, troubles, domestic matters; and never, never discuss your wife or husband. Streams of personal gossip and egotism destroy all objective discussion — of art, science, history, the day's news, sport, or whatever. Such chatter bores the listener, and the talker, repeating only what he already knows, learns nothing from others.

2. *Don't monopolize the conversation.* One of my friends was a laughing, attractive person, who told stories well — but too many of them. You roared with laughter, but after a while you grew restless and yearned for more quiet, comfortable talk with plenty of give and take. You couldn't help remembering what John Dryden said about those "who think too little, and who talk too much." Or what Sydney Smith wrote of Macaulay: "He has occasional flashes of silence, that make his conversation perfectly delightful."

3. *Don't contradict.* You may say, "I don't quite agree with

that," but flat contradiction is a conversation-stopper. One should seek to find points of agreement. In that way the subject develops in interest with each one's contribution. "That is the happiest conversation," said Samuel Johnson, "where there is no competition, but a calm quiet interchange of sentiments."

4. *Don't interrupt*. Of course when you throw a few grace notes into the talk, such as, "How wonderful!" or, "You mean she didn't know?" it doesn't put the train of conversation off the track. But to interpolate views of your own often leaves the speaker hanging uncomfortably in mid-sentence.

One perfect conversational dinner party is still alive in my memory. It was given in Boston by Mrs. James T. Fields, and there were six present — the ideal number for an intimate dinner; if you have more the conversation is apt to break up into separate side dialogues. Each of us talked and each of us listened. No one interrupted, no one contradicted, no one monologued. The affair had the charm and pleasing restfulness of music.

5. *Don't abruptly change the subject*. Some people, after patiently — and painfully — waiting for a talker to pause a moment, jump into the conversation with a totally new subject. In our Conversation Club it was an unwritten rule that after a person stopped talking there should be a brief silence in which to reflect, digest and appreciate what had been said. It is the proper tribute to anyone who has offered an idea for consideration.

6. *Show an active interest in what is said*. This brings out the best in a speaker. You need not only your ears to listen well, but your eyes, hands and even posture. I have often tested an article I have written by reading it aloud to friends. What they said about it never helped much, since one often liked what another didn't. But if their eyes went to a picture on the wall, if their fingers fiddled, I knew that the manuscript wasn't holding their interest and I marked the dull spots for revision.

There is no surer way to make people like you than to pay them the compliment of interest and sympathy. Prolong their subject, ask more about it, and they expand like flowers in the sun. Yet what usually happens is that, should you venture to describe some misfortune that has happened to you, others immediately narrate a similar mischance that they have suffered.

7. *After a diversion, bring back the subject*. Often while a subject is not yet fully considered it is lost in some conversational detour. There is no surer test of being able to converse well than to reintroduce this forgotten topic. This is not only polite and gracious, but it is the best evidence of real interest.

Of course, if it is your own story it is futile for you to bring it back to persons who have bypassed it. Let it go, but see that you don't commit their error.

8. *Don't make dogmatic statements of opinion*. The Japanese tea ceremony is perhaps the most refined social form ever practiced. It is a cult of self-effacement. One of the rules concerns conversation. It is considered vulgar to make any definite, decisive statement. One may speak of anything, but never with an expression of finality. The remark is left up in the air, for the next guest to enlarge upon, so that no one is guilty of forcing any personal opinion upon the others.

It is a good game, but difficult; try it some time with your friends. You may state facts as facts; but your application of them should be tentative, with such qualifications as "It seems to me," or "Isn't it possible that —" Those who really know things usually speak thus, "with meekness of wisdom," as St. James says, while the ignoramus is always for cut-and-dried pronouncements.

9. *Speak distinctly*. While I was a member of the executive committee of the Authors' League I was fascinated by the fact that those who spoke slowly and clearly dominated our meetings. High, hurried voices simply couldn't compete with Ellis Parker Butler's deliberate words, and his voice maintained his leadership for years. If you observe a group talking you'll find that the one with a low, controlled voice always gets the most respect. The eager, temperamental contenders dash up against it like waves against a rock, and the rock always wins.

10. *Avoid destructive talk*. We are all likely to make many unnecessary derogatory remarks. Evil, of course, must be condemned. But try to avoid the unnecessary criticism, the desire to raise a laugh through ridicule, the tendency to look on the unpleasant side of life. Cynical comments may sound clever, but they make others uncomfortable.

So much for the negative side of conversational rules. How can you create an agreeable conversation?

The secret is simple. To talk well one must think well. You must think underneath the subject, above it and all around it.

This kind of thinking is well illustrated in the conversation of baseball enthusiasts. Are they content with telling the score, the number of hits and runs? Not at all. They discuss a team's potentialities, the characteristics of the different players, the technique of the game. The same principle applies to all conversation. *Anyone who finds it hard to talk should learn to think about what he sees and hears and reads.* As you ponder, associate the subject with your own experience and observation.

To avoid falling into the rut of shop talk, enlarge your interests by making acquaintances engaged in pursuits other than your own. Develop a curiosity about what has so far been outside your range of knowledge. Read up on subjects that have interested you, that have been outside your field of view.

If you fertilize and enrich your thinking in such ways you need not worry about being able to converse well. Every new experience will make your talk more interesting and more valuable.

The Ways of the Lord . . .

This was scribbled almost a century ago by an anonymous soldier of the Confederacy:

I asked God for strength, that I might achieve — I was made weak, that I might learn humbly to obey.

I asked for help that I might do greater things — I was given infirmity, that I might do better things.

I asked for riches, that I might be happy — I was given poverty, that I might be wise.

I asked for all things, that I might enjoy life — I was given life, that I might enjoy all things.

I got nothing that I asked for — but everything I had hoped for.

Despite myself, my prayers were answered. I am, among all men, most richly blessed!   — Contributed by Oren Arnold

Try to vary the habitual tempo of your work and play

Change Your PACE

By Hilton Gregory   *Condensed from The Rotarian*

ALL OF US have experienced at one time or another the feeling of renewal that comes from a change of pace. We may be walking or driving along slowly, and something happens that makes us speed up. New sensations occur; new thoughts cross the mind. We become more alert. Or if we have been walking breathlessly beyond our pace there is a feeling of relief, even repose, in slowing down.

The pace that kills is the pace that never changes; frequent change of pace will keep us from tedium on one hand or apoplexy on the other.

For most of us a change of pace means slowing down, but in many activities we should speed up. We may walk and talk too fast but think and work too slowly.

Everyone in journalism knows that as a deadline approaches the reporter, the make-up man, the people on the copy desk all turn out better work in half the time it takes when there is no pressure. The acceleration releases latent powers. I have seen men, when there is time, bone for an hour over a title or a heading — conjuring up, as the slow mind at work will, dozens that are no good. But as the last hour approaches, when there is no time to dally, their minds click and the captions come in a flash. It is not mere speed that does the trick, but speed that follows deliberation.

Experts in charge of reading clinics point out that the best way to get something out of the printed page is to read it fast, to set about to see how quickly it can be intelligently covered, because the mind may wander when reading is too slow. The chances are that you should change your reading pace from one of leisurely inspection to one of concentrated, swift consideration. On the other hand, if you have allowed yourself to become a hit-and-run reader, you may need to give more time. No one pace is adequate in reading. There are books to be read hastily and others to be read with loving delay.

I have a nephew whose slowness is the despair of his teachers, not to mention his kin. At the age of nine he gets his work done in his own good time. The other morning his mother suggested with wisdom that he write a letter before going to school. His other letters had taken as much as a day, off and on, to compose. In this case, his time was limited to 20 minutes in which to write his grandmother everything he could think of. The result was the best letter he had ever done. It was the change of pace that did it, by putting emphasis upon the preciousness of time and the importance of using it to maximum effect.

We've been kidding ourselves too long with the notion that we are rushed to death. We are rushed with the wrong things. In these we ought to slow down, but in others speed up. "Slow and easy" is no motto for an interesting life, as some contend. Indeed slowness may be a deterrent; often a man can get further with a difficult job by plunging into it full steam.

Not infrequently a change of pace is in itself a means of learning. Years of using the typewriter steadily — added to the fact that I never learned to write as a child — recently made it almost imperative that I improve my longhand. I discovered that I had been rushing pellmell through my words. I disciplined myself to write plainly, meticulously. Associates testify gratefully that the improvement is a long step toward legibility. And what was once a chore has become a pastime.

Thus a change in tempo may increase enjoyment whether or not it improves our work. If you are doing something tedious, it may become fun if done at a changed speed. Many tasks — to mention only cleaning house and writing letters — are oppressive in part at least because they are time-consuming. But if we make them an affair of dashing cavalry our attitude changes. The job becomes an adventure, or a contest at least.

For, oddly enough, a job done at different speeds is not the same job at all. The motions and emotions connected with it are different. Many people who pine to change their jobs need only to change the pace with which they do their jobs — mix up their work and get variety into the tempo.

Change of pace is like what we call second wind; in moments of fatigue it sets up a fresh current of nervous energy. If you have been methodically moving around the house, making beds, dusting, sweeping, try shifting the flow of your energy into a different rhythm. Or in the office, vary rush typing with work at slower speed. As you work at any fatiguing task you'll find that change of tempo rewards you, like the second wind, with a glowing sense of power.

Nowhere in the simple acts of daily life does a change in pace make more difference than in eating. Most of us gulp our food, and we miss half the fun of eating. I was a fast eater, and so tried imagining that I was a slow-motion picture of myself. Then I really tasted for the first time foods I had been eating half-consciously all my life.

I live in one of the uncelebrated scenic spots of the United States. There are no travel folders to hymn its grandeur. Everyone rather accepts its charm as a matter of course, and one reason for this is that no one, save perhaps when mothering a new car, drives slowly enough to appreciate the region. Until I myself broke in a new car I never even saw an old tulip tree on the way to the station. Its top is broken by a generation of storms, some of its limbs are missing, yet it survives with a pride and strength that shame me in moments of trifling discouragement. It has been there for years but I never saw it while I was hellbent for nothing. And there is a cathedral of trees and rocks on the parkway not a mile from where I live — a place of quietness and strength. Even to glance at it thoughtfully in passing is to experience a moment of vespers. I had never been aware of this spot until I changed my pace.

Since in my work I have to talk a lot, I have fallen into the habit of talking rapidly. Lately I decided to alternate rapid speech with periods of slowing down, weighing each word, and letting its implications have full play. And this, I find, keeps the auditor's attention on edge, and makes me phrase more clearly the ideas I want to convey. But it does more — it affords me a new sense of confidence.

Haven't you, on the other hand, known dreary, hesitant people who ought to try talking fast for a change? While they fumble vaguely with facts, ideas and phrases, you'd like to jolt them into thinking a sentence swiftly through before they began it, so that words would follow one another with logical sequence and zip. Deliberate speeding up would not only add tremendously to their conversational effectiveness, but would also transform them by giving them a new and more sparkling personality.

In our method of thinking, above all, change of pace can be invaluable. The almost universal curse of worry is simply thought slowed down to a stumbling and circuitous walk. To think through and settle once for all a problem in the shortest possible time, and to act briskly and daringly on our decision, is to annihilate the problem of worry.

On the other hand, on busy days, try slowing down instead of speeding up. Linger over breakfast; pretend that you have a lifetime for the many things which must be crowded in before night. Live at slow motion. Instead of racing, make yourself stroll. And, paradoxically, when evening comes you will have actually done more work than if you had pushed yourself.

To live all one's life at *largo* would be deadly boring. The symphony you like or the musical composition that stirs you is neither fast nor slow throughout; it has as much variety in tempo as in mood. It is this in part that keeps your interest keyed to the theme.

If we are hectic and rushed it is not necessary to pull up stakes, move to the country and drive a horse to change the pace of living. It's not the city or business that wears us out; it's our response to it, our meeting life head-on without slowing down or speeding up. So if you are hitting a terrific pace, slow down. You don't have to slow down forever: it's the change you need. Or if you are going too slowly, if you are not alert but stodgy and graceless in your living, "step on it" a while. What's tedious in one speed may be delightful in another.

Three Steps to Personal Peace

By *Norman Vincent Peale, D.D.*

Pastor of Marble Collegiate Church, New York City

Condensed from "The Power of Positive Thinking"

AMERICANS are so keyed up nowadays that I, a minister, must report that it is almost impossible to put them to sleep with a sermon. It has been years since I have seen anyone asleep in church. And that is a sad situation.

Most of us don't realize how accelerated the rate of our lives has become, or the speed at which we are driving ourselves. Men and women are destroying their bodies by this pace — and, what is even more tragic, their minds and souls as well. For constant overstimulation produces poisons in the body and creates fatigue and emotional illness.

There are times when the only way to check this headlong pace is to stop — abruptly. I went to a certain city on a lecture date and was met at the train by a committee. I was rushed to a bookstore for one autographing party and then on to another. After that I rushed to a luncheon, rushed through it, and on to a meeting. After the meeting I rushed back to the hotel, where I was told I had 20 minutes to dress for dinner. While I was dressing, the telephone rang. "Hurry," the voice said, "we must get down to dinner."

"I'll be right down," I said.

I was about to rush from the room when suddenly I stopped. "What is this all about?" I asked myself.

I telephoned downstairs and said, "If you want to eat, go ahead. I'll be down after a while."

I took off my shoes, put my feet up on the table and just sat. Then I opened the Bible to the 121st Psalm: "I will lift up mine eyes unto the hills, from whence cometh my help." I read it slowly, aloud. Then I had a little talk with myself: "Come on now, slow down. God is here and His peace is touching you."

79

I shall never forget the sense of peace and personal mastery I had when I walked out of that room 15 minutes later. I had the glorious feeling of having taken control of myself emotionally. And all I had missed was the soup.

Everyone should insist upon not less than a quarter of an hour of absolute quiet every 24 hours. As Thomas Carlyle said: "Silence is the element in which great things fashion themselves." Go alone into the quietest place available and sit or lie down for 15 minutes. Think as little as possible. This may be difficult, at first, but practice will make it easier. Then try to listen for the deeper sounds of harmony and beauty and of God that are to be found in the essence of silence.

Go out some warm day and lie down on the earth. You will hear all manner of sounds, the wind in the trees and the murmur of insects; presently you will discover a well-regulated tempo. You can find it in church, and you can also find it in a factory. An industrialist in a large plant in Ohio told me that his best workmen are those who get into harmony with the rhythm of the machine on which they are working. To avoid tiredness and to have energy, feel your way into the essential rhythm that is in all things.

By the very words we use and the tone in which we use them we can talk ourselves into being nervous, high-strung, upset. Other words produce a tranquil state. The words of the Bible have a particularly therapeutic value. Drop them into your mind and allow them to "dissolve"; they will spread a healing balm over your spirit.

A salesman told me that on a business trip he had gone to his hotel room, terribly nervous. "I tried to write some letters," he said. "I paced the room, tried to read the paper — anything to get away from myself.

"Then I noticed the Bible on the dresser. I hadn't read one in years, but something impelled me — I opened the book to a Psalm. I read that one, then sat down and read another.

"Soon I came to the 23rd Psalm. I had learned it as a boy in Sunday school and was surprised that I still knew most of it by heart. I tried saying it over: 'He leadeth me beside the still waters. He restoreth my soul. . . .' I sat there repeating the words — and the next thing I knew I woke up.

"Only about 15 minutes had passed, but I was as refreshed as if I'd had a good night's sleep. Then I realized that for the first time in a long while I felt at peace."

Emotional control cannot, however, be developed by merely reading a book, although that is often helpful. The only sure method is by working at it regularly and persistently. The secret is to keep the mind quiet, avoid all hasty reactions, keep the tempo down.

Capt. Eddie Rickenbacker is a very busy man, but he manages to handle his responsibilities in a manner indicating reserves of power. I found one element of his secret quite by accident.

I was filming a program for television with him. We had been assured that the work could be done quickly, but the filming was delayed long beyond the time anticipated. The Captain showed no signs of agitation. He did not pace up and down or put in frantic calls to his office. He sat down in an old rocking chair, completely calm.

"I know how busy you are," I said. "How can you be so relaxed?"

"Oh, I just practice what *you* preach," he replied. "Come, sit down beside me." I pulled up another rocking chair and did a little relaxing on my own. Then Eddie gave me his formula to attain serenity. I now use it myself several times a day and find it effective.

First, collapse physically. Let go every muscle in the body. Form a mental picture of a huge burlap bag of potatoes. Then mentally cut the bag, allowing the potatoes to roll out. Think of yourself as the bag. What is more relaxed than an empty burlap bag?

The second element in the formula is to drain the mind of all irritation, resentment, disappointment, frustration, annoyance. To do this, think of the most beautiful and peaceful scenes you know — a mountain at sunset, a valley filled with the hush of early morning, a lake by moonlight.

Third, turn the mind to God. At least three times a day "lift up your eyes unto the hills." This keeps you in tune with God's harmony. It refills you with peace.

How To Win Friends and Influence People

A condensation from the book

by Dale Carnegie

Dale Carnegie has trained thousands of business and professional men, including some of the most famous, in public speaking and in the technique of handling people. His courses have proved so valuable in business relationships that such organizations as the Westinghouse Electric and Manufacturing Company, McGraw-Hill Publishing Company, American Institute of Electric Engineers, and the New York Telephone Company have had this training conducted in their own offices for their members and executives.

"This book," the author says, "wasn't written in the usual sense of the word. It grew and developed out of the experiences of thousands of adults in my classes." And from this extensive reservoir of experience has come the wealth of anecdote and variety of common-sense lessons in human relationships in which *How to Win Friends and Influence People* abounds.

Criticism Is Futile

In May 1931, when "Two Gun" Crowley was captured — after being besieged by 150 policemen with machine guns and tear gas — Police Commissioner Mulrooney declared that this desperado was one of the most dangerous criminals in the history of New York. "He will kill," said the Commissioner, "at the drop of a feather."

But how did "Two Gun" Crowley regard himself? While the

police were firing into his apartment, he wrote a letter addressed "To Whom It May Concern." In this letter he said: "Under my coat is a weary heart, but a kind one — one that would do nobody any harm."

A short time before this, Crowley had been having a necking party on a country road out on Long Island. Suddenly a policeman walked up to the parked car and said: "Let me see your license."

Without saying a word, Crowley drew his gun, and shot the policeman dead.

Crowley was sentenced to the electric chair. When he arrived at the death house at Sing Sing, did he say, "This is what I get for killing people"? No, he said: "This is what I get for defending myself."

The point of the story is this: "Two Gun" Crowley didn't blame himself for anything.

Is this an unusual attitude among criminals? If you think so, listen to Warden Lawes of Sing Sing: "Few criminals regard themselves as bad men. Most of them attempt to justify their anti-social acts even to themselves, consequently stoutly maintaining that they should never have been imprisoned at all."

If the desperate men behind prison walls don't blame themselves for anything — what about the people with whom you and I come in contact?

Personally I had to blunder through a third of a century before it even began to dawn upon me that, 99 times out of a hundred, no man ever criticizes himself for anything, no matter how wrong he may be; and that criticism is futile because it puts a man on the defensive, and usually makes him strive to justify himself.

Criticism is also dangerous, because it wounds a man's precious pride, hurts his sense of importance, and arouses his resentment.

When I was very young and trying hard to impress people, I wrote a foolish letter to Richard Harding Davis. I was preparing a magazine article about authors; and I asked Davis to tell me about his method of work. I had just received a letter with this notation at the bottom: "Dictated but not read." I was quite impressed. I felt the writer must be very busy and important. And as I was eager to make an impression on Richard Harding Davis, I ended my own short note, "Dictated but not read."

He never troubled to answer the letter. He simply returned it with this scribbled comment: "Your bad manners are exceeded only by your bad manners." True, I deserved his rebuke. But, being human, I resented it. I resented it so sharply that when I read of the death of Richard Harding Davis ten years later, the one thought that still persisted in my mind — I am ashamed to admit — was the hurt he had given me.

When dealing with people, remember you are not dealing with creatures of logic, but with creatures of emotion, creatures bristling with prejudices and motivated by pride and vanity. And if you want to stir up a resentment tomorrow that may rankle across the decades and endure until death, just indulge in a little stinging criticism — no matter how certain you are that it is justified.

Benjamin Franklin, tactless in his youth, became so diplomatic, so adroit at handling people that he was made American Ambassador to France. The secret of his success? "I will speak ill of no man," he said, "and speak all the good I know of everybody."

As Dr. Johnson said: "God Himself, sir, does not propose to judge man until the end of his days."

Why should you and I?

We Want To Be Important

PROFESSOR John Dewey, America's most profound philosopher, said the deepest urge in human nature is the "desire to be important." Remember that phrase, "the desire to be important." It is a gnawing and unfaltering human hunger. It was this desire that led the uneducated, poverty-stricken grocery clerk, Abraham Lincoln, to study law; that inspired Dickens to write his immortal novels. It makes you want to wear the latest styles, drive the latest car, and talk about your brilliant children.

People sometimes become invalids in order to win sympathy and attention, and get a feeling of importance. Some authorities declare that people may actually go insane in order to find, in the dreamland of insanity, the feeling of importance that has been denied them in the harsh world of reality.

If people are so hungry for a feeling of importance, imagine what miracles you and I can achieve by giving them honest appreciation. The rare individual who honestly satisfies this heart hunger will hold people in the palm of his hand.

Andrew Carnegie paid Charles Schwab the unprecedented salary of a million dollars a year. Because Schwab knew more about the manufacture of steel than other people? Nonsense. Schwab told me himself that he had many men working for him who knew more about steel than he did, and that he was paid this salary largely because of his ability to deal with people. And what is his secret?

"I consider my ability to arouse enthusiasm among the men," he said, "the greatest asset I possess, and the way to develop the best that is in a man is by appreciation. There is nothing that so kills the ambitions of a man as criticism from his superiors. So I am anxious to praise but loath to find fault. I have yet to find the man, however exalted his station, who did not do better work and put forth greater effort under a spirit of approval than under a spirit of criticism."

Sincere appreciation was one of the secrets of Rockefeller's success in handling men. For example, when one of his partners, Edward T. Bedford, lost the firm a million dollars by a bad buy in South America, John D. might have criticized; but he knew Bedford had done his best. So Rockefeller found something to praise; he congratulated Bedford because he had been able to save 60 percent of the money he had invested. "That's splendid," said Rockefeller. "We don't always do as well as that upstairs."

Ziegfeld, the most spectacular entrepreneur who ever dazzled Broadway, gained his reputation by his subtle ability to "glorify the American girl." He repeatedly took some drab little creature that no one ever looked at twice and transformed her on the stage into a glamorous vision of mystery and seduction. Knowing the value of appreciation and confidence, he made women *feel* beautiful by the sheer power of his gallantry and consideration. He raised the salary of chorus girls from $35 a week to as high as $175; and on opening night at the

Follies, deluged every chorus girl in the show with American Beauty roses.

Almost everyone considers himself important. So does every nation. Do you consider yourself superior to the Hindus in India? That is your privilege; but a million Hindus wouldn't befoul themselves by touching the food your heathen shadow has fallen across. Do you feel superior to the Eskimos? Again, that is your privilege; but would you really like to know what the Eskimo thinks of you? Well, there are a few native hoboes among the Eskimos, worthless bums who refuse to work. The Eskimos call them "white men" — that being their utmost term of contempt.

The truth is that almost every man you meet feels himself superior to you in some way; and a sure way to his heart is to let him realize that you recognize his importance. A line in *Reunion in Vienna* runs, "There is nothing I need so much as nourishment for my self-esteem." We nourish the bodies of our children and friends; but how seldom do we nourish their self-esteem!

No! I am not suggesting flattery. Flattery ought to fail and usually does. But flattery is from the teeth out. Sincere appreciation is from the heart out.

Let's cease thinking of our own accomplishments, our wants. Let's try to figure out the other man's good points. Give him honest, sincere appreciation for them and he will cherish your words years after you have forgotten them.

Emerson said: "Every man I meet is my superior in some way. In that, I learn of him."

What the Other Fellow Wants

Tomorrow you will want to persuade somebody to do something. Before you speak, remember there is only one way under high Heaven to get anybody to do anything. And that is by making them *want* to do it.

Andrew Carnegie was a past master at influencing people by talking in terms of what the other person wants. To illustrate: His sister-in-law was worried sick over her two boys at Yale, who neglected to write home and paid no attention to their mother's letters. Carnegie offered to wager a hundred dollars that he could get an answer by return mail, without even asking for it. Someone called his bet; so he wrote his nephews a chatty letter, mentioning casually in a postscript that he was sending each one a five-dollar bill.

He neglected, however, to enclose the money.

Back came replies by return mail.

This strategy appealed, of course, to a relatively low motive; but it is often possible to influence people by appealing to the highest motive possible to the situation. When the late Lord Northcliffe found a newspaper using a picture of himself which he didn't want published, he wrote the editor a letter. But did he say, "Please do not publish that picture of me any more; I don't like it"? No, he appealed to the respect all of us have for motherhood. He wrote, "Please do not publish that picture of me any more. My mother doesn't like it."

When John D. Rockefeller, Jr., wished to stop newspaper photographers from snapping pictures of his children, he didn't say: "I don't want their pictures published." No, he appealed to the desire, deep in all of us, to refrain from harming children. He said: "You know how it is, boys. You've got children yourselves. And you know it's not good for youngsters to get too much publicity."

Charles Schwab had a mill manager whose men weren't producing their quota of work. "How is it," Schwab asked, "that a man as capable as you can't make this mill turn out what it should?"

"I don't know," the man replied, "I've coaxed the men; I've pushed them; I've sworn and cussed. They just won't produce." It happened to be the end of the day, just before the night shift came on.

"Give me a piece of chalk," Schwab said. Then, turning to the nearest man: "How many heats did your shift make today?"

"Six." Without another word, Schwab chalked a big figure six on the floor and walked away. When the night shift came in, they saw the "6" and asked what it meant. "The big boss was in here today," the day men said. "He asked us how many heats we made, and we told him six. He chalked it down on the floor." The next morning Schwab walked through the mill again. The night shift had rubbed out "6," and replaced it with a big "7."

When the day shift reported for work, they saw a big "7" on the floor. So the night shift thought they were better than the day shift, did they? Well, they would show the night shift a thing or two. They pitched in with enthusiasm and when they quit that night, they left behind them an enormous, swaggering "10." Shortly this mill, that had been lagging way behind in production, was turning out more work than any other mill in the plant.

The principle? "The way to get things done," says Schwab, "is to stimulate competition. I do not mean in a sordid, money-getting way, but in the desire to excel."

Back in 1915 when Woodrow Wilson determined to send a peace emissary to counsel with the war lords of Europe, William Jennings Bryan, Secretary of State, the peace advocate, longed to go. He saw a chance to make his name immortal. But Wilson appointed Colonel House, and it was House's thorny task to break the news to Byran. "Bryan was distinctly disappointed," Colonel House records in his diary, "but I explained that the President thought it would be bad for anyone to do this officially, and that his going would attract a great deal of attention and people would wonder why he was there."

You see the intimation? House practically tells Bryan that he is too important for the job — and Bryan is satisfied. Colonel House, adroit, experienced in the ways of the world, was following one of the important rules of human relations: Always endeavor to make the other man happy about doing the thing you suggest.

Don't Argue

At a banquet one night the man next to me told a story in which he used the quotation, "There's a divinity that shapes our ends, rough-hew them how we will," and attributed it to the Bible. He was wrong. And to display my superiority, I corrected him. He stuck to his guns. From Shakespeare? Absurd! That quotation was from the Bible. An old friend of mine, seated at my left, was a Shakespearean scholar. The story-teller and I agreed to submit the question to him. My friend listened, kicked me under the table and said: "Dale, you are wrong. The gentleman is right. It is from the Bible."

On our way home that night, my friend explained: "Of course that quotation is from Shakespeare, Dale; but we were guests at a festive occasion. Why prove to a man he is wrong? Is that going to make him like you? Why not let him save his face? He didn't ask for your opinion. Why argue with him? Always avoid the acute angle."

"Always avoid the acute angle." I sorely needed that lesson because I had been an inveterate arguer. During my youth, I had argued with my brother about everything under the Milky Way. In college I studied logic and argumentation, and later taught them in New York. As a result of it all, I have come to the conclusion that there is only one way to get the best of an argument — and that is to avoid it. Nine times out of ten, an argument ends with each of the contestants being more firmly convinced than ever that he is absolutely right. You can't win an argument. You can't win because even if you win it, you lose it, for you will never get your opponent's good will.

William G. McAdoo, Secretary of the Treasury in Woodrow Wilson's Cabinet, declared that he had learned, as a result of his crowded years in politics, that "it is impossible to defeat an ignorant man by argument." You put it mildly, Mr. McAdoo. My experience has been that it is all but impossible to make *any* man — regardless of his I.Q. rating — change his mind by a verbal joust.

For example, Frederick S. Parsons, an income-tax consultant, had been disputing and wrangling for an hour with a government tax inspector. An item of $9000 was at stake. Mr. Parsons claimed that this $9000 was a bad debt, the inspector that it must be taxed.

"This inspector was cold, arrogant, and stubborn," Mr. Parsons said. "The longer we argued, the more stubborn he became. Finally I said, 'I suppose that this is a very petty matter in comparison with the really important and difficult decisions you are required to make. I've made a study of taxation myself. But I've had to get my knowledge from books. You are getting yours from the firing line of experience. I sometimes wish I had a job like yours. It would teach me a lot.' I meant every word I said. Well, the inspector straightened up in his chair, leaned back, and talked for a long time about his work, telling me of the clever frauds he had uncovered. His tone gradually became friendly; and presently he was telling me about his children. As he left, he advised me that he would consider my problem further, and give me his decision in a few days. He called at my office three days later and informed me that he had decided to leave the tax return exactly as it was filed."

This tax inspector was demonstrating one of the most common of human frailties. He wanted a feeling of importance; and as long as Mr. Parsons argued with him, he got his feeling of importance by loudly asserting his authority. But as soon as his importance was admitted, and the argument stopped, and he was permitted to expand his ego, he became a sympathetic and kindly human being.

I have quit telling people they are wrong. And I find it pays. Few people are logical. Most of us are prejudiced, blighted with preconceived notions. When we are wrong, we may admit it to ourselves. And if we are handled gently and tactfully, we may admit it to others and even take pride in our frankness. But not if someone else is trying to ram the unpalatable fact down our esophagus.

In his biography, Ben Franklin tells how he conquered the iniquitous habit of argument and made himself one of the most able diplomats in American history. One day, when Franklin was a blundering youth, an old Quaker friend took him aside and lashed him with a few stinging truths: "Ben, your opinions have a slap in them for everyone who differs with you. Your friends find they enjoy themselves better when you are not around. You know so much that no man can tell you anything. Indeed no man is going to try, for the effort would lead only to discomfort. So you are not likely ever to know any more than you do now, which is very little."

Ben Franklin was wise enough to realize that this was true, and he made a right-about-face. "I made it a rule," said Franklin, "to forbear all direct contradiction to the sentiments of others, and all positive assertion of my own. I even forbade myself the use of every expression that imported a fix'd opinion, such as 'certainly,' 'undoubtedly,' etc., and I adopted, instead,

'I conceive,' a thing to be so; or 'it so appears to me at present.' When another asserted something that I thought an error, I deny'd myself the pleasure of contradicting him abruptly, and of showing immediately some absurdity in his proposition: and in answering I began by observing that in certain cases or circumstances his opinion would be right, but in the present case there seem'd to me some difference.

"And this became at length so habitual that perhaps for these 50 years past no one has ever heard a dogmatical expression escape me. And to this habit (after my character of integrity) I think it principally owing that I had early so much weight with my fellow citizens when I proposed new institutions, or alterations in the old, and so much influence in public councils."

When You're In the Wrong

WHEN one is at fault, it is frequently disarming to admit it quickly. Ferdinand E. Warren, a commercial artist, used this technique to win the good will of a petulant art director. "Recently I delivered him a rush job," Mr. Warren told me, "and he phoned me to call at his office immediately. When I arrived, I found just what I had anticipated — he was hostile, gloating over his chance to criticize. He demanded with heat why I had done so and so. Trying a new strategy, I simply said, 'I am at fault and there is absolutely no excuse for my blunder. I have been doing drawings for you long enough to know better. I'm ashamed of myself.'

"Immediately he started to defend me. 'Yes, you're right, but after all, this isn't a serious mistake —'

"I interrupted him. 'Any mistake may be costly. I should have been more careful. I'm going to do this drawing over.'

"'No! No!' he protested. 'I wouldn't think of putting you to all that trouble.' He praised my work, assured me that he wanted only a minor change, a mere detail — not worth worrying about. My self-criticism took all the fight out of him. Before we parted, he gave me a check and another commission."

The First Person Singular

MANY of the sweetest memories of my childhood cluster around a little yellow-haired dog with a stub tail. Tippy never read a book on psychology. He didn't need to. He had a perfect technique for making people like him. He liked people himself — and his interest in me was so sincere and genuine that I could not keep from loving him in return.

Do you want to make friends? Then take a tip from Tippy. Be friendly. Forget yourself. People are not interested in you. They are interested in themselves — morning, noon, and after dinner. The New York Telephone Company made a detailed study of telephone conversations to find out which word is the most frequently used. It is the personal pronoun "I." It was used 3900 times in 500 telephone conversations. "I," "I," "I," "I," "I."

That is why you can make more friends in two months by becoming interested in other people than you can in two years by trying to get other people interested in you.

This was one of the secrets of Theodore Roosevelt's astonishing popularity. Roosevelt called at the White House one day when the President and Mrs. Taft were away. His honest liking for humble people was shown by the fact that he greeted all the old White House servants by name, even the scullery maids.

"When he saw Alice, the kitchen maid," writes Archie Butt, "he asked her if she still made corn bread. Alice told him that she sometimes made it for the servants, but no one ate it upstairs.

"'They show bad taste,' Roosevelt boomed, 'and I'll tell the President so when I see him.'

"Alice brought a piece to him on a plate, and he went over to the office eating it as he went and greeting gardeners and laborers as he passed. They still whisper about it to each other, and Ike Hoover said with tears in his eyes: 'It is the happiest day we have had in nearly two years.'"

It was this same intense interest in the problems of other people that made Dr. Charles W. Eliot of Harvard one of the most successful presidents who ever directed a university. One day a freshman, L. R. G. Crandon, went to the president's office to borrow $50 from the Student's Loan Fund. The loan was granted. "Then" — I am quoting Crandon — "President Eliot said, 'Pray be seated.' To my amazement, he continued, 'I am told that you cook and eat in your room. Now I don't think that is at all bad for you if you get the right food and enough of it. When I was in college, I did the same. Did you ever make veal loaf? That, if made from sufficiently mature and sufficiently cooked veal, is one of the best things you could have, because there is no waste. This is the way I used to make it.' He then told me how to pick the veal, how to cook it slowly, with such evaporation that the soup would turn into jelly later, then how to cut it up and press it with one pan inside another and eat it cold."

Does this attitude work in business? Does it? I could cite scores of illustrations.

Charles R. Walters, of one of the large banks in New York City, was assigned to prepare a confidential report on a certain corporation. He knew of only one man who possessed the facts, the president. As Mr. Walters was ushered into his office, a young woman stuck her head through a door and told the president that she didn't have any stamps for him that day.

"I am collecting stamps for my 12-year-old son," the president explained.

Mr. Walters stated his mission, and began asking questions. The president was vague, general, nebulous. The interview was brief and barren.

Mr. Walters didn't know what to do. Then he remembered that the foreign department of his bank collected stamps, taken from letters pouring in from every continent.

"The next afternoon I called on this man again," said Mr. Walters, "and sent in word that I had some stamps for his boy. He greeted me radiating smiles. 'My George will love this one,' he kept saying as he fondled the stamps. 'And look at this. This is a treasure.'

"We spent half an hour talking stamps, and then he devoted more than an hour of his time to giving me every bit of information I wanted — without my even suggesting it."

If we want to make friends, let's put ourselves out to do things for other people — things that require time, energy and thoughtfulness.

Be a Good Listener

I RECENTLY MET a distinguished botanist at a dinner party. I had never talked to a botanist before, and I literally sat on the edge of my chair the whole evening while he spoke of hashish and potatoes and Luther Burbank and indoor gardens. Midnight came. I said good night and departed. The botanist then turned to our host and paid me some very flattering compliments. I was "most stimulating," a "most interesting conversationalist."

An interesting conversationalist? I had said hardly anything at all. I couldn't have said anything if I had wanted to without changing the subject, for I know nothing about botany. But I had done this: I had listened intently, because I was genuinely interested. And he felt it. Naturally that pleased him. That kind of listening is one of the highest compliments we can pay to another person.

And that is the secret of success alike in social conversation and in a business interview. Remember that the man you are talking to is a hundred times more interested in himself and his wants and problems than he is in you and your problems. His toothache means more to him than a famine in China. Think of that the next time you start a conversation. And if you want people to like you, be a good listener. Encourage them to talk about themselves.

The Magic of Names

I ONCE ASKED Jim Farley the secret of his success. He said, "Hard work," and I said, "Don't be funny."

He then inquired what I thought was the reason for his success. I replied: "I understand you can call 10,000 people by their first names."

"No. You are wrong," he said. "I can call 50,000 people by their first names."

Make no mistake about it. That ability helped Mr. Farley put Franklin D. Roosevelt in the White House. During the years that Jim Farley traveled as a salesman for a gypsum concern, he built up a system for remembering names. Whenever he met a new acquaintance, he found out his complete name, the size of his family, the nature of his business, and the color of his political opinions. He got all these facts well in mind, and the next time he met that man, he was able to slap him on the back, inquire after the wife and kids, and ask him about the hollyhocks in the back yard. No wonder he developed a following!

He had discovered early in life that the average man is more interested in his own name than in all the other names on earth put together. Remember that name and call it easily, and you have paid him a subtle and very effective compliment. But forget it or misspell it — and you have placed yourself at a sharp disadvantage.

Andrew Carnegie, by the time he was ten years old, had discovered the astonishing importance people place on their own names. And he used that discovery to win coöperation. He had a nest of little rabbits, but nothing to feed them. Then he had a brilliant idea. He told the boys in the neighborhood that if they would pull enough clover and dandelions to feed the rabbits he would name the bunnies in their honor.

The plan worked like magic; and Carnegie never forgot it.

Years later, he made millions by using that same psychology in business. For example, he wanted to sell steel rails to the Pennsylvania Railroad, of which J. Edgar Thompson was then president. So Andrew Carnegie built a huge steel mill in Pittsburgh and called it the "J. Edgar Thompson Steel Works."

When the Pennsylvania Railroad needed steel rails, where do you suppose J. Edgar Thompson bought them?

When Carnegie and George Pullman were battling each other for supremacy in the sleeping-car business, the Steel King again remembered the lesson of the rabbits.

The Central Transportation Company, which Andrew Carnegie controlled, was fighting with the company Pullman owned. Both were struggling to get the sleeping-car business of the Union Pacific Railroad, bucking each other, slashing prices, and destroying all chance of profit. Both Carnegie and Pullman had gone to New York to see the board of directors of the Union Pacific. Meeting Mr. Pullman one evening in the St. Nicholas Hotel, Carnegie suggested a merger of the two companies. He pictured in glowing terms the mutual advantages of working with, instead of against each other. Pullman listened attentively, but was not convinced. Finally he asked, "What would you call the new company?" and Carnegie replied promptly: "Why, the Pullman Palace Car Company, of course."

Pullman's face brightened. "Come into my room," he said. "Let's talk it over." That talk made industrial history.

One of the simplest, most obvious, and most important ways of gaining good will and making people feel important is by remembering names. Yet how many of us do it? Half the time we are introduced to a stranger, chat a few minutes, and can't even remember his name when we say good-bye. Most people don't remember names for the simple reason that they don't take the time and energy necessary to concentrate and repeat and fix names indelibly in their minds.

Napoleon III of France boasted that he could remember the name of every person he met. His technique? If he didn't hear the name distinctly, he said, "So sorry. I didn't get the name clearly." Then, if it was an unusual name, he would say, "How is it spelled?"

During the conversation, he took the trouble to repeat the name several times, and tried to associate it in his mind with the man's features, expression, and general appearance. If the man were someone of importance, Napoleon went to further pains. In privacy he wrote the man's name down, concentrated on it, fixed it securely in his mind. Thus he gained an eye impression of the name as well as an ear impression.

All this takes time, but "good manners," said Emerson, "are made up of petty sacrifices."

Remember that a man's name is to him the sweetest and most important sound in the English language.

Sign of Good Sense

WHILE touring through New Mexico I stopped at a gas station long enough to step into the ladies' rest room. I was delighted to find it immaculately clean and neat. Then I noticed the sign tacked above the wash basin: "Have you an imagination? Won't you please pretend this is the bathroom in your own home and your mother-in-law is coming for a visit?"

— Contributed by Mrs. E. F. Guingona

¶*Even our slightest impulse toward prayer has a dynamic, beneficial effect upon our lives*

Prayer Is Power

Alexis Carrel, M.D.

PRAYER is not only worship; it is also an indivisible emanation of man's worshiping spirit — the most powerful form of energy that one can generate. The influence of prayer on the human mind and body is as demonstrable as that of secreting glands. Its results can be measured in terms of increased physical buoyancy, greater intellectual vigor, moral stamina, and a deeper understanding of the realities underlying human relationships.

If you make a habit of sincere prayer, your life will be very noticeably and profoundly altered. Prayer stamps with its indelible mark our actions and demeanor. A tranquility of bearing, a facial and bodily repose, are observed in those whose inner lives are thus enriched. Within the depths of consciousness a flame kindles. And man sees himself. He discovers his selfishness, his silly pride, his fears, his greeds, his blunders. He develops a sense of moral obligation, intellectual humility. Thus begins a journey of the soul toward the realm of grace.

Prayer is a force as real as terrestrial gravity. As a physician, I have seen men, after all other therapy had failed, lifted out of disease and melancholy by the serene effort of prayer. It is the only power in the world that seems to overcome the so-called "laws of nature"; the occasions on which prayer has dramatically done this have been termed "miracles." But a constant, quieter miracle takes place hourly in the hearts of men and women who have discovered that prayer supplies them with a steady flow of sustaining power in their daily lives.

Too many people regard prayer as a formalized routine of

words, a refuge for weaklings, or a childish petition for material things. We sadly undervalue prayer when we conceive it in these terms, just as we should underestimate rain by describing it as something that fills the birdbath in our garden. Properly understood, prayer is a mature activity indispensable to the fullest development of personality — the ultimate integration of man's highest faculties. Only in prayer do we achieve that complete and harmonious assembly of body, mind and spirit which gives the frail human reed its unshakable strength.

The words, "Ask and it shall be given to you," have been verified by the experience of humanity. True, prayer may not restore the dead child to life or bring relief from physical pain. But prayer, like radium, is a source of luminous, self-generating energy.

How does prayer fortify us with so much dynamic power? To answer this question (admittedly outside the jurisdiction of science) I must point out that all prayers have one thing in common. The triumphant hosannas of a great oratorio, or the humble supplication of an Iroquois hunter begging for luck in the chase, demonstrate the same truth: that human beings seek to augment their finite energy by addressing themselves to the Infinite source of all energy. When we pray, we link ourselves with the inexhaustible motive power that spins the universe. We ask that a part of this power be apportioned to our needs. Even in asking, our human deficiencies are filled and we arise strengthened and repaired.

But we must never summon God merely for the gratification of our whims. We derive most power from prayer when we use it, not as a petition, but as a supplication that we may become more like Him. Prayer should be regarded as practice of the Presence of God. An old peasant was seated alone in the last pew of the village church. "What are you waiting for?" he was asked; and he answered, "I am looking at Him and He is looking at me." Man prays not only that God should remember him, but also that he should remember God.

How can prayer be defined? Prayer is the effort of man to reach God, to commune with an invisible being, creator of all things, supreme wisdom, truth, beauty, and strength, father and redeemer of each man. This goal of prayer always remains hidden to intelligence. For both language and thought fail when we attempt to describe God.

We do know, however, that whenever we address God in fervent prayer we change both soul and body for the better. It could not happen that any man or woman could pray for a single moment without some good result. "No man ever prayed," said Emerson, "without learning something."

One can pray everywhere. In the streets, the subway, the office, the shop, the school, as well as in the solitude of one's own room or among the crowd in a church. There is no prescribed posture, time or place.

"Think of God more often than you breathe," said Epictetus the Stoic. In order really to mold personality, prayer must become a habit. It is meaningless to pray in the morning and to live like a barbarian the remainder of the day. True prayer is a way of life; the truest life is literally a way of prayer.

The best prayers are like the improvisations of gifted lovers, always about the same thing yet never twice the same. We cannot all be as creative in prayer as Saint Theresa or Bernard of Clairvaux, both of whom poured their adoration into words of mystical beauty. Fortunately, we do not need their eloquence; our slightest impulse to prayer is recognized by God. Even if we are pitifully dumb, or if our tongues are overlaid with vanity or deceit, our meager syllables of praise are acceptable to Him, and He showers us with strengthening manifestations of His love.

Today, as never before, prayer is a binding necessity in the lives of men and nations. The lack of emphasis on the religious sense has brought the world to the edge of destruction. Our deepest source of power and perfection has been left miserably undeveloped. Prayer, the basic exercise of the spirit, must be actively practiced in our private lives. The neglected soul of man must be made strong enough to assert itself once more. For if the power of prayer is again released and used in the lives of common men and women; if the spirit declares its aims clearly and boldly, there is yet hope that our prayers for a better world will be answered.

You Become Someone – Alone

Condensed from The Yale Review

Mary Ellen Chase

*Professor of English literature at Smith College;
author of "A Goodly Fellowship," etc.*

SOME 12 years ago I went to England, to Cornwall, all by myself. The trip was in the nature of an experiment. Frankly, although I had always loved to be alone for hours and even for days, I contemplated an entire summer in a foreign country with some uneasiness. I was assailed by all the usual anxieties: illness alone, accident alone, and above all else loneliness. But I resolutely put them out of my mind and set forth, Tourist Class, with a cabin and table to myself.

I began to realize at once the privileges of being alone. "The soul of a journey," Hazlitt writes, "is liberty to think, feel, do just as one pleases." I could read until all hours of the night. I could sing in my cabin all I liked, however tunelessly. I was free from invitations to play ship games at which I am deplorably stupid. I had time to think over events of the past year, to plan for the next. I had time to weigh one point of view against another on all manner of subjects and to determine my own honest attitude toward them. I had time to look at myself quite as though I were analyzing another person, with no necessity for deceit.

One day I spent hours attempting to remember just what I had done in what place during the summer holidays of the past 25 years. The effort brought sharply home to me how blurred most experiences become, not because of their lack of value in themselves, but merely because we have not taken time either to appreciate them while they were near at hand or to recollect and relive them in the years following. On another day I lived over my life as a young child, bringing up from the past those objects and persons, places and pastimes, which had gone into the process of making me. It was fun in the weeks afterward to come upon bits of me at five and ten and thirteen in my tastes and desires, habits and prejudices, and to recognize them as I had not done before.

When we neared Southampton, I realized suddenly and with thanksgiving that there was no one with whom I had to confer, make plans. I could linger in the New Forest a week if I liked, lie under a tree and sleep. I had never been really free before, I thought, and this intoxication continued all summer in spite of an occasional wistful hour which comes to us all and serves, by contrast, to increase rather than to diminish our contentment.

I shall always remember and cherish those long days in Cornwall. Their quiet succession added strength and personality to them as individuals. They were like rare persons upon whom we learn to depend because they are familiar and yet always new.

During the long, slow mornings I read on a cliff above the restless Cornish sea. I had brought only six books, six which could be read and re-read — *Virgil,* Plato's *Republic,* Homer's *Iliad* and *Odyssey,* the *Oxford Book of English Prose,* and Palgrave's *Golden Treasury of English Verse.* I never exhausted them. I could raise my eyes from the page whenever I liked and think quietly of what I had read, with my eyes on the distant horizon of sea and sky.

In the afternoons I walked alone through miles of gorse and heather. I bought manuals of English birds and flowers and went on journeys of new discovery. Tea was an occasion, now here, now there, in odd cottage gardens, by this stream and that.

For once in my life I held Time fast in my hands. It would steal away from me, but I would be there as it went, watching it, saying:

"You have not escaped me. You have given me your gifts, and for once I have been able to take them. This is five o'clock in the afternoon, and I shall always remember the chaffinch pecking at his bit of my tea-cake and the sunlight on the rose bay and white bedstraw by this quiet stream."

If he who travels alone wants to speak to strangers he may do so. If he prefers to avoid them no one is the wiser. The solitary traveler is far more likely to make friends than one who is obviously supplied with them. He draws the interest and attention of others, whose kindness he may accept or whose advances he is at liberty to decline.

During my solitary summer fear of being alone fled away, never to return. In its place was born the tenacious resolve to salvage from every day and at any cost at least half an hour to be spent entirely by myself. I learned that reading is rich in proportion to re-reading, that a good paragraph re-read half a dozen times does more for the mind and the spirit than any book hastily scanned. I learned that to look at a single tree for ten minutes reveals a personality hitherto completely unnoticed, that one bit of jagged coastline can be forever new as it flashes before tired eyes. I learned that merely to wait quietly, seemingly without thinking, is sure to bring its sudden and bright reward. I gained a new perspective on myself, of my assets and liabilities for my own work in the world.

I felt strangely new when I came back from Cornwall. I was physically strong and well from long walks in the sun or rain. In my mind were strongholds of security to which I could retreat whenever I felt the need: new thoughts, or old ones strengthened, new understandings, new memories. From being alone I had gained a new respect for others, their confusions and anxieties. I could look upon my friends with new appreciation, partly because of my absence from them, partly because of a new understanding of myself. For the first time I felt able to cope with the countless demands of a busy life; and, to speak humbly, I felt for the first time that I had more to give to others from the unexpected gifts which I had received.

I have never since been able to have an entire summer by myself; but I have learned that even two weeks alone can multiply their days and hours indefinitely. I allow no day to rush by without yielding me at least its half-hour of solitude. I may spend this in watching the snow fall; in saying over to myself imperishable things memorized long ago; in thinking or in not thinking. My mind is refreshed, my spirit strengthened.

Every family should grant its members periods of solitude in which to develop their individual personalities. The group around the fireplace in the evening maintains congeniality more easily if its several members spent some part of each day by themselves. Family excursions take on new excitement if occasionally the several members are encouraged to go off by themselves.

Married couples regain their identity as persons instead of pairs if each sometimes goes off alone. The adventurous partner returns with something new to talk about and with the inevitable confidence and refreshment which being on one's own always engenders. An occasional month away from one's husband or wife increases the happiness and romance of life together.

Books were written alone and must be read and considered alone. Pictures were painted alone, and no amount of dependence on the judgment of others can ever reveal them to us. Art and music will always remain a mystery to us if we run through galleries in herds or attend concerts as social functions. And the bobolinks over American fields will have no meaning for us unless we go alone to see them, soaring and singing in the sun.

Yesterday I took a long walk in the country. As I watched the fluttering bobolinks and heard their wild rippling song, I thought of the almost passionate love the English have for their skylarks — those symbols, as Santayana calls them, of the English spirit. I wondered why it is that we Americans do not have equally passionate loves for those birds and flowers and trees which are distinctly American. To the Scotsman, the heather is a portion of himself. Why do not our own arbutus, blue gentians and mountain laurel, our elms and redwoods and pointed firs, stand to more of us as signs and tokens of home, as indissoluble parts of ourselves?

Most of us never seek the riches of our American countryside by ourselves. We are as a people either unused to being alone or actually afraid of it. We have for so long talked and eaten, argued and thought, sung and even read in groups, that we are at a loss how to manage our minds or our bodies alone. We have become people, not persons. What was once individual about us has been diluted until both strength and color have disappeared. And with the disappearance of our courage has gone much of our personal dignity. We no longer trust our own judgments; before we venture to praise or to condemn a book, a picture, a person, an idea, we look furtively about to find someone ready to stand by us in case we are on the unaccepted side of the fence. We can no longer capture the essence of experiences because they are forever shared and commented upon by others: they have ceased to be our own.

To restore color to our faded personalities and vitality to our languid minds, we must learn to do things, to think things, to *become* someone, alone. If we are to gain from the world of experience and of people what that world has to offer us, we must frequently withdraw from it and find new experiences within ourselves. We need that confidence in ourselves and strength from some Power greater than ourselves which can come to us only from occasional solitude.

Modern Inconveniences

H<small>OWARD</small> M<small>AXWELL</small> of Los Angeles is a man in tune with his times. So when his four-year-old daughter Melinda acquired a fixation for "The Three Little Pigs" and demanded that he read it to her night after night Mr. Maxwell, very pleased with himself, tape-recorded the story. When Melinda next asked for it, he simply switched on the playback. This worked for a couple of nights, but then one evening Melinda pushed the storybook at her father. "Now, honey," he said, "you know how to turn on the recorder."

"Yes," said Melinda, "but I can't sit on its lap."

— Gene Sherman in Los Angeles *Times*

A<small>N</small> <small>OLD</small> <small>FRIEND</small> was living in solitary grandeur in her three-story mansion, surrounded by hundreds of new one-story houses. When her grandchildren from the West Coast came to visit her she decided to give a party and invite the children from the development. The next day I asked her how the party had gone. I knew she had planned it in the grand manner with a magician and ventriloquist.

"Times have changed even more than I ever dreamed," she said. "The children said they were sick of looking at magicians and ventriloquists on television. All they wanted to do all afternoon was slide down my banisters!"   — Contributed by Margaret B. Link

If you want the world to take stock in you —

Don't Sell Yourself Short

Condensed from Ladies' Home Journal   *Gelett Burgess*

A T A PARTY I was much attracted to a pretty girl with a charming personality. A fellow I know — doing publicity for a big diamond firm — sauntered up to her, spoke of her graceful posture and told her she was pretty. After a while he said he'd like to use her as a model for photographs to advertise some jewels. She could pose with a half-million dollars' worth of necklaces and bracelets, he said.

She laughed and said she'd love to. "But my hands are awful," she added, and sprawled them out to him, with her fingers wide apart.

Up to that moment I hadn't noticed her hands — which were a bit red and rather large. But after that uncalled-for remark I almost forgot her hair, that I had thought so fetching, and her lovely violet eyes and engaging smile. And as we went on talking I saw nothing but hands. She seemed to have so many hands. . . .

I don't say that you ought to wave flags and ring bells in an attempt to advertise your own excellence and importance. There are enough boasters, heaven knows. But if you're too modest to throw bouquets at yourself, must you throw brickbats? Why call attention to your deficiencies?

Let me tell you of a wise and a foolish virgin I met at that same party.

One of them, Alice, pulled off one of her earrings and showed it to her friend. "Pretty, aren't they?" she asked. "And just think, Eloise, I got them at a ten-cent store. Oh, they're not so nice as yours, I know. But then of course yours are expensive."

Eloise the wise virgin smiled and said nothing. But she also, I happened to know, was wearing inexpensive earrings.

You think she should have told her friend? Why? It was nobody's affair but her own where she got her things. It would have been dishonest to lie about the matter if she had been asked, but she wasn't asked. She didn't have much money but did have excellent taste. Why shouldn't she benefit by her superior judgment and allow people to think what they pleased?

What was the result of Alice's indiscretion? Well, as I was leaving the party I heard one lady say to another, "No, not the dark girl with Harry — I mean the one with the ten-cent earrings."

This incident illustrates the almost inevitable effect on hearers of any self-dispraise. When you open that personal door of familiarity, those who rush in can often be very disagreeable.

To illustrate how ill-advised most self-disparagement is, just imagine that those slurring remarks are made by someone else. You say, perhaps, "Oh, I don't care how I put on my hat. I'm too old now. Nobody notices me any more." But suppose some personal demon followed you about saying, "Oh, shove it on any which way, old gal. You're far too old to bother about your looks." How would you like it? Isn't it just as bad when you say it yourself?

If you spotlight the bad feature, all the good ones are apt to fall into a shadow. If that woman had kept her pretty mouth shut about her wrinkles and long nose and paid more attention to her dress and deportment, if she had been careful of her posture and cultivated her voice, she might easily have acquired a name for having style — and style is a kind of beauty accessible to all.

Many people make themselves unmagnetic — if not actively disliked — by always making a play for sympathy. Your mother or your sweetheart may care, but to everyone else the recital of your troubles and illnesses is usually a bore.

If, when you try to account for not looking well, you say, "I didn't shut my eyes all night; I must look awful," you've just injured yourself uselessly. Nobody is interested in the reason you're seedy, and nobody believes you anyway. If you exerted yourself to be animated and charming, if you complimented others and thought of something kind to do or interesting to say, perhaps they wouldn't notice your haggard face.

Why do so many people voluntarily disparage themselves, and reveal failings and deficiencies better left untold? For several reasons, perhaps — all mistaken. Some say, "I'm afraid this dress is awful," merely in hopes that you may say, "Why no, Ida, I think it's very pretty, and most becoming." They are merely fishing for compliments. With some it's a sort of chronic self-pity. Saying things like "I'm broke — I don't see how I'll make out till pay day," or "My husband made a terrible fuss about the household bills today," reveals a definite inferiority complex.

But most of these voluntary confessions are due to simple thoughtlessness, or an inordinate tendency to talk. For when one talks too much, you know, one is apt to talk of oneself. Some people indulge an irresistible urge, upon meeting a friend — any friend at all, a stranger, even — to pour out a sort of oral diary, telling everything that has happened to them and everything that is in their minds. And it is in the midst of such uncontrolled chatter that these little derogatory confessions slip out.

Quite apart from the practical benefits in guarding against self-depreciation, a discreet repression improves your morale. Just as a boiler that has no outlet compresses the steam and makes it more powerful, so a certain amount of reticence gives you more power. It lifts you to a higher plane of self-respect. The boy who is deformed and doesn't complain or mention it; the girl who is handicapped in beauty and is silent about it, and seeks to excel in other lines; the woman who suffers pain and never betrays it; the man who is disappointed and carries on with a smile — all are acting with a more effective mental and moral force than the one who lets his tongue wag over his troubles. They are building character; they are making themselves more valuable; they are growing in power, in wisdom and in influence.

Stories of the fortitude of actors under suffering and misfortune are classic — and mostly true. When the curtain is up, private trials must be forgotten.

I once called on a well-known star who was suffering from such an excruciating attack of arthritis that he had to remain in his dressing room at the theater night and day for almost a month. But not only did he go onto the stage at every performance and act his part so well that no one in the audience suspected his agony — that was nerve — but he positively forbade every member of his company to speak about his condition — that was intelligence.

"The show must go on!" That's the rule of the theater: it should be the rule in life as well. We, too, owe it to our friends to play our parts without apologies.

I Demand Worse Weather!

THE WEATHER around my place isn't bad enough. I wish it would get worse, like on my neighbors' land where the elements constantly go berserk. Recently, for example, during a rugged cold snap, our thermometer registered ten below zero one morning. On the train I cited this figure to Thompson, my neighbor. "That all?" he asked. "You got off lucky. Fourteen below at my place."

"We had 19 below," chimed in Jameson, who, curiously, lives across the street from us. "Was up all night with an electric heater to keep our pipes from freezing."

It's always like that. If we get snowdrifts five feet high in our driveway, the man next door gets them eight feet high. Wind that blows my hat off blows people's coats off when it leaves our property.

Occasionally, of course, an erratic cloud wets us as much as it does the neighbors — above ground, that is. But not in our cellar. We're continually being humiliated by the puny floods we get there. If the water's up to our ankles, it's up to Jameson's knees. If mice are swimming around in ours, the Thompsons have beavers.

I'm beginning to suspect the trouble. We've got a leak somewhere that lets the water out. I'm going to locate that leak and plug it up with the best cement. Then, for the next cloudburst, I'm going to install a giant blower in the cellar.

Waves? Brother, we're going to have whitecaps!

— Parke Cummings in *This Week*

Sweeping aside ancient accumulations of notions, nostrums and
nonsense, scientists have established new solid facts
about this elusive subject

Sleep and How to Get More of It

Condensed from Life

Robert Coughlan

A GALLUP POLL of eight North Atlantic nations in
1948 showed that Americans are the champion
insomniacs: 52 percent said they had trouble
part or all of the time going to sleep at night.
They and their friends, the people who wake up
in the night and the people who can't sleep past a fixed hour in
the morning, are the sleeping-pill customers. Last year they
bought 3,360,000,000 pills, an average of 24 for every American.

Insomnia has never killed anyone. But to the people who
suffer from it, insomnia is as debilitating as anemia, as nagging as an ulcer, uncomfortable as a leg in a cast. And chronic
insomnia has the peculiar distinction of being its own cause.
The advanced insomniac approaches his bed in a state of anxiety and spends the next hours awake because he is fearful
that he will do just that.

No one really knows what sleep is or exactly what causes it
or exactly why it is needed. The process can only be described.

After a normal period of relaxation (up to 30 minutes) the
prospective sleeper reaches a stage of semiconsciousness which
is neither sleeping nor waking. It is a feeling of "floating" or
being "disembodied." If all goes well, sensation ends and the
subject floats over the borderline to unconsciousness. The pas-
sage takes only a few seconds and is marked at the end by an
abrupt shift in the origin of brain waves (minute electrical
charges) from the back part of the head to the front. This shift

was discovered last year by Dr. Mary A. B. Brazier at the Massachusetts General Hospital, and there is no theory yet to explain why it takes place. It is a triumph to have discovered it, however, since heretofore sleep investigators have been handicapped by not knowing the exact dividing line between sleep and waking.

With the reversal in the source of brain waves sleep has come, bringing with it mysterious and rather alarming transformations. The sleeper breathes slowly. His eyeballs turn out and up. His fingers grow cold and his toes grow warm. His senses fade. The blood does not leave his brain, contrary to popular belief, but his blood pressure falls rapidly, becoming weakest about three hours after sleep begins. His heart rate also decreases, but often rises again to reach a peak in two or three hours, after which it slackens and becomes slowest about four hours later. His body temperature falls about one half a degree Fahrenheit. The sleeper has at first lain quietly, but soon he begins to move — an arm, a leg, now his whole body, shifting from side to side and front to back. In the morning he may declare with perfect honesty that he slept "like a log," but an observer would have recorded that he changed position between 20 and 60 times. It is possible to "sleep like a log" only if one is anesthetized or dead-drunk or feeble-minded.

After a certain time, depending on the sleeper's normal sleep span, the initial process is reversed. Sleep becomes lighter, consciousness flickers, fails, flickers, the brain charge is reversed — the sleeper is awake. Perhaps he yawns, thereby inhaling extra oxygen to lower the proportion of carbon dioxide that has accumulated in his body as a result of his muscular inactivity during sleep.

This, then, is normal sleep, "tired nature's sweet restorer," the insomniac's goal. Why is it so often so difficult to attain?

In general, insomnia is a price man pays for having become man. Sleep is not a problem for earthworms, tadpoles, bears or even monkeys, and only rarely for young babies. These lower forms of life lack the intelligence required for insomnia — which means, physiologically, that they lack the highly developed cerebral cortex of the adult human.

Aside from purely physical causes such as disease and organic malfunctionings, it is one word — anxiety — in all its complexities of cause and effect, which explains most sleep aberrations. It usually is anxiety that causes nightmares and "night terrors" in children, and it is the most frequent cause of sleepwalking and sleeptalking. The cure therefore is obvious: stop worrying, especially at bedtime.

That, however, is easier urged than done. It is not enough, for example, to tell a battle-shocked soldier who relives his war experiences at night to forget them; obviously he would like nothing better. The same is true of the ordinary insomniac. Countless nights have reverberated to his ancient cry, "If I could only stop thinking!" In advanced cases the only cure may be psychotherapy, but for most of humanity there are techniques which can be applied in the privacy of one's own bedroom.

The first and obvious one is to direct the mind by an effort of will away from personal matters. If one must think, let it be about objective rather than subjective things: not about one's own love problems but about the bees and the flowers. Along with this must be a high degree of muscular relaxation. Complete relaxation is, of course, impossible (nor is it necessary; people go to sleep while driving, and exhausted soldiers fall asleep while actually on the march). But the insomniac should aim for as much of it as he can get, with special attention to the muscles of the head, neck and chest. The reason for this is simply that a greater area of the brain is devoted to the incoming and outgoing signals of these muscles than to those of all the others combined. After the eye muscles, the ones to discipline most firmly are the speech muscles. The ability to think is intimately connected with the ability to talk. It is, in fact, almost impossible to maintain coherent thought without activity (minute, to be sure, but present and measurable) in the voice muscles. It follows that if the muscles having to do with speech are relaxed, the mind, in bafflement, will at last give up. The best way to do this is to let the jaw and whole face go slack in an expression of complete stupidity.

Mental vacuity and physical inertness are thus the uncomely handmaidens of sleep. They can be acquired by practice, but not easily: sometimes a year of conscientious application is necessary. They can be helped along by various palliatives, which will be useful to the light and troubled sleepers as well as to the true insomniac.

There are no uniformly effective rules for the best way to sleep. Room temperature, bed coverings, ventilation are all matters of individual preference or habit. Most people sleep better alone. The admonition against lying on one's left, or "heart," side is pure superstition, since the heart is approximately in the middle of the upper body cavity and since, in any case, the normal turnings of the sleeper will inevitably land him on the left side several times during a night. Provided the sleeper enjoys normal digestion, a big meal helps rather than hinders sleep, and for some people the process may be helped along by a cup of good coffee to stimulate the digestive processes. And there is also much to be said for the "nightcap" as a soporific.

Other forms of bedtime nourishment seem to have little effect. Tests at the University of Chicago showed no significant differences whether the subjects did or did not take one or two sandwiches or hot or cold milk before retiring. If a snack, a bath and 15 minutes of music seem to form a satisfying pre-sleep ritual, then they are useful.

Women, on the average, get more sleep than men, partly because they carry around relatively fewer problems and partly also because of their custom of creaming their faces, brushing their hair and spending a good deal of time in similar pre-bed activities. The ritual itself comes to be associated with sleep and thus helps to bring it. The same associative value applies to the bed itself and speaks against making reading in bed a part of the ritual, especially the reading of mystery novels.

It is helpful to establish a regular time for going to bed and getting up. This can as well be late to bed and late to rise as the other way around, but it should be consistent. The reason lies in the workings of what Dr. Nathaniel Kleitman, University of Chicago physiologist who has spent 30 years probing the mysteries of sleep, calls "the diurnal sleep cycle." Everyone undergoes a rise and fall of body temperature over a 24-hour period. The average swing is a little over one degree, although swings of twice that are not uncommon. The drop in temperature brings with it a natural period for sleeping and this drop can be induced by repetition to arrive at a certain time. Thus the problem sleeper, by going to bed at a regular hour, can establish a temperature cycle which automatically will make him sleepy at that time. He may choose any hour around the clock. Some persons can establish a cycle easily; others may take months and must count on a long period of nightly restlessness before the cycle clicks into place.

Temperature cycles differ. There is the kind that climbs steeply as its owner wakes up, causing him to jump out of bed eagerly. He is a "morning person"; his temperature keeps going up and reaches a peak around noontime, when he is at his most wide-awake. When it begins to fall soon after, he begins to feel less energetic. His temperature continues to fall, reaching the "drowsiness level" fairly early in the evening.

The "evening person's" temperature rises very slowly and does not reach its peak until late afternoon, when he feels at his best. He dislikes getting up, and feels groggy and out-of-sorts in the morning. By the time the "morning person" is looking forward to bed the "evening person" may be wound up and going strong. Dr. Kleitman is fond of saying: "More marriages are broken up by temperature than by temperament."

Dr. Kleitman's tests show that in both mental and physical tasks performance and resistance to fatigue are best when temperature is high, worst when it is low. Consequently it is a good idea to arrange important affairs so that they can be handled during the daily period of maximum temperature.

In the past many experimenters have supposed that fatigue created various "waste products" and "poisons" that numb the brain, and that sleep was needed to eliminate them from the body. There were several drawbacks to this theory. One was that no one could ever find any such poisons in the blood stream. Another was the evident truth of the familiar expression, "too tired to sleep"; there comes a stage when fatigue is a hindrance rather than a help to slumber. Also Dr. Kleitman discovered that people of all types usually are least efficient after a night's sleep; it was no longer possible to imagine sleep as a cleanser of poisons. Sleep can take place without fatigue. A completely rested person can fall asleep if he relaxes enough.

On the other hand, "healthy fatigue" is an aid to relaxation.

The sleeping pill should be the last resort of an insomniac. The standard barbiturate drugs are not harmful in themselves if taken in medically prescribed doses. But, says Dr. Harris Isbell, director of research at the U. S. Public Health Service Hospital, Lexington, Ky., "taken regularly in large doses, they can be habit-forming, and the addiction can be more painfully difficult to break and more dangerous than morphine addiction."

Suppose that the chronic insomniac has tried all the suggestions given here — in vain. What then?

He shouldn't lose any sleep over it. For it is certain that if he keeps at it he will learn the trick, and it is equally true that it will do him no serious harm if he takes a long time to do it. Chronic "undersleeping" is widely supposed to lead to mental and physical breakdown, but almost certainly it can do neither. Experiments show that protracted sleeplessness seems to have no pronounced effect on the fundamental physiological processes of the body. For tasks requiring short periods of physical or mental coördination, lack of sleep leaves performance as good as ever. In tasks calling for sustained effort, loss of sleep causes performance to fall off drastically. And it does increase sensitiveness to pain.

The common belief that one cannot "pay back" a sleep debt is untrue; the debt can be liquidated in one long sleep.

There is no absolute answer to the question: "How much sleep should people get?" It depends on age, health and activity. Laboratory tests show that sleep needs tend to decline each year from birth to senility. But a 50-year-old mathematician probably will need more sleep than a 25-year-old ditchdigger, for physical workers usually can get along on about two hours less a night than people who work with their brains. If Jones feels good on three hours' sleep, he needs no more; if Smith doesn't feel good on eight hours', chances are that he needs nine or ten.

Happily for the insomniac, rest can take place without sleep, and so long as he lies down and gets a measure of relaxation in mind and body, he can keep going almost indefinitely. Probably he will feel awful; but that will be the worst of it.

HOW TO SAY NO

Condensed from Future
Vance Packard

MANY OF US are harassed in daily life by an inability to utter a firm but gracious no. Often our difficulty is caused by a desire to be a good fellow.

A relative of mine, Edgar Wright, is a small-town business-man. Edgar is serving on 17 committees, mostly because he just can't say no. He goes to bridge parties which bore him. When his hostess offers him chocolate cake, for which he has an allergy, he eats it politely and is sorry later.

Edgar's wife, Ella, is just as bad. A few weeks ago an acquaintance who sells cosmetics by home demonstration asked her to sponsor a "cosmetic party." Ella tried to say no, but the woman kept coaxing until she said yes. Ella persuaded 20 of her friends to come; they couldn't say no either. Edgar estimates that the "party" cost him and the other husbands $148.

Almost every day many of us are caught in positions where we should logically say no, but don't. However, there are several reasonable and friendly ways of saying no. You may find one of them useful the next time you are faced with the problem.

Put it on an impersonal basis.

One of the most serene housewives I know says she achieved her serenity when she licked the problem of saying no. She explained: "I go by rules."

When an acquaintance asks her to wrap packages for unfortunates in Mozambique she says simply: "Sorry, I can't. This year I'm confining myself to two things, the Girl Scouts and the polio drive, and trying to do them right."

When a salesman knocks at her door, she is polite but firm: "My husband won't let me buy anything at the door."

Make it clear that you would like to say yes.

Tim Gammon, at the Liberty Mutual Insurance Co., is in charge of adjusting claims made against clients the company has insured. Though his office approves millions of dollars in payments each year, Gammon often has to say no. However, he always shows sympathy for the claimant. He explains that morally he may agree with him, but legally his hands are tied. In this case the company's legal department has ruled that the insured has no liability. He adds, regretfully, "We are unable to make a voluntary payment."

"People usually go away," he says, "feeling that at least we would like to be helpful."

Show that you have given the request real thought.

And *do* give it real thought. It is the brush-off that causes resentment. As Clarence Lyons, at the Industrial Bank of Commerce of New York, explains: "You must make the person see that you understand his problem, even if you have to say no."

Joe Stauffer, of N. W. Ayer & Son advertising agency, has to turn down many amateur ideas submitted for radio and television programs. He observes, however, that "most of the people seem satisfied if they simply get a chance to tell their story."

Say no by helping the person say no to himself.

One of my neighbors is an interior decorator. He never says no to clients when they want to incorporate impractical ideas into their homes. Instead he educates them to say yes to what he wants them to do.

He told me about a couple who built a modern home with floor-to-ceiling windows and open layout. The day came when the wife was to pick curtain material. She preferred flowery chintz — most inappropriate to the house.

The decorator suggested: "Let's go through the house and see just what you want your curtains to do." As they walked he talked about the functions the curtains would serve in each room, and what fabrics would harmonize best with the modern *décor*. By the time they were through, the woman had forgotten her enthusiasm for chintz.

In saying no, show what needs to be done to get a yes.

Should you try to cash a check at a Statler Hotel without sufficient identification, the clerks will not merely say no. They will helpfully suggest some way that you can obtain identification locally.

Dr. William Reilly, author of *Successful Human Relations,* is a management consultant. Here is how he advises business executives to handle the man who wants a raise but doesn't deserve it.

"Yes, George, I understand your need for a raise. However, to give it to you we will have to make you more valuable to the company. Now let's see what we need to do. . . ."

Say no by showing that the request isn't reasonable.

By asking questions you may turn up circumstances which give you a legitimate excuse for saying no. Asking questions also gives you time to think up a graceful refusal.

Here is how a smart executive will say no, gently, to a poor idea without discouraging future ideas: "John, your suggestion has merit, but what would you decide if you were in my place?" He then weighs the pros and cons to show why the answer must be no.

Most important, say your no in the nicest way you can.

I learned one of my best lessons in the art of saying no nicely from my four-year-old daughter, Cindy. A few days ago a rather effusive elderly woman decided to become Cindy's pal. After fussing over the child a while she asked: "Cindy, would you like to come up to my house and play tomorrow?"

I held my breath as Cindy considered the proposal. I would have stumbled all over myself trying to reject such an invitation. Cindy's face broke into a big warm grin as she gave her one-word answer. She said, "No."

Her no was friendly and appreciative and good-humored. But it was so unmistakably firm that the woman did not pursue the matter.

+++++++++++++

A FRIEND of Clara Barton, founder of the American Red Cross, once reminded her of an especially cruel thing that had been done to her years before. But Miss Barton seemed not to recall it.

"Don't you remember it?" her friend asked.

"No," came the reply. "I distinctly remember forgetting it."

—Think

ADD YEARS TO YOUR LIFE

Condensed from The American Mercury

Francis and Katharine Drake

Just how young you will be at 70 depends largely on how well your health has been preserved between 40 and 60. Almost all of us begin slowing down, physically, after 40 — despite the fact that our bodies are capable of reaching 100 without wearing out in any vital part. Now, thanks to geriatrics — that branch of medicine concerned with the body's aging process — we have an excellent chance to advance vigorously into the 70's and 80's.

This depends on two things: the guidance of an experienced geriatrician and initiative on the part of the "patient" in having regular health checkups and following instructions.

The importance of this simple program is shown by the physical condition of most Americans passing the 60-year milestone. Twenty-eight percent are far overweight, and 99 percent of such overweight is due to injudicious eating. At any age, overweight people die at the rate of nearly two for one by comparison with persons of normal weight. Most people of 60 have from one to eight diseases or deficiencies; three out of four lack minimum healthful amounts of calcium, protein, iron or vitamins. Fully 25 percent of those over 65 are anemic.

By contrast, the record of those who have had regular health checkups is outstanding. In a pioneer geriatric clinic in Rhode Island, less than one percent of the patients have required hospitalization in the past ten years. In a Connecticut insurance center, over a five-year test period, there were 44 percent fewer deaths among medically supervised employes than among those who refused the service. When surgery is unavoidable, geriatric patients have been found to be incomparably better risks.

After 40 our illnesses generally come from many causes, and seldom give definite warning of arrival. Before they reach the "symptom" stage — pain, fever, nausea, etc. — disorders of middle-life may already have sabotaged a perfectly sound organ far removed from the original trouble site. For example, that heart attack which hospitalized Mrs. Jones for months was not due to a faulty heart; it was caused by a steadily increasing traffic-jam of fat in her arteries, which forced the heart to increase its pumping load so far above the legal limit that it revolted. In common with countless "heart" sufferers, Mrs. Jones had long been taking too many sweets and fats with her daily fare.

The aging of human organs is a highly individual thing. As Dr. C. Ward Crampton, Chairman of the Sub-Committee on Geriatrics of the Medical Society of New York County, says, "a 60-year-old man may have a 40-year-old heart, 50-year-old kidneys and an 80-year-old liver and be trying to live a 30-year-old life."

The geriatrician's first job is to establish the top health potential of each patient. This he determines by a complete physical examination and by informing himself of his patient's background, family, work, worries, responsibilities and the like. If the over-all picture is good, the patient can go his way rejoicing for another year. But if anything is functioning poorly, the geriatrician brings into play every art of medical science to lift the patient's over-all condition as near maximum efficiency as possible — and keep it there.

Although it is prudent to conserve health by checking up at 40 rather than at 60, much can be done at any age, even in cases of chronic illness. For instance, if the heart is organically weak, the geriatrician also checks the other organs and the nutritional resources of the patient. Vitality may be stepped up with iodine or iron, resistance fortified with proteins, skin and tissues refreshed with selected vitamins, arteries relieved by diet, blood enriched with liver extract. Improving the whole system automatically reduces the strain on the heart.

The big saboteurs of health after 40 are our pet theories of what, and how much, we should eat. In this country we are surrounded by excellent food in endless variety, yet clinical records show that about 75 percent of the senior half of the population suffers from malnutrition. Doctors find as many dietary deficiencies among the well-to-do as among the lower-income groups. One geriatrician cites the case of a 60-year-old millionaire, half starved by his belief that proteins, especially meat, were "bad for anyone over 40."

What, then, should men and women over 40 eat, and how much? Nutritional needs vary, but some basic food rules hold good for everybody. Calcium, iron and protein head the list of needs — without an abundance of each, the body withers. Calcium poverty keeps bones from knitting properly after a break; iron poverty — the most frequent health impairment found in adults — brings anemia and that exhausted feeling; protein poverty may make us a setup for ulcers of the stomach.

Calcium, which nourishes the blood, bones and tissues, is in leafy green vegetables, cheese, milk. Iron, which helps to make blood, is in lean meat, liver, green vegetables, eggs, oysters, dried peas and beans, apricots, raisins. Rich in proteins, which furnish energy, restore tissues and repel disease, are lean meat, eggs, lima beans, peanuts, poultry, fish, milk and cheese.

Raw fruit and vegetables are right for everyone, with qualifications: (a) if you chop them to pieces, you reduce their vitamin values, (b) if they contain seeds or fibers, they can irritate delicate intestines.

Liquids are indispensable to proper body balance — between one and two quarts a day after 40, in such forms as water, milk, tea, coffee, soup.

Here is a doctor's table of basic daily food that will take care of a person's minimum needs after 40:

Milk: 1 pint (may be in soups, cooking, etc.).
Orange, grapefruit or tomato juice; 1 liberal serving.
Green vegetable: 1 serving.
Other vegetable: 1 serving.
Eggs: one or more.
Meat or fish: 1 serving.
Butter or margarine: two or three pats.

This list must be supplemented in accordance with each person's daily requirements, and it is here, in calorie mathematics, that the unsupervised majority make the dangerous mistakes. A man of 60 needs 35 percent fewer calories than a man of 30, even if both are performing identical work. After 40, the gradually slowing down human powerplant cannot keep up its former pace of converting calories into energy. Result: unconverted calories begin to get dumped — around the waistline or, worse still, around arteries and organs. Many people who eat light meals fall into the insidious "snack" habit. One geriatrician traced the mounting avoirdupois of a matron with a "birdlike appetite" to the salted nuts she had nibbled evening after evening for years.

Not to begin cutting down on fats, sugars and starches after 40 is to invite disaster. These are the snipers that end so many lives prematurely by a stroke, a blinding stab of angina, hardening of the arteries and coronary artery disease. Life-insurance figures show that fat people with high blood pressure are 12 times as susceptible to heart disease as people of normal weight. Doctors deny the popular belief it is "natural" to gain weight during the middle years — the potbelly and the middle-aged spread in virtually every case come from improper diet.

Other important controls on the geriatric health program may include a switch from too strenuous exercise to safer routines, instructions for rest or massage or different shoes. Medical records show that after geriatric care the vast majority of people become more vigorous than they were before, their aging processes definitely retarded.

Typical is the history of the Smiths, a couple who might pass for 50 but are actually 62 and 60. Some years ago Smith sought medical help because colds, digestive and kidney distresses and heaviness in the chest were causing him to lose more and more workdays. "Nothing the matter except age, I guess," he told the geriatrician. But examination showed high blood pressure, a faint whisper over the heart, neglected infections in both sinuses, one kidney damaged by a long-congested prostate and insufficient acid in his stomach juices for proper digestion.

Mrs. Smith, height five feet four, weight 152 pounds, breathing heavily after the short walk to the doctor's office, was pretty well, she thought. It was just that she hadn't any pep, caught colds easily, found things getting on her nerves. The geriatric analysis showed that almost all of her troubles stemmed from faulty diet — not enough liquids, too many starches and a dangerous shortage of thiamine, the age-fighting vitamin which the nervous system needs increasingly after 40.

Nowadays the couple's friends exclaim, "What *have* you been doing to yourselves?" Smith has not lost a day's work in a year, his infections, knocked out by penicillin, have not returned, he digests whatever he eats, his blood pressure is down to 143. Mrs. Smith is buying the size 14's she wore at 30; her metabolism rate, thanks to iodine, is back to normal; and she feels as gay as she looks. Both are grateful to medical science for a totally unlooked-for revival of vigor and interests. In reply to their friends' questions, the Smiths say: "Eat less, drink more, get a calorie chart, a good pair of scales — and leave the rest up to the doctor. That's the way to forget about birthdays — and make sure they forget about you."

MARTIN BUXBAUM, editor of *The Southern Dairy,* kissed his wife hello one evening and asked: "Well, how was everything today?"

"Pretty good. The latest issue of *Parents' Magazine* was a big help in straightening out a couple of young ladies who were acting up."

"What was the article?" asked Buxbaum.

"No article. I just rolled up the magazine and shellacked them good and proper."

— Bill Gold in Washington *Post*

As A YOUNG Frenchman pushed his son's carriage down the street, the youngster howled with rage. "Please, Bernard, control yourself," the father said quietly. "Easy there, Bernard, keep calm!"

"Congratulations, monsieur," said a woman who had been watching. "You know just how to speak to infants — calmly and gently." Then she said, "So the little fellow's named Bernard?"

"No, madame," corrected the father. "He's named André. *I'm* Bernard."

— Pierre-Jean Vaillard in *L'Anneau d'Or*

Spoken at the right time in the right way —

There is Magic

in a Word of Praise

By Fulton Oursler

A BROADWAY COMEDIAN once had an excruciating nightmare: he dreamed he was telling stories and singing songs in a crowded theater, with thousands of people watching him — but no one laughed or clapped.

"Even at $100,000 a week," he says, "that would be hell on earth."

It is not only the actor who has a deep, primal need for applause. Without praise and encouragement any one of us can lose self-confidence. Thus we all have a double necessity: to be commended and to know *how* to commend.

There is a technique in giving a compliment, a right way to go about it. It is no real compliment, for instance, to praise a man for some obvious attainment. Use discernment and originality. "That was a wonderfully convincing speech you made tonight," a gracious woman once said to a businessmen. "I could not help thinking what a fine lawyer you would have made." The merchant flushed like a schoolboy at the *unexpected* character of the tribute. As André Maurois once remarked: "The general did not thank me when I talked to him of his victories, but his gratitude was unbounded when a lady mentioned the twinkle in his eye."

No one, great or obscure, is untouched by genuine appreciation. Yale's renowned English professor, the late William Lyon Phelps, relates: "One hot summer day I went into a crowded railroad dining car for lunch. When the steward handed me the menu, I said, 'The boys in the kitchen certainly must be suffering today!' The steward looked at me in surprise. 'People come in here and complain about the food, kick about the service and growl about the heat. In 19 years you are the first person who has ever expressed any sympathy for the cooks back there in the kitchen.' What people want," Mr. Phelps concluded, "is a little attention as human beings."

In that attention, sincerity is essential. For it is sincerity — unmixed with the possibility of flattery — which gives potency to a compliment. The man coming home after a hard day's work, who sees the faces of his children pressed against the windowpane, waiting and watching for him, may water his soul with their silent but golden opinion.

The simple principles of the art of praise — to realize the human need for it, to compliment sincerely, and to train ourselves to look for the praiseworthy — help rub off the sharp edges of daily contact. And nowhere is this more true than in marriage. The wife or husband who is alert to say the heartening thing at the right moment has taken out valuable marriage insurance.

Women seem to have an instinct for such things; they look at life, so to speak, through their hearts. Lyon Mearson, the author, and Rose, his wife, were married on February 23. "Well," remarked Lyon, "I will never forget our wedding anniversary. It will always be the day after Washington's Birthday." "And I," his bride answered, "will never forget Washington's Birthday. It will always be the day before we were married."

One night Sir Max Beerbohm went with his aging wife to a theatrical party in London. As they entered the room he was ambushed by a horde of stage and film beauties, all eager to impress the great critic and caricaturist. Beerbohm turned to the lady on his arm: "My dear, let's find a quiet corner. You are looking so charming tonight that I want to talk to you alone."

Children especially are hungry for reassurance, and the want of kindly appreciation in childhood can endanger the growth of character; it can even be a lifetime calamity. A young mother told the Rev. A. W. Beaven of a heartaching incident:

"My little daughter often misbehaves and I have to rebuke her. But one day she had been an especially good girl, hadn't done a single thing that called for reprimand. That night, after I tucked her in bed and started down the stairs, I heard her sobbing. Turning back, I found her head buried in the pillow. Between sobs she asked, 'Haven't I been a *pretty* good girl to-day?'

"That question," said the mother, "went through me like a knife. I had been quick enough to correct her when she did wrong, but when she had tried to behave I had not noticed it. I had put her to bed without one word of appreciation."

The same principle — using the kind word — is potent in all human relationships. In my boyhood in Baltimore, a new drug-store opened in the neighborhood, and old Pyke Barlow, our skilled and long-established pharmacist, was outraged. He accused his young rival of selling cheap drugs and of being inexperienced in compounding prescriptions. Finally the injured newcomer, contemplating a suit for slander, consulted a wise lawyer, Thomas G. Hays. "Don't make an issue of it," Hays advised. "Try kindness."

Next day, when customers reported his rival's attacks, the new druggist said there must be a mistake somewhere. "Pyke Barlow," he told them, "is one of the finest pharmacists in this town. He'll mix an emergency prescription any hour, day or night, and the care he takes with them sets an example for all of us. This neighborhood has grown — there's plenty of room for both of us. I'm taking Doc's store as the pattern for mine."

When the older man heard these remarks — because compliments fly on the winds of gossip quite as fast as scandal — he could not wait to meet the young fellow face to face and give him some helpful advice. The feud had been wiped out by sincere and truthful praise.

Wherever human beings gather, thoughtfulness is needed. In a group conversation the kind person will help everyone to feel a part of the discussion. A friend once paid this tribute to Prime Minister Balfour as a dinner host: "He would take the hesitating remark of a shy man and discover in it unexpected possibilities, would expand it until its author felt he had really made some contribution to human wisdom. Guests would leave, walking on air, convinced that they were bigger men than they had thought."

Why must most of us leave unuttered some pleasant truths that would make others happy? It would help if we remem-

bered more often that "a rose to the living is more than sump-
tuous wreaths to the dead." A charming old gentleman used to
drop in occasionally at an antique shop near Conway, N. H.,
to sell merchandise. One day after he left, the antique dealer's
wife said she wished they had told him how much they enjoyed
his visits. The husband replied, "Next time let's tell him so."
The following summer a young woman came in and introduced herself as the daughter of the salesman. Her father, she
said, had died. Then the wife told her of the conversation she
and her husband had had after her father's last visit. The
visitor's eyes filled with tears. "How much good that would
have done my father!" she exclaimed. "He was a man who
needed to be reassured that he was liked."

"Since that day," says the shop-owner, "whenever I think
something particularly nice about a person, I tell him. I might
never have another chance."

As the painter, the musician and all other artists find joy in
giving beauty to others, so anyone who masters the art of
praising will find that it blesses the giver quite as much as the
receiver. It brings warmth and pleasure into commonplaces and
turns the noisy rattle of the world into music.

Something good can be said about everyone. We have only
to say it.

The Searching Question

At Columbia College they still remember the time the late Professor Raymond Weaver gave his first class in English literature
their first quiz. A whistle of joy went up from the group, which
had been trying to make things hard for the new instructor, when
Weaver wrote on the blackboard, "Which of the books read so
far has interested you least?"

But then Weaver wrote the second and last question: "To what
defect in yourself do you attribute this lack of interest?"

— Joseph Wood Krutch in *The Nation*

Why We All Have
"Ups and Downs"

Condensed from Redbook   Myron Stearns

F OR years psychologists have known — as you know yourself — that people react differently, on different days, to the same things. One day the Boss is genial; his secretary's small mistakes don't bother him. On other days her work must be letter-perfect or he'll bite her head off. Every mother knows that on some days her youngster is affectionate and obedient, while on others he seems "possessed." On some mornings your husband sings in his shower: on others he is glum.

"Ups and downs" are commonplace. You take it for granted that a run of bad luck will get you "down." Good news, on the other hand, raises you to the top of the world. You're sure of it.

Now along comes science to tell you you're wrong. Dr. Rexford B. Hersey of the University of Pennsylvania, who has been studying the rise and fall of human emotions for more than 17 years, has found that with all of us high and low spirits follow each other with a regularity almost as dependable as that of the tides. Outside circumstances merely advance or postpone slightly our regular periods of elation or depression. Instead of lifting you out of a slump, good news will give your spirits only a brief boost. And, conversely, bad news is less depressing when you're in an emotional "high." About 33 days after your particularly low or high spots, you're likely to find yourself feeling the same way again, for that is the normal length of the human "emotional cycle."

Research into the best working conditions for railroad repair-shop men led to Hersey's discovery of emotional cycles in 1927. Checking 25 repair-shop men every day, four times a day for more than a year, he made charts based on what they said, how they acted, their physical condition and state of mind.

Presently, to his astonishment, he found that all the charts fell into a fairly regular pattern. For each worker one week in every period was much lower than the rest, and the intervals were remarkably steady. Between the low points there was a rise to relatively high spirits.

One man lost an arm in an auto accident. It occurred during his high period, and for the first weeks of his stay at the hospital he remained cheerful. "You can't keep a good man down!" he'd say. "Maybe I'll get me a better job!"

It worked out exactly that way. Returning to work, he was given a job as a minor supervisor, with more authority and pay than he'd ever had. But by that time he was in a low period; instead of being elated, he became so depressed that he broke off his engagement to an attractive girl who was genuinely in love with him. "She'd regret it," he said. "She's just being sorry for me."

An elderly mechanic claimed he was not subject to ups and downs of any sort. "I'm always cheerful," he said. But Hersey's chart showed that about every fifth week he became much more critical of his superiors, refused to joke with his companions, and didn't want to talk with anybody.

Almost without exception, the men failed to recognize any particular changes within themselves. Outside conditions, they felt, were responsible. The reason for feeling poorly was always immediate and plausible: a man hadn't slept well, or he'd had a spat with his wife, or it was the nasty weather.

Wanting more information as to *why* our spirits go up and down and how we can use the constant ebb and flow of well-being more efficiently, Hersey made a detailed investigation of his own ups and downs.

In his low periods, he soon learned, he became more critical than at other times, and more irritable. He didn't want to be bothered by talking to people. He planned his schedule so that during his periods of depression he could devote himself to research, avoiding anything that required much self-confidence. During his high periods he scheduled his consultations and lectures.

Then he made a long-drawn-out investigation of his own internal processes to ascertain the physiological basis for his emotional changes. Joining forces with Dr. Michael J. Bennett, endocrinologist of the Doctor's Hospital in Philadelphia, he underwent every week, for over a year, a searching physical examination.

He found that the work and output of his thyroid glands, his pituitary glands, his liver and other internal production plants varied markedly from week to week. The number of his red blood corpuscles, his blood cholesterol, each had — as with all of us — its own particular rhythm. The thyroid output, which to a greater extent than any other single factor determines the total "emotional cycle" rhythm, usually makes a round trip from low to high and back in from four to five weeks. Together, Hersey and Bennett decided, all the different factors work out to a "normal" cycle length of between 33 and 36 days.

Basically this emotional cycle consists of an over-all upbuilding and giving-out of energy. But the production and use of energy do not parallel each other quite evenly. First, we gradually build up more energy than we use. That makes us feel better and better, and we become more and more active and high-spirited. So we begin to use more energy than our system is producing. This keeps on until exhaustion of our surplus energy induces a reaction. We slump, often quite sharply, into feeling tired, depressed, discouraged.

We feel on top of the world for some time after our store of energy created for best conditions has begun to diminish. And conversely we feel low for some time after the rebuilding process has started up again. When everything seems hopeless we have already turned the corner.

Bringing more and more people under observation, Drs. Hersey and Bennett concluded that variations from the 33-day cycle are largely caused by unusual thyroid activity. If you are a hyperthyroid case, your cycle may be as short as three weeks. If you have a low, or hypothyroid, output, your cycle may be several weeks longer than average. Hersey has noticed that his own emotional cycles lengthen as he gets older.

There seems to be no difference in cycle length between men and women. With women, however, the results are confused by the menstrual cycle, which has its own ups and downs. When the emotional low of the menstrual cycle and the low of the basic emotional cycle coincide, an abnormally bad state of nervousness or anxiety may develop. Many unnecessary marital separations have unquestionably, Hersey and Bennett believe, been started at such a time.

You can see at once how tremendously important these findings can be to you personally. First of all, you can lessen any discouragement you may feel from temporary setbacks, any worry or anxiety about the future you experience when you are blue, by the realization that your depression may be a perfectly natural phase of living, soon to be followed by days or weeks of greater strength, assurance and optimism. No matter how dismal the outlook may seem to be, you simply won't be able to avoid feeling better presently.

Next, you can keep track of your emotional cycles, so you will know when to expect a high or a low period. Simply mark on a calendar the days when you feel unusually discouraged or depressed. Your low days give you more accurate dates to go by than your high periods, because the "happiness" portions of your curve are usually more long-drawn-out; low periods seldom run more than a week and usually occur with regularity.

After you have found when to expect your high and low emotional tides, you can take advantage of both by planning your work intelligently. With a little experimenting you may find yourself able to plan the tough, constructive jobs, which require energy and confidence, for your high periods. At the bottom of your cycle, your powers of observation, coördination and memory seem less acute; that is the period for easy routine.

One great danger is that during low periods minor crises or mishaps seem unduly important.

"Be sure," Dr. Hersey advises, "not to let unimportant troubles be magnified just because you are 'down.'"

Try Giving Yourself Away

Condensed from Forbes

Anonymous

LIKE MOST people, I was brought up to look upon life as a process of getting. The idea of giving myself away came somewhat by accident. One night, lying awake in my berth on the Twentieth Century Limited en route to New York, I fell to wondering just where the Centuries passed each other in the night. "That would make a good subject for one of the New York Central's advertisements," I thought to myself — "Where the Centuries Pass." Next morning I wrote the New York Central System, outlining the idea and adding, "no strings attached." I received a courteous acknowledgment, and the information that the Centuries passed near Athol Springs, N. Y., nine miles west of Buffalo.

Some months later I received a second letter informing me that my idea was to be the subject of the New York Central calendar for the new year. You may recall it: a night picture of the oncoming locomotive of one Century and the observation platform of the other, a scene rich in color and railroad romance.

That summer I traveled a good deal, and in almost every railroad station and hotel lobby and travel office I entered, even in Europe, hung *my* calendar. It never failed to give me a glow of pleasure.

It was then that I made the important discovery that anything that makes one glow with pleasure is beyond money calculation in this world where there is altogether too much grubbing and too little glowing.

I began to experiment with giving-away and discovered it to be a lot of fun. If an idea for improving the window display of a neighborhood store flashes to me, I step in and make the suggestion to the proprietor. If an incident occurs, the story of which I think the local Catholic priest could use, I call him up and tell him about it, though I am not a Catholic myself. If I run across an article some Senator might want to read, I mail it to him.

It has come to a point where I sometimes send books to virtual strangers when I feel sure they would be interested in some "find" I have made. Several fine friendships have been started in that way.

Successful giving-away has to be cultivated, just as does successful getting. Opportunities are as fleeting as opportunities for earning quick profits. But you will find that ideas in giving are like some varieties of flowers — the more you pick them, the more they bloom. And giving-away makes life so much more exciting that I strongly recommend it as a hobby. You need not worry if you lack money. Of all things a person may give away, money is the least permanent in the pleasure it produces and the most likely to backfire on the giver. Emerson was wise and practical when he wrote, "The only gift is a portion of thyself."

People have different things to give. Some have time, energy, skill, ideas. Others have some special talent. All of us can give away appreciation, interest, understanding, encouragement — which require no money expenditure unless for a postage stamp or a telephone call.

The giver-away should "major" in the items in which he is "long," and fill in with the rest. Having no special talent myself, I specialize in ideas and appreciation and assorted surprises. If I am buying popcorn at a popcorn wagon and a couple of urchins are watching longingly, without looking at the children I order three bags, pay for them, hand the urchins their two bags and walk away without a word. It never fails to make the world more exciting for three people.

Of course you will be tempted to backslide. An idea popped into my head one day which I thought some department store might be able to use profitably. "Now *this* idea is worth money," I said to myself. "I'll try to sell it."

"You'll do nothing of the kind," said my wiser self. "You'll not spend your time peddling an idea; you'll give it away and get it out of your system."

So I wrote a letter to one of the world's most famous department stores, outlining the idea. It was immediately adopted with appreciation, and now I have a big department store as a friend.

I have made several discoveries about giving-away. The first is that to be successful at it one must act fast, while the impulse is fresh. Another is that little gifts are as potent as big ones in producing surprise and inducing a glow of pleasure. Simple appreciation, for example, is one of the most acceptable forms of giving-away. I have found that authors, actors, musicians, editors, lecturers, playwrights, public servants — even the biggest of them — are hungry for genuine expressions of approval. We think of them as being smothered with appreciation, whereas all too often they live on crumbs. The manufactured publicity that is created to promote them does not warm their hearts. What they crave is the spontaneous, human, friendly appreciation of the people they are trying to serve.

The other noon I was in a hotel dining room where an orchestra was playing. It was a good orchestra, offering well-chosen selections, well played. On the way out impulse prompted me to stop and say, "Gentlemen, I have thoroughly enjoyed your playing." For a second they looked almost startled. Then all of their faces broke into smiles and I left them beaming over their instruments. My own afternoon went off better for it, too.

Another discovery I have made is that it is almost impossible to give away anything in this world without getting something back — provided you are not trying to get something. Usually the return comes in some utterly unexpected form, and it is likely to be months or years later.

For example, one Sunday morning the local post office delivered an important special delivery letter to my home, though it was addressed to me at my office, and the post office had discharged its obligation by attempting to deliver it there. I wrote the postmaster a note of appreciation. More than a year later I needed a post-office box for a new business I was starting. I was told at the window that there were no boxes left, that my name would have to go on a long waiting list. As I was about to leave, the postmaster appeared in the doorway. He had overheard our conversation. "Wasn't it you who wrote us that letter a year ago about delivering a special delivery to your home?"

I said it was.

"Well, you certainly are going to have a box in this post office if we have to make one for you. You don't know what a letter like that means to us. We usually get nothing but kicks."

I had a box within the hour. Bread upon the waters!

After years of experience, this is how I have come to feel about my hobby: I have a job which pays me a living, so why should I try to drive a sharp bargain with the world for the extra ideas and impulses that come to me? I say let the world have them if they are of any value. I get my compensation out of feeling that I am a part of the life of my times, doing what I can to make things more interesting and exciting for other people. And that makes life more interesting and exciting for me, and keeps my mind keener.

As if this were not enough, I find that friends multiply and good things come to me from every direction. I've decided that the world insists on balancing accounts with givers-away — provided their hands aren't outstretched for return favors.

Marriage Matters

WHEN General Mark Clark was asked what was the best advice he ever got, he answered, "To marry the girl I did."

"Who gave you that advice, General?"

"She did."

— Tex McCrary and Jinx Falkenburg in New York *Herald Tribune*

AGATHA CHRISTIE, the detective-story writer, lives most of the time in Bagdad, where her archaeologist husband is working on important excavations. "An archaeologist," she says with conviction, "is the best husband any woman can have. The older she gets, the more he is interested in her."

— *Gothenburg Trade and Shipping Journal*, quoted by Alec de Montmorency, NANA

You're Smarter

Than You Think

By John Kord Lagemann

"Women know everything," my grandfather once told me, "and Heaven help us if they ever find it out." He was referring, of course, to feminine intuition — that mysterious faculty which enables women to answer questions before they're asked; predict the arrival of unexpected guests; identify social climbers, alcoholics and rivals as if they were plainly labeled; know without being told when their husbands have quarreled with the boss or daydreamed — just day-dreamed, mind you — about another woman.

Ever since Eve took the first bite out of the apple, man has been asking woman how she knows all these things without any apparent reason for knowing. Nothing infuriates him more than to be told: "I just know, that's all."

Does intuition really exist? And if so, is it feminine? I decided to put the question to science.

Intuition, I learned, is a normal and highly useful function of human intelligence. This fact has been confirmed by each of the half dozen authorities I consulted. Though associated with high IQs in both sexes, it is more characteristic of women than of men.

Why? As Dr. Helene Deutsch, author of *The Psychology of Women,* points out, in adolescence a boy is interested primarily in asserting himself in action, while a girl's interests center around feelings, her own and others. Dr. Deutsch compares the adolescent girl to "someone listening in the dark and perceiving every noise with special acuteness." From the understanding she gains of her own emotions she is able by analogy to relive the emotions of others.

Women don't pay nearly as much attention as men to what people say, but they are apt to know a great deal more about the way people feel. One winter when I was living in New Hampshire my friend Mr. White coveted a corner pasture which his neighbor Mr. Perry stubbornly refused to sell. The men were no longer on speaking terms, but their wives went right on visiting over the phone. One night after a long and rambling party-line visit — in which the land issue was never mentioned — Mrs. White said to her husband, "I think Mr. Perry will sell that corner lot if you still want it." When I saw the Whites a few months later the deal had been completed.

Reduced to simplest terms intuition is a way of thinking without words — a short cut to the truth, and in matters of emotion, the only way of getting there at all. Dr. Carl Jung defines it as "a basic psychological function which transmits perceptions in an unconscious way." This perception is based on the evidence of our physical senses. But because it taps knowledge and experience of which we aren't aware it is often confused with telepathy, clairvoyance or extrasensory perception. We all know the "psychic" card player who seems to read another's hand; actually he notes a telltale flutter of your eyelid or lip, a hesitation in speech, the tightening of a wrist muscle when your hand touches a card. He may not be aware himself of the clues he follows.

Civilization has substituted words and various other abstractions for the direct experience of seeing, hearing, smelling, tasting, touching and feeling. But our neglected senses still go right on operating, far better than we realize. Take the sense of smell, perhaps the least developed of the senses. We used to laugh at backwoods doctors who diagnosed certain diseases by sniffing the air near the patient. Then we discovered that these diseases really did produce chemical changes resulting in characteristic odors. Experiments have shown that the odor of a person's breath actually varies with changes in his emotional attitude. The distance over which we can unconsciously pick up the scent of another human being is unknown, but it is almost certainly greater than the length of a room. How can an odor of which you are not even aware mean anything to you? If you've ever been awakened slowly and deliciously by the aroma of coffee and bacon, you know the answer.

Last summer I saw an example of how the senses coöperate to produce intuition. On the boat from Woods Hole to Martha's Vineyard my wife nodded toward a young woman sitting nearby and remarked, "I'm sure I know her. Yet I can't remember having seen her before."

Impulsively we introduced ourselves and mentioned my wife's feeling. After the young woman had spoken, my wife said, "Now I know. You take phone calls for Dr. Miller."

"Why, yes, I do," the girl answered.

Why did my wife feel there was something familiar about the girl? "But don't you see?" she explained to me later. "She *looked* just the way she sounded over the phone." Simple as that. Come to think of it, though, can't almost any teen-ager spot a blind date from the way he or she sounded on the phone?

Most women are quite good at guessing age, particularly if the subject is another woman. If you don't believe it, try it sometime at a party. The difference between a girl of 23 and a girl of 25 is far too subtle to put into words. Men try to reason it out and usually their guesses are not better than chance or gallantry will allow. Yet with the aid of almost imperceptible clues women can often spot the difference.

One of the few attempts to observe intuition systematically was made by Dr. Eric Berne, a former staff psychiatrist with the Army Medical Corps, now a practicing psychoanalyst at Carmel, Calif. While interviewing men at an Army Separation Center, Dr. Berne and his colleagues tried to guess, before the patient had spoken, what his occupation had been in civilian life. All the patients were dressed in standard maroon bathrobes and cloth slippers. The doctors' guesses averaged well above chance. "On one occasion," Dr. Berne reports, "the occupations of 26 successive men were guessed correctly." Clues unconsciously detected in the men's eyes, gestures, facial expressions, speech, hands, and so on, probably explain this success.

As psychiatry and common sense have actually proved, you know a lot more than you are aware that you know. The mind tunes into consciousness only a few of the impressions which flow in from your sense organs. But your brain does not waste these impulses. It stores them up in your unconscious mind where they are ready to be used. Some physicians, for instance, have only to glance at a patient to diagnose correctly a disease which others cannot identify without painstaking examination. These intuitive doctors note many faint clues and match them with relevant information accumulated over a lifetime.

Likewise, every intuitive person knows how to draw on his reserve of unconscious knowledge and experience in coping with the problems of everyday life. The American Chemical Society questioned 232 leading U. S. scientists, found that 83 percent of them depended on intuition in their research after intense conscious effort had failed to produce results. A similar study by Dr. Eliot Dole Hutchinson revealed that intuition played an important part in the creative work of 80 percent of a sample of 253 artists, musicians and writers.

The unconscious part of your brain never stops working. So when you're faced with a perplexing job, work on it as hard as you can. Then if you can't lick it, try sleeping on it or taking a walk or relaxing with friends. If you have primed yourself with all available facts, the answer is likely to "dawn" on you while your mind is seemingly at rest.

In the case of a purely personal decision, the important facts are your own deep feelings, and in this case you know intuitively what to do without the need for long preliminary deliberation. Dr. Sigmund Freud once told a friend, "When making a decision of minor importance I have always found it advantageous to consider all the pros and cons. In vital matters, however, such as the choice of a mate or a profession, the decision should come from the unconscious, from somewhere within ourselves. In the important decisions of our personal lives we should be governed by the deep inner needs of our nature."

Life is much more interesting for the intuitive person than for the nonintuitive. People mean more when you understand them from the inside out — and because of this, you mean more to them. That is what intuition is, really — finding new and deeper meanings in people and events, making more sense out of life. How can you develop your intuitive powers? Like any other form of thinking, intuition requires an alertness, sensitivity and discipline of mind which have to be cultivated.

Take off the blinders of habit and open your mind to what's going on around you. See people as they really are, not as you think they ought to be. Don't let prejudices distort your vision. Half the trick is to let people tell you about themselves unconsciously. The way a person stands, sits, shakes hands, smokes or sips a drink will be, to the intuitive man or woman, important clues in sizing up character.

Intuition isn't the enemy, but the ally, of reason. Effective realistic thinking requires a combination of both.

A World of Challenge

DURING a discussion of "The World We Want" at the New York Herald Tribune Youth Forum, Johnny B. Antillon, 18-year-old delegate from the Philippines, made the following contribution:

"Usually, when I discuss with people the kind of world we want, they astonish me by describing a Utopia without cares. As for me, I like this world we have. I like living in this century — so full of strivings and plans that I feel part of a wonderful and exciting experiment. I like the suspense which gives to life its only true zest. Let me have this world, with dreams for me to dream and problems for me to solve.

"If I had lived before the A- and H-bombs I might be less optimistic of the future. But today I have great hope that we shall enjoy peace, for I feel deeply that no nation will start a war which none can possibly survive.

"I believe that this world we have deserves a vote of confidence. With its dirt and cleanness, its ups and downs and its total unexpectedness, it has given, through variety, more pleasure than pain. Whatever else it may be, this particular century is still the broadest, the most exciting, the most promising of all.

"May this world always be as challenging as it is. May it always have something to be solved, patched or mended. But above all, may this world never be a soft place for soft people with soft heads. For I want a world where a man, by facing his troubles, can prove his manhood. With a world of such challenge and scope, our lives will never be complacent, but they will certainly be worth living."

Obey That Impulse

Condensed from a CBS Broadcast

William Moulton Marston

For years as a psychologist I have sought in the careers of great and of everyday people the inner springs that make for successful living. There are two which seem to me of prime importance: The first is hard work, governed by cool, logical thoughtfulness. The other is sudden, warm, impulsive action.

Admitting that I can't name a single person of true accomplishment who hasn't forged success out of brains and hard work, I still hazard the sweeping assertion that most of the high spots and many of the lesser successes in their careers stem from *impulses* promptly turned into action.

Most of us actually stifle enough good impulses during the course of a day to change the current of our lives. These inner flashes of impulse light up the mind for an instant; then, contented in their afterglow, we lapse back into routine, feeling vaguely that sometime we might do something about it or that at least our intentions were good. In this we sin against the inner self, for impulses set up the lines of communication between the unconscious mind and daily action. Said William James, "Every time a resolve or fine glow of feeling evaporates without bearing fruit, it is worse than a chance lost; it works to hinder future emotions from taking the normal path of discharge." Thus we fail to build up the power to act in a prompt and definite way upon the principal emergencies of life.

In 1915 William Moulton Marston developed at the Harvard psychological laboratory the technique of testing deception by recording blood-pressure changes and other physical reactions. Used in the investigation of spy cases for the U. S. Army during the World War, his apparatus later became the basis of the Lie Detector machines now used in business and police work. Among Dr. Marston's books are *The Lie Detector Test, Try Living,* and *March On.*

Once, in Hollywood, where Walter B. Pitkin and I were retained by a motion-picture studio, a young promoter presented an ambitious production idea to us. The plan appealed to both of us. It was, I thought, distinctly worth considering; we could think it over, discuss it and decide later what to do. But even while I was fumbling with the idea, Pitkin abruptly reached for the phone and began dictating a telegram to a Wall Street man he knew. It presented the idea in the enthusiasm of the moment. (As delivered it was almost a yard long.) It cost money, but it carried conviction.

To my amazement, a ten-million-dollar underwriting of the picture project came as a result of that telegram. Had we delayed to talk it over we might have cautiously talked ourselves out of the whole idea. But Pitkin knew how to act on the spur of the moment. All his life he had learned to trust his impulses as the best confidential advisers he had.

Behind many an imposing executive desk sits a man who is there because he learned the same lesson. You've probably seen him in action more than once. Somebody is presenting to him a new idea, say in employe relations. It calls for extensive changes in office routine. And, deciding instantly, he calls an associate and gives instructions to make the change — then and there, not next week or next month.

We envy such men the ease with which they make up their minds and swing into action. But this ease is acquired over a long period of years. Rather than being, as we sometimes think, a privilege of their position, it is a practice that has led to their success. First in small matters and then in larger ones, they have acquired the do-it-now habit.

Calvin Coolidge remains an enigma to political commentators because the reasons for his actions were seldom apparent and the source of his astuteness could not be traced. No one could seem less impulsive than Coolidge, yet all his life he trained himself to rely on "hunches." He was not afraid of his impulses, and the celebrated Coolidge luck followed a pattern of action based on them. As a young attorney in a country law firm Coolidge was interviewing an important client one day when a telephone message informed him that the county political boss was in town. It occurred to Coolidge that he ought to see the local bigwig at once and propose himself as a candidate for the legislature. Without hesitation, this usually shy young lawyer cut his legal conference short, left the office and hunted up the county leader. That impulse bore fruit, and from then on the inner urges of Coolidge led him consistently to political success.

It should be clear from Coolidge's case that the person who follows his impulses is not necessarily flighty. The timid soul, however, is fearful lest impulse lead him into all manner of mistakes. But mistakes are inevitable — we are bound to make them no matter which course we take. Some of the worst mistakes in history have followed consciously reasoned decisions. If we're right 51 percent of the time in our impulsive actions we aren't doing badly by any standard.

The mistakes of inaction, flanked by heavy reasoning, are likely to be worse than the mistakes of genuine impulse. For one thing, they make our inertia worse day by day. Not long ago a woman whose husband had left her came to seek my advice. The difficulty between them appeared to be one of temperament which could be easily adjusted. And the woman told me that what she really wanted to do was simply to call her husband up and talk with him. I told her to follow that inclination. She left me somewhat at peace. But she didn't make the call; and in a few days she was back again. Once more she left with the impulse to call her husband. Unhappily, she never did. And a domestic rift that a few impulsive words on the phone might have healed finally ended in Reno. From childhood she had made time after time the mistake of letting her impulses die a-borning, and when the time came for a simple, direct decision in a situation that mattered, she was unable to act.

We all know people who go through agonies of indecision before taking any important step. There are always arguments for and against, and the more we think about them the more they seem to offset each other, until we wind up in a fretful state of paralysis. Impulsive action, which originates in a swift subconscious appraisal of the situation, might have saved all that worry. And when a painfully thought-out decision proves wrong, how often we remember an original hunch that would have been right!

The way to get things done is to bring mind and muscle and

voice into play at the very second a good impulse starts within us. I know a writer who was once engaged on a major project and was resolved that nothing could divert him from it. But he saw an announcement of a contest for the ten best rules for safe driving. The announcement flashed a light on the panel of his mind. Here was something he knew about. He interrupted his job long enough to get to a library and study up. He wrote 250 words. He turned in his entry in his own typing, not wanting to stop his stenographer from the bigger job. Months later that obeyed impulse netted him an award of $25,000. The project from which he turned aside for a moment finally brought him $600.

Or consider the young college instructor who sat listening one day to a commencement address by Woodrow Wilson, then governor of New Jersey. The instructor had written a book on political science, but had sought a publisher in vain. It embodied his innermost convictions and its apparent failure had caused him to despair of the future of his teaching.

Something Mr. Wilson said made the instructor feel that he ought to seek the governor's advice. He had heard that Wilson was cold and hard to approach; but at the end of the address he let his impulse carry him forward through the crowd; he grasped Mr. Wilson's hand, and said rapidly, "Your speech was wonderful! I've written a book maintaining that . . ." In a few pithy sentences he stated his theory.

Wilson shook his head. "No," he said. "You're wrong. I'll tell you why. See me after lunch at the Faculty Club." There for two hours Wilson talked earnestly. And under the inspiration Wilson gave him, the instructor wrote a new book. It sold more than 100,000 copies and launched him on a distinguished educational career. The first vital impulse, half-hesitantly obeyed, was the starting point.

The life stories of successful people are chock-full of such episodes that have marked major turning points in their careers. True impulses are intelligent. They show the path we can most successfully follow because they reveal the basic interests of the unconscious mind.

There is in all of us an unceasing urge toward self-fulfillment. We know the kind of person we want to be because our impulses, even when enfeebled by disuse, tell us. Impulsive action is not to be substituted for reason but used as a means of showing the direction reason is to take. Obviously the path is not without pitfalls. To start suddenly throwing ourselves around on impulse might be hazardous. But at least we can begin responding oftener to inner urges that we know we can trust.

We *know* that in the midst of reading we ought to stop and look up a word if the meaning is not clear. We know that we ought to speak more words of unpremeditated praise where they are due. We know that we ought to wriggle out of selfish routine and take part in civic activities, that we ought to contribute not merely money but time to the well-being of the neighborhood.

Such separate moments of achievement are cumulative and result in enriched living, a consciousness of daily adventure, a long-term sense that life is not blocked out and cut-and-dried but may be managed from within. The man whose philosophy is summed up in the feeble and indecisive motto, "Well, we'll see about it," misses the savory moments of experience, the bounce and gusto of life.

Thumb back over the pages of your own experience and note how many of your happiest moments and greatest successes have followed spur-of-the-moment actions and decisions. They are reminders that only from the depths of your inner self can you hope for an invincible urge toward accomplishment. So, obey your best impulses and watch yourself go!

Children — Seen and Heard

AN EIGHT-YEAR-OLD taken to the hospital to see a new baby was asked what she thought of him. Disappointed but polite, she stammered, "He's — he's — just my favorite shade of red!"

— Contributed by Laura Rountree

THE COCKTAIL PARTY was in full swing, when the host's small daughter pulled at her father's sleeve. "Daddy," asked the puzzled youngster, "haven't we had this party before?"

— Bob Considine, King Features

HOW TO HELP
SOMEONE IN SORROW

April 26. 2008

Condensed from The Christian Advocate   Howard Whitman

MOST OF US want to be helpful when grief strikes a friend, but often we don't know how. We may end up doing nothing because we don't know the right — and helpful — things to say and do. Because that was my own experience recently, I resolved to gather pointers which might be useful to others as well as to myself.

Ministers, priests and rabbis deal with such situations every day. I went to scores of them, of all faiths, in all parts of the country.

Here are some specific suggestions they made:

1. *Don't try to "buck them up."* This surprised me when the Rev. Arthur E. Wilson of Providence, R. I., mentioned it. But the others concurred. It only makes your friend feel worse when you say, "Come now, buck up. Don't take it so hard."

A man who has lost his wife must take it hard (if he loved her). "Bucking him up" sounds as though you are minimizing his loss. But the honest attitude, "Yes, it's tough, and I sure know it is," makes your friend feel free to express grief and recover from it. The "don't take it so hard" approach deprives him of the natural emotion of grief, stops up the safety valve God has given him.

2. *Don't try to divert them.* Rabbi Martin B. Ryback of Norwalk, Conn., pointed out that many people making condolence calls purposely veer away from the subject. They make small talk about football, fishing, the weather — anything but the reason for their visit.

The rabbi calls this "trying to camouflage death." The task of the mourner, difficult as it is, is to face the fact of death, and go on from there. "It would be far better," Rabbi Ryback suggested, "to sit silently and say nothing than to make obvious attempts to distract. The sorrowing friend sees through the effort to divert him. When the visitor leaves, reality hits him all the harder."

3. *Don't be afraid to talk about the person who has passed away*. Well-intentioned friends often shy away from mentioning the deceased. The implication is that the whole thing is too terrible to mention.

"The helpful thing," advised Rabbi Henry E. Kagan of Mount Vernon, N. Y., "is to talk about the person as you knew him in the fullness of his life, to re-create a living picture to replace the picture of death."

Once Rabbi Kagan called on a woman who had lost her brother. "I didn't know your brother too well," he said. "Tell me about him." The woman started talking and they discussed her brother for an hour. Afterward she said, "I feel relieved now for the first time since he died."

4. *Don't be afraid of causing tears*. When a good friend of mine lost a child I said something which made his eyes fill up. "I put my foot in it," I said, in relating the incident to the Rev. D. Russell Hetsler of Brazil, Ind. "No, you didn't," he replied. "You helped your friend to express grief in a normal, healthy way. That is far better than to stifle grief when friends are present, only to have it descend more crushingly when one is all alone."

Fear of causing tears, probably more than anything else, makes people stiff and ineffective. Visiting a friend who has lost his wife, they may be about to mention a ride in the country when they remember the man's wife used to love rides in the country. They don't dare speak of peonies because they were her favorite flower. So they freeze up.

"They really are depriving their friend of probably the greatest help they could give him," Pastor Hetsler commented. "That is, to help him experience grief in a normal way and get over it." Medical and psychological studies back up the pastor's contention that *expressing* grief is good and *repressing* it is bad. "If a comment of yours brings tears," he concluded, "remember — they are healthy tears."

5. *Let them talk*. "Sorrowing people need to talk," explained the Rev. Vern Swartsfager of San Francisco. "Friends worry about their ability to *say* the right things. They ought to be worrying about their ability to *listen*."

If the warmth of your presence can get your friend to start talking, keep quiet and listen — even though he repeats the same things a dozen times. He is not telling you news but expressing feelings that need repetition. Pastor Swartsfager suggested a measuring stick for the success of your visit: "If your friend has said a hundred words to your one, you've helped a lot."

6. *Reassure — don't argue*. "Everybody who loses a loved one has guilt feelings — they may not be justified but they're natural," Rabbi Joseph R. Narot of Miami pointed out. A husband feels he should have been more considerate of his wife; a parent feels he should have spent more time with his child; a wife feels she should have made fewer demands on her husband. The yearning, "If only I had not done this, or done that — if I only had a chance to do it now," is a hallmark of grieving.

These feelings must work their way out. You can give reassurance. Your friend must slowly come to the realization that he or she was, in all probability, a pretty good husband, wife or parent.

7. *Communicate — don't isolate*. Too often a person who has lost a loved one is overwhelmed with visitors for a week or so; then the house is empty. Even good friends sometimes stay away, believing that people in sorrow "like to be alone."

"That's the 'silent treatment,'" remarked Father Thomas Bresnaham of Detroit. "There's nothing worse." Our friend has not only lost his loved one — he has lost us too.

It is in that after-period, when all the letters of sympathy have been read and acknowledged and people have swung back into daily routine, that friends are needed most.

Keep in touch, Father Bresnaham urges. See your friend more often than you did before. See him for any purpose — for lunch, for a drive in the country, for shopping, for an evening visit. He has suffered a deep loss. Your job is to show him, by implication, how much he still has left. Your being with him is a proof to him that he still has resources.

8. *Perform some concrete act.* The Rev. William B. Ayers of Wollaston, Mass., told me of a sorrowing husband who lost all interest in food until a friend brought over his favorite dish and simply left it there at suppertime. "That's a wonderful way to help, by a concrete deed which in itself may be small yet carries the immense implication that you care," Pastor Ayers declared.

We should make it our business, when a friend is in sorrow, to do at least one practical, tangible act of kindness. Here are some to choose from: run errands with your car, take the children to school, bring in a meal, do the dishes, make necessary phone calls, pick up mail at the office, help acknowledge condolence notes, shop for the groceries.

9. *Swing into action.* Action is the symbol of going on living.

By swinging into action with your friend, whether at his hobby or his work, you help build a bridge to the future. Perhaps it means painting the garage with him, or hoeing the garden. Or spending an afternoon with a woman friend mending the children's clothes, or browsing through antique shops.

In St. Paul, Minn., the Rev. J. T. Morrow told me of a man who had lost a son. The man's hobby had been refinishing furniture. When he called on him Pastor Morrow said, "Come on, let's go down to the basement." They sanded a table together. When Pastor Morrow left, the man said, "This is the first time I've felt I could go on living."

Sorrowing people, Pastor Morrow pointed out, tend to drop out of things. They're a little like the rider who has been thrown from a horse. If they are to ride again, better get them back on the horse quickly. *pilet the same way after crush*

10. *"Get them out of themselves,"* advised Father James Keller, leader of the Christophers. Once you have your friend doing things for himself, his grief is nearly cured. Once you have him doing things for others, it *is* cured.

Grief runs a natural course. It will pass. But if there is only a vacuum behind it, self-pity will rush in to fill it. To help your friend along the normal course of recovery, guide him to a new interest.

Volunteer work for a charity, enrollment in a community group to help youngsters, committee work at church or temple are ways of getting people "out of themselves."

If you and I, when sorrow strikes our friends, follow even a few of these pointers, we will be helpful.

Ministers, priests and rabbis have a spiritual job to do; they can do that better than we can. But we have a practical job of helpfulness; we can do that better than they.

One of the clergymen I met on my rounds, the Rev. Loyal M. Thompson of Kewanee, Ill., carried with him for years — until it was worn to shreds — a bookmark which a woman had embroidered for him. On visits to people in sorrow he would show them the back of the embroidery, a senseless mass of threads going every which way. Then he would turn it over to the right side, and the threads spelled out "God Is Love."

We may not be able to explain what often seems senseless about death. But by our helpfulness we can give living proof of the right side of the embroidery.

Courage

The courage that my mother had
    Went with her, and is with her still:
Rock from New England quarried;
    Now granite in a granite hill.

The golden brooch my mother wore
    She left behind for me to wear;
I have no thing I treasure more:
    Yet, it is something I could spare.

Oh, if instead she'd left to me
    The thing she took into the grave! —
That courage like a rock, which she
    Has no more need of, and I have.

—Edna St. Vincent Millay, *Mine the Harvest:*
A Collection of New Poems (Harper)

You Won't Be Snubbed

By
Henry Morton Robinson

ROUND ME, a bright-muffled throng of winter-sports enthusiasts loafed in the white Adirondack sunshine. Lean ski jumpers puffed at blunt brown pipes; bobsledders tossed challenges and snowballs at each other; wind-burned débutantes, whose color was at least half their own, basked in deck chairs. The thin northern air crackled with frost and gaiety; everyone was having fun.

That is, everyone but me. The deck chair beside me was vacant, yet no one sat down in it. For years, no one ever *did* sit down by me voluntarily. For some reason I had always been unable to draw other human beings into warm personal contacts.

But the whole picture changed on that snow-brilliant day when David Jessup sat down in the deck chair beside me. I had particularly observed this man; it was a joy to watch him approach a stranger and melt the icy cellophane that most human beings come wrapped in. I saw him do it dozens of times, so gently and so *right* that even the chilliest glaze of hostility was quickly transformed into a lubricating warmth between two human beings. I envied him his easy approach to others, yet I would have gone to my grave (so stern were the proprieties of my New England upbringing) before speaking to him or any stranger first.

But evidently my high-fenced reserve was no barrier to Jessup, for he turned his friendly gray eyes on me, and smiled with genuine good nature. There were no inanities about the weather, no self-conscious preliminaries. Like a man imparting news of interest to an old friend, he said without tension or embarrassment: "I saw you watching that bronzed chap mending his snowshoes. He's the Rhodes Scholar from New York. He stroked the Cornell crew last year and was president of the debating club besides. Don't you think he's a splendid type to represent American youth at Oxford?"

Jessup's opening remarks led us at once into a discussion of Cecil Rhodes' dream of cementing Anglo-American friendship. From that take-off, our talk continued through many fields of common interest and special information. When we stopped an hour later we were friends. It was something of a miracle, and I asked Jessup point-blank how he did it.

"Your happy knack of speaking to strangers — how do you manage it? Personally, I'm limited in my human acquaintance, which is confined to a small circle of friends, all of the same type. All my life I've wanted to mingle with strangers who could widen my interests and quicken my sense of being alive, yet I've always hung back, afraid of a rebuff. How does one overcome this fear of being snubbed?"

Jessup waved his hand inclusively at the throng around us. "My fear of being snubbed," he said, "completely disappears when I remember that the dearest friends I have were once strangers. So when I see a young woman arranging a cluster of holly boughs, or a group of men tinkering with a bobsled, they needn't belong to my private collection of acquaintances before I speak to them. If I speak, perhaps they *will* belong to that collection, and I shall be the richer for knowing them."

"But," I persisted, "how about being misunderstood?"

"If you approach your fellow man with honest sympathy and a desire to be humanly friendly," said Jessup, "he is not likely to misread your motive. I have met men of the most formidable self-importance, and found them all responsive, eager to visit with me. Rarely have I encountered even the slightest hint of a snub. No, my friend, you mustn't let fear be the basis of your seclusion. The new, the unusual, is no more dangerous than the familiar, and it has the advantage of being decidedly more exciting."

Subsequent experiences with David Jessup proved how right he was. Wherever he went, he would enter into conversation with all manner of people, and was forever turning up strange new types and odd, stimulating information. On one of our trips together we passed a granite quarry in which a number of men were walking about on tiptoe, carrying red flags and acting like advance messengers of doom. Instead of hurrying past, Jessup spoke to one of the flag-carriers, and in a few moments the man was telling us a hair-curling story. It seems that many years ago, engineers had drilled 50 holes in this quarry, packed the holes with dynamite, then wired them up for a blast. But some of the wiring was defective, and as a result only half of the dynamite exploded! For 20 years workmen could not be persuaded to go near the quarry; it had to be abandoned, and was now being reopened by men who received double pay because of the attendant danger.

Another time, on the shore of a beautiful lake in a state park, Jessup noticed a man making sketches. Skillfully engaging the man in conversation, Jessup discovered that he was a marine horticulturist with a new idea called "pond-scraping." "On the lakes surrounding the ancient Aztec capital," said the sketcher, "were many floating islands covered with feathery trees and rare flowers. I believe that I have rediscovered how such islands can be constructed and kept in motion, and am now making some sketches to interest the park commission in my idea."

On the way home I remarked, "That was one of the most interesting things that ever happened to me. Both the man and his drawings were fascinating."

Jessup agreed, then added slyly: "And you wouldn't have met him in a thousand years if you had waited for an introduction, would you?"

"Don't rub it in, please. I've always known that I was missing a great deal, but I never knew how to get people started."

"To talk to a stranger," advised Jessup, "begin with a remark that penetrates to the core of his interest. Usually it will be something that applies to his work. Inane general remarks or fussy little questions only irk the busy man. One must be genuinely interested in what the stranger is doing, make an intelligent comment, then wait for him to respond. And he *will* respond, for the simple reason that most human beings are overjoyed when another person shows interest in their work. Take that floating-garden chap for instance: if we had seemed bored he wouldn't even have begun to talk, for no man likes to expose his treasures to the indifferent. But when he saw that we were really deriving pleasure from his conversation, he tried to reward our interest and prolong our pleasure. Why should he do this? Simply because no one has ever yet discovered a keener happiness than giving pleasure to others."

I was always expecting Jessup to be snubbed, but the snub never came. Once while touring with him, a trio of noisy roughs boarded our bus and began to annoy the passengers with a display of downright coarseness. Dignified, serious, Jessup got up and went back to them. "Here," thought I, "my friend is riding for a fall." But I was wrong. What Jessup said to those fellows I never knew, but within five minutes he had engaged the three of them in an earnest discussion of labor conditions throughout the country and their own chances of employment.

I've seen Jessup address women bred in the strictest code of convention, and often wondered how he avoided being cut by them. He explained it in this way: "If in speaking to a woman you reveal that you are primarily interested in her personally or as a member of the opposite sex, she will instantly resent it, as she has every right to do. In effect, you are insulting her by the assumption that her attention may be so cheaply won. But speak to her as one human being to another, as one interested in the same scenery, the same music, or the same social problems, and she will extend her ready fellowship. Both men and women love to use their minds, and women especially regard it as a distinct compliment to be met on the intellectual plane that both sexes hold in common."

Since knowing David Jessup, the stranger at my elbow has become the most interesting and approachable thing in life. No longer do I ride for hours in cold dumbness beside him rather than risk one tentative remark. For I have grown to believe that he is just as eager to know me — to know why I wear ear muffs and smoke a calabash pipe — as I am to know similar things about him. And I have finally learned that if I approach him unaffectedly, without a false sense of toploftiness on the one hand, or advantage-grabbing on the other, there is no danger of my being snubbed.

For ultimately we are not so different from one another.

Training and tradition may have cast us in dissimilar molds, but the basic stuff of our humanity is pathetically the same. It is this realization that now makes every stranger accessible to me. He may be a barber or a banknote-engraver, but it is almost certain that he can tell me something that will heighten my mental stature or increase my spiritual gauge. I may like him or I may not; if he bores me, I can be off. But the thing that constantly surprises me is the scarcity of people who are really boresome or offensive. By far the larger part of our human race is composed of unexpectedly interesting and friendly members, all pitifully eager to know each other. And I have yet to see the man or woman who did not become more attractive and more *alive* for laying aside their too-prized reserve and mingling on equal terms with other members of our common, struggling, hungering human family.

My Father's Legacy

From an Elsa Maxwell CBS Broadcast

I HAD a wonderful father. I was his only child. In 1907 my father sent for me and said, "I'm going to die and I've nothing to leave you. You've got to go out into the world and make your own living. How are you going to do it? You're nothing much to look at, never will be. You have no name. You haven't any money. But I'm going to leave you a legacy. It's three simple rules.

"First, never be afraid of 'they.' People are more afraid of 'they' than anything else in the world. Strong generals with great armies will face courageously the most outrageous foes yet be terrified of what 'they' might say, 'they' might do, 'they' mightn't like.

"The second rule," he said, "is even more important. Never collect inanimate objects. You can't do it, for they collect you." So I thought the more you own the more you are possessed; therefore I own nothing but essentials. I'm free as air, and it's wonderful.

And the third one, which suited me rather well, he said was, "Always laugh at yourself first. Everybody has a ridiculous side and the whole world loves to laugh at somebody else. You laugh at yourself first, and the laughter of others falls off harmlessly as if you were in golden armor." I have always followed that, too.

— *Talks*

Turn Your Sickness into an Asset

Louis E. Bisch, M.D.   Author of "Be Glad You're Neurotic"

O NLY YESTERDAY you were marching in health and vigor; sickness was a far-off shadow. Then suddenly illness unhinged your knees, brought you limply to bed. And now you are a horizontal citizen of the sickroom, an unwilling initiate in the fellowship of pain.

Your reaction is to rail fretfully against fate, to resent bitterly such untimely interference with life's routine. Yet your illness can confer substantial benefits — and not just in the realm of Job-like piety, either. An enforced holiday in bed blamelessly releases us from a too-busy world, sharpens our mental and spiritual perceptions, and permits a clearer perspective on our lives. Any serious illness should be regarded as an opportunity to gather dividends and generate energies that mere health cannot possibly bestow.

I am not speaking of those chronic sufferers whose illness dooms them to a life of invalidism, and whose heroic readjustments lift them above the rank of ordinary men. The great American historian Francis Parkman is a triumphant prototype of all such conquerors of pain. During the greater part of his life, Parkman suffered so acutely that he could not work for more than five minutes at a time. His eyesight was so wretched that he could scrawl only a few gigantic words on a manuscript. He was racked by major digestive trouble, terrific rheumatism and agonizing headaches. Physically, almost *everything* was wrong with him, yet he contrived to write nearly 20 magnificent volumes of history.

But our interest here centers on the ordinary mortal stricken for the first time. These sick-chamber casuals rarely learn to make the most of illness, regarding it only as a visitation of bad luck. Yet thousands actually have found themselves for the first time during sickness. The "beloved physician," Dr. Edward Livingston Trudeau, was sent, as a young doctor, to the mountains where he expected to die of tuberculosis. But he did not die. As he lay in bed he had a vision of a great hospital where he could rebuild other sufferers. Flat on his back, he examined patients not as ill as himself. He raised money and labored until his dream became the great sanatorium at Saranac that helped thousands of tuberculosis patients. Trudeau's affliction turned an unknown doctor into a physician of world-wide fame.

Eugene O'Neill was an utter drifter with no plan of life until he was 25. A serious breakdown gave him the requisite leisure, he says, "to evaluate the impressions of many years in which experiences had crowded one upon the other, with never a second's reflection." It was in the hospital that he first began to write the plays that revolutionized American drama.

Like any major experience, illness actually changes us. How? Well, for one thing we are temporarily relieved from the terrible pressure of meeting the world head-on. Responsibility melts away like snow on an April roof; we don't have to catch trains, tend babies, or wind the clock. We enter a realm of introspection and self-analysis. We think soberly, perhaps for the first time, about our past and future. Former values are seen to be fallacious; habitual courses of action appear weak, foolish or stubborn. Illness, it seems, gives us that rarest thing in the world — a *second chance,* not only at health but at life itself!

Illness knocks a lot of nonsense out of us; it induces humility, cuts us down to our own size. It enables us to throw a searchlight upon our inner selves and to discover how often we have rationalized our failures and weaknesses, dodged vital issues and run skulkingly away. Mistakes made in our jobs, marriage and social contacts stand out clearly. Especially when we are a bit scared is the salutary effect of sickness particularly marked; typhoid and pneumonia have reformed drunkards, thieves, liars and wife-beaters. If a stiff bout of illness brings us near to death's door — perhaps so much the better. For only when the way straitens and the gate grows narrow, do some people discover their soul, their God, or their life work.

Florence Nightingale, too ill to move from her bed, reorganized the hospitals of England. Semiparalyzed, and under the constant menace of apoplexy, Pasteur was tireless in his attack on disease. Innumerable illustrations might be cited. And the testimony from humbler sources is just as striking. A young man in a hospital for two weeks discovered that he had always wanted to be a research worker in chemistry. Till then he had been "too busy" as a drug salesman. Today he is making a splendid go of his new job. While recuperating from scarlet fever a woman in her 40's vanquished the terrors she had felt about approaching middle life. "I am not going to return to my former state of feeling superfluous," she resolved. "My children are married and can take care of themselves. I'm going to start a millinery shop and make them like it." She did, and needless to say, they do!

In talking with patients, I find that many who have sojourned in "the pleasant land of counterpane" say that for the first time they learned the true meaning of friendship, often undecipherable in the complex pattern of this modern world. They say also that they discovered secret depths of their own life-stream. "After a few days in bed," writes one of them, "time becomes an unimagined luxury. Time to think, time to enjoy, time to create, time at last to express the best and deepest part of human nature. Illness is one of the great privileges of life; it whispers that man's destiny is bound up with transcendental powers. Illness pares and lops off the outer parts of life and leaves one with the essence of it."

Even pain confers spiritual insight, a beauty of outlook, a philosophy of life, an understanding and forgiveness of humanity — in short, a quality of peace and serenity — that can scarcely be acquired by the "owner of pure horse flesh." Suffering is a cleansing fire that chars away much of the meanness, triviality and restlessness of so-called "health." Milton declared, "Who best can suffer, best can do." The proof is his *Paradise Lost* written after he was stricken blind.

In illness you discover that your imagination is more active than it ever has been; unshackled by petty details of existence, you day-dream, build air castles, make plans. As your physical strength returns, your fantasies are not dulled; rather they become more practical, and you definitely decide upon the things you will put into action when you recover.

Your concentration improves tremendously. You are astonished to find how easily you can think a difficult problem through to its solution. Why? Because your instincts of self-preservation are speeded up, and all non-essentials are eliminated. It is interesting too that your reactions to what you see and hear are more acute. A robin at the window, a fleeting expression on a friend's face, are delicately savored as memorable experiences. Illness *sensitizes* you; that is why you may be irritable. You may even weep at the least provocation. But this sensitivity should be turned to better uses. Now is an excellent time to develop yourself along a special line, to read widely, or to create original ideas. Contrary to an old belief, a sick body does not necessarily make a sick mind, except in those who try to make their illness an excuse for laziness. No one honestly can use his illness, whatever its nature, as an excuse for ineffectualness or failure.

Artists and lovers have always known that suffering confers a radiant beauty upon the afflicted. Such beauty has nothing to do with make-up or negligee. Rather it is an inner loveliness, illuminating the spirit and features of those who have learned to look upon illness as a challenge that must be met with hope and courage.

If you have never been sick, never lost so much as a day in bed — then you have missed something! When your turn comes, don't be dismayed. Remind yourself that pain and suffering may teach you something valuable, something that you could not have learned otherwise. Possibly it may change for the better the entire course of your life. You and those around you will be happier if you can look upon any illness as a blessing in disguise, and wisely determine to make the most of it. You *can* turn your sickness into an asset.

BECAUSE of the housing shortage near the military base where he was stationed, a young doctor and his wife and three children had to live in cramped quarters in a hotel. A friend said to the doctor's six-year-old daughter, "Isn't it too bad that you don't have a home?"

"Oh, we have a home," the youngster replied quickly. "We just don't have a house to put it in." — Contributed by M. Elizabeth Lynch

You can enhance your personality and broaden your
opportunities by learning to speak effectively

Put Your
Best Voice Forward

Condensed from The American Magazine

Stephen S. Price

Have you ever heard how your voice
sounds to others? If not, go to a
corner of the room. Face closely into the corner, cup your ears
and speak a few words. That stranger you hear talking is you.

It is this voice which has been labeling you in people's minds.
It labels you every time you meet someone at a party, greet a
new customer, express an opinion at a meeting or talk on the
telephone.

Is it a voice that gives warmth and assurance, that helps you
make the right impression?

There is no one who cannot make his or her voice more
appealing. In acting as voice counselor to thousands of people
in the past 21 years I have found five major vocal shortcomings.
To check up on them in yourself, ask yourself these questions:

"Is my speech slurred rather than clear?"

Do people frequently misunderstand you or ask you to repeat? Say this sentence aloud several times: "Leaves, frost
crisped, break from the trees and fall." If it makes you feel a
little tongue-tied you are probably lip lazy. Vowels are easy to
say, but we get power and clarity into our speech with conso-
nants. To pronounce these properly you must use the tongue,
lips and teeth energetically.

A father asked me to help his 19-year-old daughter, whose
speech was listless and mumbling. She was moody and unhappy. I encouraged her to spend 30 minutes each day in front

of a mirror energetically repeating the alphabet, and five minutes whistling. Whistling is a good corrective for lip laziness. Within two months people began noticing a change in her.

If you need to make your enunciation clearer, practice talking like Gary Cooper, through clenched teeth. This makes you work your tongue and lips harder. With teeth closed tightly, read aloud, slowly at first, then rapidly. Repeat such phrases as, "He thrust three thousand thistles through the thick of his thumb." You'll find you have to exert more power in your breath, and your speech will be more energetic.

"Is my voice harsh rather than agreeable?"

Shrill, grating or brassy voices stem from tension in the throat and jaw. Foreigners often comment on the harsh voices of American women. (Tension shows up more in a woman's voice.)

To relax your throat muscles, slump forward in your chair. Let your head drop, your jaw sag and your arms flop. Slowly and gently roll your head in a circle. Continue circling three minutes. Then yawn a few times, opening your mouth wide and then say such words as "clock," "squaw," "gong," "claw."

For at least a few minutes every day concentrate on talking slowly and gently to people — as if talking to a baby or a puppy. Gradually, gentleness will pervade all your talk.

"Is my voice weak?"

Your diaphragm, the band of muscle a few inches above your midriff, is the bellows that blows fire into your speech and adds oomph to your personality. If your diaphragm is weak you probably have a thin, uncertain, shy voice. People don't pay much attention when you talk.

A young research expert with a wispy voice said to me, "In a group I rarely get a chance to finish a sentence. Someone always butts in." I put my hand on his diaphragm and asked him to say loudly, "Boomlay, boomlay, boomlay, boom!" His diaphragm muscle barely fluttered. A well-developed diaphragm will really bounce when you say "boom."

To give him a vigorous diaphragm I prescribed boxing lessons and daily "deep-breathing walks." I also told him to lie on the floor breathing deeply, with a heavy book on his diaphragm. Then to shout several times, "Hay! he! ha! hi! ho!

who!" Then to sit up, inhale and blow out through a tiny hole formed by pursed lips. After these exercises he was to pick up a newspaper and see how long he could read aloud with one breath. As his diaphragm strengthened he was able to read for 15, and later 20, seconds in one breath (25 is excellent).

But it is breath control, not mere lung capacity, that gives you an outstanding voice. To check your breath control, hold a lighted candle four inches from your mouth and say, "Peter Piper picked a peck of pickled peppers." If you blow out the flame you have poor breath control.

Whispering aloud is an excellent way to develop breath control and voice power. Have a friend stand across the room, then whisper loudly to him. As soon as he can hear you clearly, have him move into another room, and then go as far away as your whisper can reach him.

"Is my voice flat rather than colorful?"

Many persons talk in a droning, boring monotone. A prim New England woman with a cold, listless voice once came to me. I asked her if she knew anyone who got a big kick out of life. She said, "Yes, the Italian who helps with our gardening." She envied his exuberance. To help bring warmth to her voice, I suggested she spend a few hours each week working along with him. I also instructed her to laugh out loud, up and down the musical scale — first using "ho," then "ha," "he" and "hoo." She was to do it slowly at first and then faster and faster. In two months her voice took on warmth and feeling.

A widespread cause of flatness is "talking through the nose" in a twangy manner, a common quality in American speech. To check for this defect, hold your nose and say "meaning." Notice how strangely muffled it sounds. Feel the vibration. That is because the sounds "m," "n," and "ng" (and only those three basic sounds) are resonated mainly in the nose. Say, "Father Manning." You should feel vibration in your nose only when you say "Manning." If any other letters sound muffled, you are probably nasal in your speech.

To stop talking through your nose and add richness to your voice, use your mouth, throat and chest. The farther you open your mouth, the richer, fuller and lower your tones will be. Try saying "olive" by opening your lips only slightly. Now repeat it while really opening your mouth and see the difference. To add vibrance to your voice, hum your favorite songs at odd moments every day.

"Is my voice high-pitched?"

You cannot actually "lower" your voice, but you can increase the use of your lower register by practicing sounds that can be resonated in the chest, such as, "Alone, alone, all, all alone. Alone, alone on a wide, wide sea."

Say, "Hello, how are you?" The first time, put your hand on your forehead and pitch your voice toward your hand. Now put your hand on your chest and low-pitch your words to the chest. Notice the greater depth and richness? You also can develop the warm lower tones of your voice by breathing more deeply as you talk and striving to speak softly, even when under stress.

A few general suggestions: Join in group singing. Read aloud classics such as the Bible. This will challenge and improve your articulation and rhythm. After a month or so of regular practice, your new way of speaking will begin to be automatic. When you sound better you can't help feeling better, and you will not only enjoy increased self-respect but people will look at you in a new way.

COURAGE begins when we can admit that there is no life without some pain, some frustration; that there is no tragic accident to which we are immune; and that beyond the normal exercise of prudence we can do nothing about it.

But courage goes on to see that the triumph of life is not in pains avoided, but in joys lived completely in the moment of their happening. Courage lies in never taking so much as a good meal or a day of health and fair weather for granted. It lies in learning to be aware of our moments of happiness as sharply as our moments of pain. We need not be afraid to weep when we have cause to weep, so long as we can really rejoice at every cause for rejoicing.

— Victoria Lincoln in *The Arts of Living* (Simon and Schuster)

HOW TO STOP SMOKING

Condensed from the book   Herbert Brean

IF YOU SMOKE, and wish you didn't, a wonderful experience lies ahead of you: the experience of freeing yourself from a burden — of rediscovering that you are your own boss. It won't come without effort. But if you make the effort you will win.

Why do people smoke? Medically speaking, tobacco is not habit-forming; it does not worm its way into your physique and psyche, as opium or cocaine does. But it *is* habit-forming in the same way that three meals a day, or eight hours' sleep, or wearing clothes, are habit-forming. If you go without any one of them for a while you become uncomfortable.

But how comfortable are you with tobacco? Smoke a cigarette. Does it really satisfy you — in the way that a big meal does when you're hungry, or a warm coat when you're cold? You know better.

Light it, smoke it, taste its bitterness, put it out. Even as you do, you know that you'll soon want another. Not that you enjoy it. You simply want it.

Why? When you smoke, nicotine, carbon monoxide, small amounts of hydrocyanic acid, pyridine and various phenols and aldehydes are absorbed into your lungs and mouth, and then

---

THE METHOD set forth in this small book has been of enormous help to thousands of unwilling smokers. Now in its tenth printing, *How to Stop Smoking* is sold with the guarantee that the purchaser's money will be refunded if, after reading the book and following the author's advice, he is unable to break the habit.

various things begin to happen. Your nervous system is momentarily stimulated. You start to salivate. Your blood pressure goes up. Your pulse rate increases. Tremors may appear in your hands and arms, and your extremities usually show a drop in temperature. (You notice none of these things, of course, though they are plainly detectable in the laboratory.)

Most important of all, your blood vessels undergo a constriction. The effect on them is like putting a flowing garden hose in a vise and tightening the vise a few turns. It "slows you down."

That is, after the momentary stimulation, smoking depresses, for a far longer period, both the sympathetic and the central nervous systems of the human body, as well as the endings of the motor nerves which activate the voluntary muscles.

This means that when you smoke you are artificially slowing down your body's normal activities. Now, suppose you are suddenly confronted with an emotional or psychological emergency: adrenalin is pumped into your blood stream, your muscles tense, you breathe faster and get edgy, jittery — "nervous." Tobacco smoke retards these natural processes by constricting your arteries, slowing down the blood circulation and thus "calming you down." You find a smoke is "good for your nerves."

If that were as far as it went there would be no occasion for worry. In fact, if you smoked only at times of real emotional stress it might be a good thing for you. But smoking goes much further than that.

If you smoke a pack and a half of cigarettes a day, you smoke an average of one cigarette every 32 minutes of your waking hours. That many crises don't arise every day. You need cigarettes simply because your body has come to expect this depressant effect every so often. If it doesn't get it you begin consciously to want a cigarette. When your body becomes habituated to tobacco you want a smoke fairly regularly. You are unhappy if you *don't* have it.

There is little pleasure in smoking — until you so inure your body to it that it puts up with the harsh taste, the hot dryness, the mouth bite, for the sake of tobacco's mild narcotic effect. If it were possible for you to go without cigarettes for the next 24 hours, and then light one, you would find out how distasteful and noxious tobacco smoke really is. After two deep inhalations of the first cigarette your head would be swimming, your legs and arms shaky. You might even feel faint and have to sit down. If you think that is an exaggeration, try it.

Or think back to the time many years ago when you smoked your first cigarette. Divorced from all the glamour and excitement of your first smoke, how did it *taste?* Gaseous, strong, biting, wasn't it?

Yet this is the experience that you give your system 30 to 60 times a day. You are able to do it because the human mechanism is a marvelously adjustable piece of machinery which can get used to living amid coal dust, or 110-degree heat, or doing the work of a truck horse. You can get used to almost anything.

Very well, you say, smoking is a bad habit. We've heard that before. What do we do about it?

It ought to encourage you to know that you have already taken one big step toward giving up smoking. For you have already read this far — which means that, for that long at least, you have been *thinking* about smoking and about giving it up. And that is an important rule. If you want to stop smoking, *think about giving it up.*

Think of it coolly and calmly, without fear or hopelessness. Many others have done it. You can, too. Consider the whole idea objectively for a little while. If you are not smoking at this minute, maybe it would be a good idea to take out a cigarette or pipe and light up. Analyze what you do and what you taste and smell. Drag the smoke into your lungs slowly and slowly exhale it. Just how good is it, really? Does it have the fragrance and goodness the copywriters claim?

Think for a moment of how much you get out of it, of how pleasurable it really is — aside from the negative pleasure of easing an otherwise painful craving. Then think of what it would be like not ever to *have* to smoke.

For giving up smoking isn't all asceticism and self-denial; there are compensations. In fact, there are so many that when you give yourself a chance to appreciate them you will never want to go back to nicotine.

When you give up smoking your food will taste much better. Your nose and throat and lungs will not be continuously permeated with smoke and smoke's residue, soot. You will begin to *smell* the world around you. When you walk into a garden you will *smell* as well as *see* flowers; as you come home at night your nose will tell you what's for dinner.

Your teeth will look cleaner because they *are* cleaner, and they will not require a dentist's cleaning so often. The yellow stain on your fingers will disappear in a few days or a week. When you get up in the morning you won't find your throat clogged with phlegm, and you won't cough or clear your throat so often.

You will actually feel far less nervous. That's hard to believe — and during the first days of nonsmoking you *will* be nervous. The depressant effect smoking has exerted on your body for years suddenly ends, and the unfamiliar effect is almost overwhelming. You will possibly be more emotional, laughing at trivial things, and, for a while, tense, jumpy. But gradually the nervousness diminishes. When you are over it, you will be surprised what experiences you can meet and live through without reaching for a cigarette.

You'll be calmer, more poised, and you may well find that there now are more hours in the day. For, when you stop slowing down your body and cutting your energy with tobacco, you will find that you have much more energy; you sleep better and feel better adjusted. So there seems to be more time to get things done.

A word of caution here. It is generally believed that a reformed smoker gains weight. If you are of normal weight or underweight, there is nothing to worry about. If you have trouble with your waistline, remember this: When you stop smoking you will probably gain. Don't worry about it — face it! Actually you will not gain more than a few pounds. For when you stop smoking you will have a great increase in *energy;* and in using up that *energy* you will burn away a lot of the weight that you put on.

If you have read this far you probably think you are about ready to swear off. But don't do it. Think about it — during the day and just a moment as you go to bed at night. Tentatively, like this: *One of these days, when I feel like it, maybe I'll try going without smoking and see what happens.* Just as an experiment, as a little change of pace in my regular routine.

Watch and wait until some time when your life is on a fairly even keel. Don't try it when you are leaving on an important business trip or preparing to give a big party, or when you are facing some personal emergency. Don't postpone it too long, either, or you will lose the momentum you are gradually building up.

But some morning — maybe on a week-end — you will wake up feeling especially good. You will have had a good night's sleep; you feel fit for anything, and the sun is shining sweetly. The idea of stopping smoking will pop into your head.

Why foul up a swell morning with the noxious fumes of burning nicotine? Why shoulder for another day the burden you've been carrying for years? Somehow it will not seem quite so impossible as it might at other times. Maybe this is the day.

Decide, then and there, quietly and firmly, that you're through with it! This is the moment, intelligently selected and properly prepared for, when you can get off with the running start of feeling good!

Now that we're on our way, let's take along some advice by a great psychologist, William James, whose observations on habits and their making and breaking are of extraordinary value to us right now.

James formulated several principles to get rid of habits. We can apply three of them to smoking.

One: Start yourself off on the new way of life with as much momentum as you can.

Tell your friends that you have given up smoking. Don't be smug or complacent or boastful, but let people know what you are doing. At some point when you are seriously tempted to smoke, the thought of all the derisive laughter you'll get for giving in may well carry you over the crisis, which is the reason to tell others about what you are doing.

Most smokers have fixed ideas about the occasions when a smoke tastes best. The first cigarette after breakfast, or the one with a cocktail before dinner. If such associations are likely to tempt you to smoke, try to avoid them for a few days. If that is impossible, brace yourself in advance for such temptations; tell yourself that such an occasion is coming, and you must be prepared to want to smoke badly yet not give in to that want. If you hold out only for a moment, that sudden strong temptation will die almost as quickly as it arose.

Two: Don't permit yourself to make a single exception to your new rule until the nonsmoking habit is firmly implanted (and that will be a long time).

If a habit is not fed, it dies relatively quickly, but it can subsist for a long time on the slightest food. If you occasionally let yourself have one cigarette or pipe on the ground that "just one won't hurt," you will keep alive the desire to smoke. Just as one drink is too many for an alcoholic, one cigarette is too many for the heavy smoker who is trying to reform. Every time you say no to the temptation to smoke, you are making the next "no" easier.

The tough moments come only one at a time, and they get easier as you defeat them one at a time. Win the battle of the moment, and forget about an hour from now, or a day from now, or a week from now. Defeat one temptation, and the next one won't be quite so tempting.

Three: Deliberately expose yourself to small temptations and conquer them.

Just as a fighter conditions himself for a major fight by road work and sparring, you can develop your determination by deliberate "workouts." Go out of your way at least once every day to demonstrate how you have forsworn tobacco. Carry matches and light cigarettes for your friends. If you are accustomed to riding in the smoking car, continue to do so, and look at all the people around you who are riding there by necessity and not choice, as you are doing. They can't give up smoking. You have!

If you thus deliberately try to make it tough, it will seem far less so, and you will much sooner get over the worst of it, which usually lasts about a week.

Baby yourself in everything else. Most of us are inclined to launch sudden, widely ambitious programs of self-improvement which defeat their own purpose. We try to do more than we can reasonably expect of ourselves. Don't increase the difficulties of stopping smoking by simultaneously adding others. On the contrary, indulge yourself. Eat what you want and enjoy it. Have an occasional cup of coffee or soft drink when you feel the desire to smoke. Make it a habit to carry mints and gum.

This is especially important. Don't worry about getting the gum or candy habit. As the desire to smoke dies, so will the desire for a substitute. But during the first few weeks keep such substitutes on hand — and pop one into your mouth whenever you feel the urge to smoke.

Let your sleep work for you. On the night of the first day that you give up smoking, go to bed as usual and think for a moment of how today you did not smoke. Think of the various times during the day when you were tempted to, yet did not give in. Then tell yourself, "Tomorrow I am not going to smoke." Repeat it to yourself as you get drowsy. This will be the last thing in your conscious mind as you drop off to sleep.

When you wake in the morning, remind yourself that you are going to get through this day, too, without smoking. Don't clench your teeth or tense your muscles or make a big issue of it. Just — briefly — say: "This day I don't smoke." And see what happens. Even if you don't follow the other rules set down here, this exercise in "controlled sleep" could get you over the hump.

We have scarcely touched on one great help in giving up the smoking habit: the knowledge, which you will gain as you go along, that you *can* do it. Added to all the physical pleasures which nonsmoking brings is the sudden sense of freedom, and self-assurance that results from simply going a half day, and then a day, and then two days without tobacco. That is a sharp and continuing pleasure, and every minute you live with it helps to strengthen you against the next minute's temptation.

And above and beyond that pleasant, heartening knowledge is the awareness that you are doing something which you will be proud of — not to mention healthier and happier for — during the rest of your life. Six months or six years from now, when someone offers you a cigarette, you will refuse it, but not weakly or defensively. You will say, "Thanks — I used to smoke, but I gave it up." And you will be looked at with a glimpse of wistful envy, like a freshman looking at a senior who has been through the mill.

I Found Freedom from Fear

Condensed from
Independent Woman

Margaret Lee Runbeck

WHEN I was graduating from high school I was a very
self-conscious and awkward child. But by reason of sheer
brute scholarship I found myself on the platform during the
earth-shaking commencement exercises with the valedictory
speech seething in my frightened little head.

Our class was ranged along the stage of the auditorium, and
down below us in a dizzy, blurred sea of drowning faces were
our parents. Among them were mine, my mother's blessed fore-
finger still pricked from the thousands of tiny handstitches she
had put into my graduating dress, my father spending one of his
precious day's leaves in order to witness the great event. If I
disgraced them today — as I most likely should — I couldn't
possibly forgive myself.

It had been arranged that we four dry-mouthed performers —
the class prophet, the valedictorian, the class poet and the grind
who was to be given a university scholarship — were to sit in
conspicuous segregation in the center of the stage. Having to
mumble a speech was horror enough, but having to sit there
where all could gaze upon my plumpness and the fever blister
which had popped out from sheer terror was agony unbearable.

To make the whole thing worse, next to me was an empty
chair for the invited speaker who was to deliver our Commencement Address. My English teacher had said firmly that I must
chat cordially with him during the few minutes before the

exercises started. It would show the audience how completely at ease everyone was, she said. This, of course, was the final ordeal, for what could I possibly find to say to a strange grownup?

When he came swinging gracefully onto the stage, while the high school orchestra was scraping through *The Blue Danube,* my despair reached its climax. But my English teacher nodded imperatively at me, so I smiled deliriously at our speaker and tried to give a pantomime impression that all was well.

"I'm supposed to talk wittily to you," I gulped in a breathless croak, "but . . . but . . . I haven't a thing to say. I'm scared to death."

"I'm scared, too," he said. "I've got a speech written down, but I don't think it's much good, and besides —"

"But *you* don't have to be afraid," I said in amazement.

He looked at me carefully, not as a man looking at a child but as one human being measuring another to see where help might be given.

"Neither do you," he said. "I'll tell you a secret; then you'll never need to be scared again. Everyone on earth is shy, self-conscious and unsure of himself. Everybody's timid about meeting strangers. So if you'll just spend the first minute you're in the presence of a stranger trying to help *him* feel comfortable, you'll never suffer from self-consciousness again. Try it."

In his handsome face I saw a kindness that made me suddenly aware of what a fine thing a man with sympathy and insight in his soul can be.

"I *will* try it," I said, very loudly, from the bottom of my heart.

Then suddenly, to my horror, I realized that *The Blue Danube* had come to its end, and that my voice had blazed out like a bullet in the silence. Our principal, a stern narrow-faced little man, was staring at me, and all my classmates were gazing openmouthed. It was a moment which easily could have toppled into neighborhood disgrace.

But the man beside me laughed with assurance, and reached out and patted my shoulder in such a friendly way that everyone in the hall felt good, and pleased, and friendly. In spite of myself, I had done exactly what my English teacher had said

I must do — I had talked pleasantly with our honored guest, so that everyone would feel at ease.

I don't remember how the speeches went off, either his or mine. But I do remember how happy I was, and how wonderful the whole occasion seemed. Most of all I remember the advice of the man who generously gave a frightened, unattractive child his secret for getting over discomfort by losing self in helping a stranger.

I've used his secret thousands of times; I've watched it work with all kinds of strangers; and increasingly I've been grateful to the man who gave it to me. I often wished I could remember who he was so that I could tell him of my gratitude.

Recently I had to dispose of an attic full of valueless treasures and trivia hoarded through the years. In a box with a few old letters I found the Commencement Day Program of Eastern High School, Washington, D. C. It has a blue-and-silver seal on the front, and a line which says:

Commencement Address, by the Honorable Franklin D. Roosevelt, Assistant Secretary of the Navy.

It is too late now for me to tell him of my gratitude. But I can pass along his secret to help others, as he passed it along to me.

Applied Psychology

SEEKING counsel from Dr. George W. Crane, the psychologist, a woman confided that she hated her husband and intended to divorce him. "I want to hurt him all I can," she said.

"In that case," said Dr. Crane, "I advise you to start showering him with compliments. When you have become indispensable to him — when he thinks you love him devotedly — then start the divorce action. That's the way to hurt him."

Some months later the wife returned to report that she had followed the suggested course. "Good," said Crane. "Now's the time to file for divorce."

"Divorce!" exclaimed the woman indignantly. "Never! I've fallen in love with him."

— William F. McDermott in *The Rotarian*

On Being
A REAL PERSON

A condensation from the book

By Harry Emerson Fosdick, D.D.

It's Up to You

THE central business of every human being is to be a real person. We possess by nature the factors out of which personality can be made, and to organize them into effective personal life is every man's primary responsibility.

Without exaggeration it can be said that frustrated, unhappy people, who cannot match themselves with life, constitute the greatest single tragedy in the world. In mansion and hovel, among the uneducated and in university faculties, under every kind of circumstance people entrusted with building their own personalities are making a mess of it, thereby plunging into an earthly hell.

Three elements enter into the building of personality: heredity, environment and personal response. We are not responsible for our heredity; much of our environment we cannot control; but the power to face life with an individual rejoinder — *that* we are responsible for. When acceptance of this responsibility involves self-condemnation, however, an alibi almost invariably rushes to the rescue. All of us resemble the lawyer in the New Testament story, concerning whom we read: "But he, desiring to justify himself, said . . ." A college president says that after long dealing with students he is unsure whether the degree B.A. stands for Bachelor of Arts or Builder of Alibis.

On the lowest level this desire to escape blame expresses itself in emphasis upon luck. Fortunate people "get the breaks," men say; personal failure is due not so much to mistake as to mischance. That luck represents a real factor in human experience is evident, and he who does not expect ill fortune as one of the ingredients of life is trying to live in fairyland. But nothing finer has appeared on earth than unlucky people who are real persons. The determining element in their experience is not so much what happens to them as the way they take it.

Glenn Cunningham, who once ran the fastest mile on record, was crippled in boyhood in a schoolhouse fire. The doctors said that only a miracle could enable him to walk again — he was out of luck. He began walking by following a plow across the fields, leaning on it for support; and then went on to tireless experimentation to see what he could do with his legs, until he broke all records for the mile run.

Pilgrim's Progress came from a prison, as did *Don Quixote,* Sir Walter Raleigh's *History of the World* and some of the best of O. Henry's stories.

Bad luck is a poor alibi if only because good luck by itself never yet guaranteed real personality. Life is not so simple that good fortune suffices for it.

Many escape a sense of personal responsibility by lapsing into a mood of emotional fatalism. This is, curiously, one of the most comfortable moods in which a man can live. If he is an automaton, he is not responsible for anything.

On its highest level man's desire to escape responsibility expresses itself in ascribing all personal qualities to heredity and environment. This is a popular theory today. From intelligence quotients within to crippling environments without, it offers defenses for every kind of deficiency, so that no botched life need look far to find an excuse.

But consider the individual of superior inheritance and favorable circumstance. Must he necessarily be an admirable personality? Is *that* fate, willy-nilly, forced upon him? Certainly it does not seem so. The disastrous misuse of fine heredity and environment is too familiar a phenomenon to be doubted.

Handling difficulty, making the best of bad messes, is one of life's major businesses. Very often the reason victory is not won lies inside the individual. The recognition of this fact, however, by the individual concerned is difficult. At times we all resemble the Maine farmer laboriously driving his horses on a dusty road. "How much longer does this hill last?" he asked a man by the roadside. "Hill!" was the answer. "Hill nothing! Your hind wheels are off!"

The world is a coarse-grained place, and other people are often unfair, selfish, cruel. Yet, after all, we know the difference between a man who always has an alibi and the man who *in just as distressing a situation* habitually looks inward to his own attitudes and resources — no excuses, no passing of the buck. In any circumstance he regards himself as his major problem, certain that if he handles himself well that is bound to make some difference. Anyone can recognize the forthright healthy-mindedness of the youth who wrote home to his father after an unsuccessful football game, "Our opponents found a big hole in our line, and that hole was me."

When we succeed, when by dint of decision and effort we achieve a desired end, we are sure we had a share in *that*. We cannot slough off responsibility when we fail. We cannot eat our cake and have it too.

The beginning of worth-while living is thus to confront ourselves — unique beings, each of us entrusted with the makings of personality. Yet multitudes of people wrestle with every conceivable factor involved in the human situation before they face their primary problem — themselves. Our commonest human tragedy is correctly represented in a recent cartoon: A physician faces his patient with anxious solemnity, saying, "This is a very serious case; I'm afraid you're *allergic to yourself*."

Our Many Selves

THE common phrase, "building a personality," is a misnomer. Personality is not so much like a structure as like a river — it continuously flows, and to be a person is to be engaged in a perpetual process of becoming.

The tests of successful personal living, therefore, are not neatly identical when applied to two persons in different situations or to the same person at different ages. Concerning one criterion, however, there is common agreement. A real person

achieves a high degree of unity within himself. The often conflicting elements of personal experience, such as impulses, desires, emotions, must be coördinated.

Each of us deals continually with the underlying problem of
a disorganized life. The ruffled man badly flurried because he
has mislaid a pair of glasses, the hurried person trying to do
something with too great haste and becoming flustered, the
frightened person fallen into a panic, the choleric individual
surprised by a burst of temper into loss of self-control — such
examples from ordinary life remind us how insecure is our personal integration.

No virtue is more universally accepted as a test of good character than trustworthiness. Obviously, however, dependability is
possible only in so far as the whole personality achieves a stanch
unity that can be counted on.

Many of us frequently act "out of character." The general
pattern of our lives may involve honesty, truthfulness and similar qualities — but not always. This is evident even with regard
to a virtue like courtesy. How common is the person whose
courtesy is unreliable! We all know him — polite today, morose
and uncivil tomorrow; obliging and well bred in business,
crabbed and sulky at home; affable with one's so-called
"equals," gruff and snobbish with one's servants, or those one
considers "inferior."

In a man with character, the responses to life are, in their
quality, established and well organized; one can count on them.
His various emotions, desires and ideas are no mere disparate
will-o'-the-wisps. He has become a whole person, with a uni-
fying pattern of thought and feeling that gives coherence to
everything he does.

A "well-integrated" life does not mean a placid life, with all
conflicts resolved. Many great souls have been inwardly tor-
tured. Florence Nightingale had a desperate time finding herself, and wrote in her diary, "In my 31st year I see nothing
desirable but death." Dwight L. Moody said, "I've had more
trouble with D. L. Moody than with any other man I know."

In all strong characters, when one listens behind the scenes,
one hears echoes of strife and contention. Nevertheless, far from
being at loose ends within themselves, such persons have organ-

ized their lives around some supreme values and achieved a powerful concentration of purpose and drive.

The process by which real personality is thus attained is inward and spiritual. No environmental changes by themselves can so *push* a personality together as to bring this satisfying wholeness within. Even so fortunate an environment as a loyal and loving family cannot dispense a man from confronting himself. Thus Novalis said: "Only so far as a man is happily married to himself, is he fit for married life." As for material prosperity, that often disorganizes life rather than unifies it. Indeed, nervous prostration is a specialty of the prosperous. Wealth, by increasing the number of possible choices, is often far more disrupting than satisfying.

A MODERN novelist describing one of his characters says, "He was not so much a human being as a civil war." Every human being sometime faces a situation where on the one side is his actual self, with his abilities and circumstances, and on the other are ideal pictures of himself and his achievements; and between the two is a gulf too wide to be bridged. Here inward civil war begins.

To hold high ideals and ambitions is man's glory, and nowhere more so than in the development of personality. This faculty, however, can function so abnormally that it tears life to pieces.

No well-integrated life is possible, therefore, without an initial act of self-acceptance, as though to say: I, John Smith, hereby accept myself, with my inherited endowments and handicaps and with the elements in my environment that I cannot control, and, so accepting myself as my stint, I will now see what I can do with *this* John Smith. So Emerson put it: "There is a time in every man's education when he arrives at the conviction that envy is ignorance; that imitation is suicide; that he must take himself for better, for worse, as his portion."

Alec Templeton entertains millions over the radio with his music and amuses them with his whimsicalities. He is stone blind. The first natural response to such crippling disadvantage is an imagination thronged with pictures of the unattainable, and from the contrast between them and the actualities commonly spring resentment, self-pity, inertia. The human story, however, has nothing nobler to present than handicapped men and women who, accepting themselves, have illustrated what Dr. Alfred Adler called "the human being's power to turn a minus into a plus."

Tension between our existent and our desired selves often arises from high moral ideals, and nowhere is it more likely to be mishandled. Unselfishness and loyalty, for instance, are major virtues, but a daughter under the thralldom of a possessive mother can so picture herself as in duty bound to be unselfish and loyal that, without doing her mother any real good, her life is blighted and her personality wrecked.

Ethical ideals in their application are relative to the individual. One man may have a calm, equable temperament that need never be ruffled; another may have to say, as Dr. Stephen Tyng did to one who rebuked him for asperity, "Young man, I control more temper every 15 minutes than you will in your whole lifetime."

WHEN self-acceptance is not achieved and the strain between the actual and the dreamed-of self becomes tense, the result is an unhappy and sometimes crushing sense of inferiority. One study of 275 college men and women revealed that over 90 percent suffered from gnawing, frustrated feelings of deficiency. They gave all sorts of reasons — physical incompetence, unpleasant appearance, lack of social charm, failure in love, low-grade intellectual ability, moral failure and guilt.

To be sure, the feeling of inferiority can never be taken at its face value as an indication of real lack. The runner-up in a championship tennis match may suffer wretchedly from a sense of inadequacy. However, the importance of the problem itself is made evident by the unhealthy ways in which it is commonly handled.

Some deal with it by the smoke-screen method. Feeling miserably inferior, and not wanting others to know it, the shy become aggressive, the embarrassed effusive, and the timid bluster and brag. One man, hitherto gentle and considerate in his family, suffered a humiliating failure. At once he began to grow harsh and domineering. Paradoxical though it is, when he felt superior he behaved humbly, as though he felt inferior; when he felt inferior he began to swagger as though he were superior.

Others, like the fox in Aesop's fable, call sour all grapes they cannot reach. The frail youth discounts athletics; the debauchee scoffs at the self-controlled as prudes; the failure at school scorns intellectuals as "high-brows." A major amount of cynicism springs from this source. Watch what people are cynical about, and one can often discover what they lack, and subconsciously deeply wish they had.

Still others find excuses based on an exaggerated acknowledgment of their inferiority. So one student who was struggling with failure said: "I have thought it over carefully and I have come to the conclusion that I am feeble-minded!" Far from being said with despair, this was announced with relief; it was a perfect excuse; it let him out from all responsibility. Yet, factually it was absurd, and emotionally it was abnormal.

A MONG the constructive elements that make self-acceptance basic in becoming a real person is the principle of compensation. Deficiency can be a positive stimulus, as in the classic case of Demosthenes. Desiring to be an orator, he had to accept himself as a stammerer. He did not, however, conceal his humiliation with bluster and brag, nor decry eloquence as worthless trickery, nor resign himself to stammering as an excuse for doing nothing. He took a positive attitude toward his limitation, speaking against the noise of the waves with pebbles in his mouth until he could talk with confident clarity. To say that Demosthenes became a great orator *despite* his stammering is an understatement; the psychologist would add that he became a supremely effective orator *because* he stammered.

Some form of compensation is almost always possible. The homely girl may develop the more wit and charm because she is homely; the shy, embarrassed youth, with the temperament of a recluse, may be all the more useful in scientific research because of that.

Involved in such successful handling of recognized inferiority is the ability to pass from the defensive to the offensive attitude toward our limitations. John Smith accepts John Smith with his realistically seen limitations and difficulties, and positively starts out to discover what can be done with him.

Captain John Callender of the Massachusetts militia was guilty of cowardice at the Battle of Bunker Hill. George Washington had to order his court-martial. Callender re-enlisted in the army as a private, and at the Battle of Long Island exhibited such conspicuous courage that Washington publicly revoked the sentence and restored to him his captaincy. Behind such an experience lies a basic act of self-acceptance — open-eyed, without equivocation or excuse — along with a shift from a defensive to an offensive attitude, that makes John Callender an inspiring person to remember.

IN ACHIEVING self-acceptance a man may well begin by reducing to a minimum the things that mortify him. Many people are humiliated by situations that need not be humiliations at all. To have what Ko-Ko called "a caricature of a face," to lack desired ability, to be economically restricted — such things are limitations, but if they become humiliations it is because inwardly we make them so. One man developed an inferiority complex that haunted him all his life and ruined his career because he had curly hair of an unusual shade of red. Napoleon accepted himself — five feet two inches tall, and 43rd in his class at the *École Militaire*. He never liked himself that way. Considering his imperial ambitions, his diminutive stature was a limitation, but had he made of it and his scholastic mediocrity a humiliation, he probably never would have been Napoleon.

Life is a landscaping job. We are handed a site, ample or small, rugged or flat, whose general outlines and contours are largely determined for us. Both limitation and opportunity are involved in every site, and the most unforeseeable results ensue from the handling — some grand opportunities are muffed, and some utterly unpromising situations become notable. The basic elements in any personal site are bound to appear in the end no matter what is done with them, as a landscape still reveals its size and its major shapes and contours, whatever the landscape architect may do. These basic elements, however, are to be accepted, never as humiliations, commonly as limitations, but most of all as opportunities and even as incentives.

One of the ablest women in this country, now the wife of a university president, was brought up in poverty. She recalls an occasion when, as a girl, she complained of her hardships to her mother. "See here," said the mother, "I have given you life; that is about all I will ever be able to give you. Now you stop complaining and do something with it."

Our most intimate and inescapable entrustment lies in our capacity to be real persons. To fail at that is to fail altogether; to succeed is to succeed supremely. Says Noah in the play *Green Pastures*, "I ain' very much, but I'se all I got." That is the place to start. Such self-acceptance is realistic, humble, self-respectful.

Getting Ourselves Off Our Hands

A CERTAIN "Charm" School, promising to bestow "personality" on its clients, prescribes in the first lesson that one stand before a large mirror and repeat one's own name in a voice "soft, gentle and low" in order to impress oneself with oneself. But obsession with oneself can be one of life's most disruptive forces. An integrated personality is impossible save as the individual finds outside himself valuable interests, in devotion to which he forgets himself. To be whole persons we must get ourselves off our hands.

Self-centeredness is natural in early childhood. Many, however, never outgrow it. At 50 years of age they still are living on a childish pattern. Moralists censure them as selfish, but beneath the ethical is a psychological problem — they are specimens of arrested development. A novelist says of one of her characters: "Edith was a little country bounded on the north, south, east and west by Edith." Edith suffers from a serious psychological affliction. Egocentricity is ruinous to real personality. At the very best, a person completely wrapped up in himself makes a small package.

Being a real person is arrived at not so much by plunging after it as by indirection. A man escapes from himself into some greater interest to which he devotes himself, and so forgets himself into consecutive, unified, significant living.

Practical suggestions as to ways and means of getting out of ourselves must start close at home with the body. Many miserably self-centered folk need not so much a psychiatrist to analyze them or a minister to discuss morals with them as common sense in handling the physical basis of a healthy life.

The modern man needs constantly to be reminded that he cannot slough off his biological inheritance. Our bodies were made to use in hard physical labor. Any man who has found his appropriate recreation or exercise where he can let himself go in the lusty use of his major muscles knows what a transformation of emotional tone and mental outlook such bodily expenditure can bring.

One of the most durable satisfactions in life is to lose oneself in one's work. This is why more people become neurotic from aimless leisure than from overwork, and why unemployment is one of the worst of tragedies, its psychological results quite as lamentable as its economic ills.

THE PROBLEM of finding external interests weighs more heavily on some temperaments than on others. The "extrovert" readily takes part in objective practical affairs, is emotionally spontaneous and outgoing, is relatively toughminded when he is disapproved by others. The "introvert" is sensitive to disapproval, is given to introspection and self-criticism, and in general is more aware of the inner than of the outer world.

While everybody can recognize these two types, and each man can judge to which of them he himself is more closely akin, they do not constitute two mutually exclusive temperaments. Nor is the advantage altogether on either side. The balanced man is a synthesis of the two.

Abraham Lincoln had a tragic struggle with himself. In his early manhood he was not a unified and coherent person but a cave of Aeolus, full of storms, with the makings of neurotic ruin in him. In 1841 he said, "I am now the most miserable man living. If what I feel were equally distributed to the whole human family, there would not be one cheerful face on earth." He could easily have been an extreme example of the morbid "introvert," but he was not. He solved his obsessing inner problems by outflanking them. The amazing development of his latter years into great personality came not so much by centering attention on himself as by forgetting himself. His devotion to a cause greater than himself transformed what he had learned in his long struggle with himself into understanding, sympathy, humor, wisdom. We cannot call him in the end either "introvert" or "extrovert." He combined them.

T HE PERSONAL counselor constantly runs upon self-focused lives, miserably striving to find happiness through "self-expression." Popularly, self-expression has meant: Let yourself go; knock the bungs from your emotional barrels and let them gurgle! As a protest against petty moralisms, this is easily explicable, and as a means of release to some individuals, tied hand and foot by senseless scrupulosities, it has had its value. The wise counselor wants self-expression too; but he wants it to be practiced in accord with the realistic psychological facts. Merely exploding emotions for the sake of the momentary self-centered thrill gets one nowhere, and in the end the constant repetition of such emotional self-relief disperses life and leaves it more aimless than it was before. Even in the sexual realm this is true. Says an eminent psychiatrist: "From the point of view of cure, the advice to go and 'express your instincts' is foolish. In actual experience I have never known a true neurosis cured by sexual libertinism."

Adequate self-expression is a much deeper matter than self-explosion. Its true exponent is not the libertine but the artist, the scientist, the fortunate mother absorbed in her family, the public-spirited businessman creatively doing something for his community, the teacher saying as Professor George H. Palmer did, "Harvard College pays me for doing what I would gladly pay it for allowing me to do." Such personalities, in eminent or humble places, really express themselves, and their common quality is not self-absorption but self-investment.

A T LEAST two practical consequences follow from such successful expansion of the self.

For one thing, it gives a person a saving sense of humor. In anyone afflicted with abnormal self-concern, a deficient sense of humor is an inevitable penalty. Only people who live objectively in other persons and in wide-flung interests, and who therefore can see themselves impartially, can possibly have the prayer answered:

> O wad some Pow'r the giftie gie us
> To see oursels as ithers see us!

The egocentric's petition is habitually otherwise:

> O wad some Pow'r to others gie
> To see myself as I see me.

Nast, the cartoonist, one evening in a social group drew caricatures of each of the company. The result was revealing — each one easily recognized the caricatures of the others but some could not recognize their own. This inability to see ourselves as we look to others is one of the surest signs of egocentric immaturity.

Aristophanes, in his drama *The Clouds,* caricatured Socrates, and when the play was produced all Athens roared with laughter. Socrates, so runs the story, went to see the play, and when the caricature came on he stood up so that the audience might the better enjoy the comic mask that was intended to burlesque him. He was mature. He had got himself off his hands.

An extended self also results in power to bear trouble. In those who rise to the occasion and marshal their forces to deal with it, one factor commonly is present — *they are thinking about someone else besides themselves*. So one young American officer in the first World War wrote home: "You can truly think of me as being cheerful all the time. Why otherwise? I have 38 men with me. If I duck when a shell comes, all 38 duck, and if I smile, the smile goes down the line."

A person who has genuinely identified himself with other persons has done something of first-rate importance for himself without intending it. Hitherto he has lived, let us say, in a mind like a room surrounded by mirrors. Every way he turned he saw himself. Now, however, some of the mirrors change to windows. He can see through them to new interests.

Using All There Is in Us

ONE WAY or another we must do something with all the emotional drives native to our constitution. Such emotional urges as curiosity, pugnacity, fearfulness, self-regard, sexual desire are an essential part of us; we can either be ignobly enslaved by them or master them for the enrichment of our personality.

Curiosity is an emotional urge in all normal people, and its manifestations are protean. Peeping Toms, prying gossips, inquisitive bores, open-minded truth-seekers, daring explorers, research scientists are all illustrations of curiosity. Some uses of it produce the most despicable persons, while others produce the most admirable, but there is no escaping it. From this fact, which holds true of all our native drives, a double lesson comes: first, *no basic emotional factor in human nature is to be despised;* and second, *each of them can be ennobled by its use.*

Pugnacity is one of the most deeply rooted emotional drives in human nature, and combativeness is necessary to the continuance and advance of human life. The fighting spirit expresses itself in hard work, in bravely facing personal handicaps, in the whole range of attack on entrenched social evils.

If, however, we give this indispensable emotional drive gangway, the results are shattering. A chronic hatred or even a cherished grudge tears to pieces the one who harbors it. A strong feeling of resentment is just as likely to cause disease as is a germ. If one is so unfortunate as to have an enemy, the worst thing one can do, not to the enemy but to oneself, is to let resentment dig in and hatred become chronic.

When Edward Everett Hale in his later years said, "I once had an enemy, a determined enemy, and I have been trying all day to remember his name," he gave evidence not only of rightmindedness but of healthy-mindedness. So, too, Lincoln, rebuked for an expression of magnanimity toward the South during the Civil War, and told bitterly that he should desire rather to destroy his enemies, was not only morally but emotionally sound when he answered, "What, madam? Do I not destroy them when I make them my friends?"

F<small>EAR</small> is another indispensable element in the human make-up. Even in its simpler forms we cannot dispense with it; on the streets of a modern city a fearless man, if the phrase be taken literally, would probably be dead before nightfall. And fear can be a powerfully creative motive. In a profound sense schools spring from fear of ignorance, industry from fear of penury,

medical science from fear of disease. But fear's abnormalities —
hysteria, phobia, obsessive anxiety — tear personality to pieces.

Human life is full of secret fears, thrust into the attics and
dark corners of personality. Fear of the dark, of cats, of closed
places, of open places; fear of responsibility, of having children,
of old age and death; guilty fears, often concerned with sins
long passed; religious fears, associated with ideas of a spying and
vindictive God and an eternal hell; and sometimes a vague fearfulness, filling life with anxious apprehension — such wretched-
ness curses innumerable lives.

The disruptive effect of such secret, chronic fearfulness is
physically based. The adrenal glands furnish us in every fright-
ening situation with "a swig of our own internal fight-tonic." A
little of it is stimulating; too much of it is poison. Habitual
anxiety and dread constitute a continuous false alarm, turning
the invaluable adrenal secretion from an emergency stimulant
into a chronic poison.

To get our fear out into the open and frankly face it is of
primary importance. As infants we started with fear of two
things only — falling and a loud noise. All other fears have been
accumulated since. To find out where and how we picked them
up, to trace their development until we can objectively survey
them as though they were another's and not our own, is half the
battle. Often they can then be laughed off the scene.

Sometimes, however, the fear we find ourselves confronting
is justified. In that case we are commonly defeated by the fallacy
that dangerous situations are necessarily undesirable, whereas
the fact is that there is *stimulus* in hazardous occasions.

Love of danger is one of the strongest motives in man. When
life does not by itself present men with enough hazard, they go
out looking for it. They seek it in their more active sports, in
risky researches and explorations, in missionary adventures, in
championing unpopular causes. To stand up to a hazardous
situation, to let it call out in us not our fearfulness but our love
of battle, is a healthy, inspiriting experience.

One of the sovereign cures for unhealthy fears is action. Dr.
Henry C. Link gives this homely illustration from a mother:
"As a young wife I was troubled with many fears, one of which
was the fear of insanity. After the birth of our first child, these

fears still persisted. However, we soon had another child and ended up by having six. We never had much money and I had to do all my own work. Whenever I started to worry about myself, the baby would cry and I would have to run and look after him. Or the children would quarrel and I would have to straighten them out. Or I would suddenly remember that it was time to start dinner, or that I must run out and take in the wash before it rained, or that the ironing had to be done. My fears were continually interrupted by tasks into which I had to put my back. Gradually my fears disappeared, and now I look back on them with amusement."

This story furnishes one explanation for the prevalence of emotional ills among prosperous and leisurely people. They have time to sit around, feeding their imaginations. In wartime they can listen over the radio to every news broadcast and commentator until, unlike a healthy soldier who has a job to do that he can put his back into, they become morbidly distraught over dangers concerning which they do nothing practical. In ordinary peacetime such people are the prey of endless imaginary woes, so that it is commonly true that those worry most who have least to worry about.

The dual nature of fear, as both good and evil, is nowhere better illustrated than in a man who dreads so much falling short of his duty that he dreads much less the cost of doing it. If one has anything positively to live for, from a child, or a worthwhile day's work, to a world delivered from the scourge of war, *that* is what matters.

Self-regard likewise is not to be despised or suppressed but educated and used.

When Charles Lamb said, "The greatest pleasure I know is to do a good action by stealth, and to have it found out by accident," he revealed how omnipresent is the wish for notice and attention that enhance self-esteem.

The cynic says that at the fountainhead of every so-called "unselfish" life are self-regarding motives. The cynic is right — but in his cynicism about it he is wrong. We all start as individual children, with self-regarding instincts. The test of us, however, lies in the objective aims and purposes which ultimately capture these forces in us and use them as driving power.

A wise personal counselor, therefore, never tells anyone that he ought not to wish to feel important, but rather endeavors to direct that powerful wish into constructive channels.

From self-regard when it goes wrong spring vanity and avarice. Some people live habitually in the spirit with which Mascagni dedicated his opera *The Masks:* "To myself, with distinguished esteem and unalterable satisfaction." Yet we neither can nor should stop caring for ourselves. Our initial business in life is to care for ourselves so much that *I* tackles *Me,* determined to make out of him something worth while.

P ROBABLY it is in the realm of *sexual desire* that "sublimation" — redirection to a higher ethical level — is talked about most and understood least. Not all demands of the human organism can be sublimated. In satisfying physical hunger there is no substitute for food. When sex is thought of in its narrowest sense, it belongs in this class.

To the youth troubled by this elemental biological need, many sensible things can be said: that chastity is not debilitating and that sexual indulgence is not necessary to health; that interest in competing concerns is good therapy; that the general unrest accompanying unsatisfied sexual tension can often be relieved by vigorous action, fatiguing the whole body; that sexual desire is natural and right, to be accepted with gratitude and good humor as part of our constitutional equipment, and not sullied with morbid feelings of guilt at its presence; that nature, when left to itself, has its own ways of relieving the specific sex-tension.

Sex, however, is far more deep-seated and pervasive in personality than at first appears. All the relationships of the family — maternal, paternal and filial — are grounded in this larger meaning of sex, all fine affection and friendship between brothers and sisters, and men and women, and all extensions of family attitudes to society at large, as in the love and care of children.

When one's life is thus thought of as a whole, sublimation of sex becomes meaningful. It is possible for one to choose a way of living that will channel one's devotions and creative energies into satisfying courses so that the personality *as a whole* finds contentment, even though specific sexual desires are left unful-filled. So an unmarried woman, denied motherhood, can dis-cover in nursing, teaching or social service an outlet for her maternal instincts that brings to her personality an integrating satisfaction.

That there must be some restraint on all our native drives is obvious. Picture a life in which all the native urges explode themselves together — self-regard, pugnacity, sexual desire, fear; obviously pandemonium would reign. The popular idea, there-fore, that the restraint of basic emotional drives is in itself un-healthy is nonsense. The choice before us is not whether our native impulses shall be restrained and controlled but how that shall be done in the service of an integrated life.

THE MULTIPLE possibilities of use and misuse in handling our native drives root back in the essential quality of all emo-tional life, *sensitiveness*. One of the most important subjects of self-examination concerns the way we handle this primary qual-ity. Let a man discover what he is characteristically touchy about and he will gain valuable insight into his personal problem.

Many people are extremely touchy to criticism. Their *amour-propre* squirms under adverse judgment. Sensitiveness to the opinion of others, without which social life could not go on at all, has in them been perverted into a disease.

Such abnormal persons take appreciation for granted and regard criticism as an impertinence. The normal person comes nearer taking criticism for granted and regarding appreciation as velvet. Emerson once made a speech that a minister sitting on the platform deeply disliked. The minister, in delivering the closing prayer, prayed, "We beseech Thee, O Lord, to de-liver us from ever hearing any more such nonsense as we have just listened to." When Emerson was asked afterward what he thought about it, he remarked, "The minister seems a very con-scientious, plain-spoken gentleman." Such healthy-mindedness is a necessary factor in a well-integrated personality.

Mastering Depression

ONE OF the commonest causes of personal disorganization is despondency. Some despondency is physically caused, but the moody dejections most people suffer are not altogether beyond their control.

A first suggestion for dealing with this problem is: *Take depression for granted*. One who expects completely to escape low moods is asking the impossible. To take low moods too seriously, instead of saying, This also will pass, is to confer on them an obsessive power they need not have.

A second suggestion is of daily importance: *We can identify ourselves not with our worse, but with our better, moods*. Deep within us all is that capacity. The ego, the central "I," can choose *this* and not *that* mood as representing the real self; it can identify itself with hopefulness rather than disheartenment, with good will rather than rancor.

All slaves of depression have this in common: They have acquired the habit of identifying their real selves with their low moods. Not only do they have cellars in their emotional houses, as everybody does, but they live there. While each of us has depressed hours, none of us needs to be a depressed person.

This leads to a third suggestion. *When depression comes, tackle yourself and do not merely blame circumstance*. Circumstances are often so tragic and crushing as to make dejection inevitable. Nevertheless, to deduce from the presence of misfortune the right to be a despondent person is a fatal error.

Life is an assimilative process in which we transmute into our own quality whatever comes into us. Walter de la Mare's lines have a wider application than at first appears:

> It's a very odd thing —
> As odd as can be,
> That whatever Miss T. eats
> Turns into Miss T.

Depressed persons can make depression out of any circumstances whatsoever. This truth is especially pertinent in a tragic era when the world is upset by catastrophic events. Not to be depressed by present calamities would reveal an insensitive spirit. Nevertheless, many today blame their emotional disorganization on the sad estate of the world, whereas their real problem is within themselves. As D. H. Lawrence wrote concerning one of his characters, "Poor Richard Lovatt wearied himself to death struggling with the problem of himself, and calling it Australia."

The fourth suggestion goes beyond self-tackling and says: *Remember others.* Emotions are contagious. One depressed person can infect a whole household and become a pest even to comparative strangers. If, therefore, Ian Maclaren's admonition is justified, "Let us be kind to one another for most of us are fighting a hard battle," good cheer and courage are among the most important kindnesses that we can show.

The fifth suggestion calls for deep resources of character: *Remember that some tasks are so important that they must be gone through with whether we are depressed or not.* Strong personalities commonly solve the problem of their despondency not by eliminating but by sidetracking it. They have work to do, a purpose to fulfill, and to *that,* whether or not they feel dejected, the main trunk line of their lives belongs.

The Ultimate Strength

To pull a personality together takes inner reserves of power — of power assimilated from beyond oneself.

No more pathetic cases present themselves to the personal counselor than those whose only technique in handling their problems is to trust in the strength of their own volition. Soon or late they face problems to which such a technique is utterly inapplicable. When bereavement comes, for instance, bringing with it profound sorrow, to appeal to the will to arouse itself and solve the problem is an impertinence.

Such moments call for another technique altogether — the hospitable receptivity of faith.

Many people ask, "How does one get faith, if one does not have it? One cannot *will* to have faith." But faith is not something we *get;* it is something we *have.* Moreover, we have a surplus of it, associated with more curious objects than tongue can tell — faith in dictatorship or astrology or rabbits' feet, in one economic nostrum or another. That we have more faith than we know what to do with is shown by the way we give it to every odd and end that comes along.

No man can really become an unbeliever; he is psychologically shut up to the necessity of believing—in God, for example, or else in no God. When positive faiths die out, their place is taken by negative faiths — in impossibilities rather than possibilities, in ideas that make victims rather than masters of life.

A friend once wrote to Turgenev: "It seems to me that to put oneself in the second place is the whole significance of life." Turgenev replied: "It seems to me that to discover what to put before oneself, in the first place, is the whole problem of life." Whatever one does put thus before oneself is always the object of one's faith; one believes in it and belongs to it; and whether it be Christ or Hitler, a chosen vocation or a personal friend, when such committal of faith is heartily made, it pulls the trigger of human energy.

Confidence that it is worth while constructively to tackle oneself, and the determination so to do, depends on faith of some sort. Distraught and dejected people almost inevitably ask: "Why should we bother to try to create an integrated and useful personality? Of what importance are we anyway?" These miserable folk perceive nothing worth living for, and the only cure for their futilitarian attitude is a positive faith.

Even though one goes no further than Robert Louis Stevenson in saying, "I believe in an ultimate decency of things," such faith has inestimable value. If one can go beyond Stevenson's affirmation, religion presents the most stimulating faith in human experience. It has said to every individual: Whatever you may fail at, you need not fail at being a real person; the makings of great personal life include handicaps, deficiencies, troubles and even moral failures; the universe is not a haphazard affair of aimless atoms but is organized around spiritual purposes; and personality, far from being a chance inadvertence, is the fullest and completest way of being alive and the most adequate symbol we have of the nature of God.

Thus religion is a basis for hopeful adventure and a source of available power in trying to make the most of our natural endowments and become what we ought to be. And he who undertakes that task is on the main highroad of creation's meaning and is accepting the central trust of life.

"Do the Thing You Fear—"

The Secret Dale Carnegie Has Taught to Thousands

Condensed from Your Life

J. P. McEvoy

OES it scare you to death to talk on your feet? Does your
tongue get thick, your voice get thin, your throat dry up?
Dale Carnegie says that this is natural, but that you can
cure yourself of the fear of speaking — *by speaking*. According
to Carnegie: "You are not afraid to talk. You fear that you will
fail. So you fail — and the next time you fail because you failed
before, so you build the habit of failure." Carnegie should know.
He has listened to and criticized 150,000 speeches in the last
40 years.

A Wall Street man who started taking Carnegie's course
under an assumed name became so terrified when called on
to speak that he ran out of the class. Later he was offered a
U.S. ambassadorship which he wanted desperately. Knowing he
would have to make public addresses, he came to Carnegie for
help. Soon he was attending classes three and four nights a
week. He became so fascinated with the thrill of hearing himself speak in public that he awoke his wife early one Sunday
morning to ask: "Is there any place in New York where I can
make a talk today?" She sleepily reminded him that anyone
could speak in a Quaker Meeting House if the Spirit moved
him. He went to a meeting and the Spirit moved him so might-
ily that he spoke for 20 minutes.

And there was the board chairman of a tire company who
told Carnegie: "The moment I stand up to speak at a board
meeting all connection between my brain and my body is

severed. I feel like a fool and talk like one. I fear my case is hopeless."

Asked why he had come if he felt that way, the man replied: "For years my accountant has been timidly sneaking into his office, hardly daring to speak to anyone. But now he walks in, head up, chest high, and booms 'good morning.' I said to him the other day: 'Who has been feeding you meat?' He told me that it was you — that he was now speaking before civic groups and enjoying it."

Four months later this executive addressed a mass meeting of 3000 people. Asked to talk for three minutes, he talked nine; and if the chairman hadn't shut him up, would have talked 90.

Carnegie likes to quote Emerson's advice to "Do the thing you fear and the death of fear is certain." He didn't know when he started to teach public speaking that this would be the secret of his fabulously successful method. "I had been taught in college by lectures," he says, "so I expected to teach the same way. Fortunately, after lecturing to my first class for 30 minutes I ran out of anything to say. To fill the time I asked the students to stand up and talk about their troubles. Without knowing what I was doing, I stumbled on the best method for conquering fear."

This was long ago — 1912, at the 125th Street YMCA in New York. "The 'Y' had so little faith in my public-speaking course," says Carnegie, "that it refused to risk $5 a night — a teacher's salary in those days. So I said 'I will work on a profit-sharing basis. From the first money that comes in, you pay for your printed matter and postage. If there is any profit we can divide it any way you like.'" Within two years Carnegie was teaching nightly classes in YMCA's in New York, Philadelphia, Baltimore and Wilmington, and was making $30 and $40 a night in commissions.

Today Carnegie licenses his method in over 300 cities in the United States and foreign countries. He trains his teachers, personally checks their performances and collects a small royalty from an average $100 fee from 35,000 students a year. The students take one lesson a week for 16 weeks. They range in age from 14 to 80, and in occupation from housewives and stenographers to truck drivers, engineers, business executives and psychiatrists.

The first night the instructor asks the students to sit at a long table, six at a time, facing the audience. This gives them moral support. They are asked such questions as: What is your name? Where do you live? What kind of work do you do? Why are you taking this course? How do you expect to use this training in your business or profession?

The second night, students answer such questions as: What is the first incident of your life you remember? How did you earn your first dollar? Get your first job? For the third night, they are asked to bring an exhibit; if possible, something that will explain their work. Holding up an exhibit and talking about it helps the speaker get his mind off himself. Only after the third night do the teachers encourage the students to stand up to speak.

Carnegie emphasizes that teachers must use encouragement rather than criticism. They must find something to praise in every student.

"A student's performance can't be entirely hopeless," Carnegie tells his teachers. He quotes the example of the student who could blurt out only a few short sentences before fear choked him off. The instructor complimented him: "Some of the world's most famous speakers have not had the judgment you have just shown. You made your point and sat down immediately. You know when to stop."

Carnegie says almost anyone can make a fair talk if he will follow these five rules:

1. Get excited about what you have to say. If you are enthusiastic about your subject, your delivery will probably be natural, sincere and moving, and you won't bother about how you stand, gesture, breathe, or use your voice. You will forget yourself into good speaking. If you stumble or stutter or make mistakes, ignore them — nobody cares but yourself.

2. Talk about something that you know through experience. Don't get your subjects out of newspapers or magazines. Dig them out of your own life, such subjects as "My biggest regret," "The most important lesson I ever learned," etc.

3. Make a few notes of what you intend to say, but don't

memorize your talk word by word, ever. You will sound cold and mechanical.

4. Fill your talk with illustrations and rehearse it by conversing with your friends. A talk should be merely an enlarged conversation. Talk to your audience as you would to a dozen people in a room, with the same natural gestures.

5. Your attitude is contagious. Unless you have a good time talking, your audience won't have a good time listening.

A Columbia University psychologist who took Carnegie's course told him: "We humans are very largely what we conceive ourselves to be. You take your students by simple, easy stages to a point where they no longer think of themselves as being afraid. They are changed human beings because their conception of themselves is changed."

Carnegie believes that you and your friends can get together informally and overcome your fear of talking — simply by talking to your own group. Little by little you will gain confidence from your own success and from the success of your friends.

"There is no magic about the method," says Carnegie, "but there is about the result. Many parents who have taken this training become active in civic affairs to set an example of self-confidence and courage for their offspring. Leave your children courage," he says, "and you will be leaving them an asset more valuable than dollars. They won't be courageous merely because you tell them to be, but they will unconsciously absorb your example of courage — or fear."

Recipe for Romance

MY BROTHER put off telling his motherless daughter the facts of life as long as possible. But when she fell in love for the first time at 16, he realized that he had to talk to her. I overheard his concluding remark, "Jean, the best advice I can give you is written on the top of a mayonnaise jar." That night, when I mixed the salad for dinner, these words on the mayonnaise jar leapt up at me: "KEEP COOL BUT DON'T FREEZE."

— Contributed by Mrs. J. A. W.

When You Talk to a Child

*Condensed from
Mental Hygiene*   *by Emily Rautman and Arthur Rautman*

WHEN introduced to a five-year-old child, many adults show the uneasiness observable otherwise only when a well-fed man is confronted with a tiger on half rations. Time and again we have been amazed to see how inept many otherwise competent people become when they encounter a live child.

Some of our acquaintances, for instance, are struck speechless when we introduce our young nephew. But far more of a problem are the garrulous adults who insist upon taking over the whole show from the moment they cast their eyes upon "the little darling," leaving us with a youngster who requires an hour of heavy handling before he becomes a reasonably civilized creature once more.

It is no unusual experience for us to be sitting in a restaurant with everything quite under control, only to have some well-meaning stranger walk up, ruffle the child's hair with a loving hand, make sundry remarks as to where he got his lovely curly hair, what beautiful brown eyes he has, and so on — with half of the people in the room beaming approval — and then, well satisfied with her work of destruction, walk out. Before this session of appreciation, we were enjoying our food and each other's company. Now the well-behaved boy has been transformed into an excited show-off, and the rest of the day is on precarious ground.

Some of our friends carry a liberal supply of candy or gum in their pockets to give to the youngster the moment they see him. "Go on and eat it. Your aunt won't mind!" They seem to assume it is possible to gain a child's affection by training him, like a horse, to come for a lump of sugar.

What, then, *should* an adult do when he meets a youngster? Above all, remember that a child is an individual, not a toy or a thing, and address him as a person. Don't stick your thumbs into his ribs to make him hysterical. This kind of romping, although it has its place, is difficult for it usually is impossible for the excited child to recognize where the socially acceptable boundary of such activity lies. He becomes quite unable to stop. What you started as innocent fun almost invariably changes the youngster into an irritating nuisance who persists in interrupting your conversation with his parents. The end is usually punishment for the child.

Don't talk baby talk! In spite of the fact that you know better you probably do it more often than you think. It is an insult to anyone to be taunted with his own imperfect speech. The child wants to learn *your* way of speaking, not to see how well you can imitate and mock his infantile pronunciation.

Don't try to be silly. When confronted with a child, most adults are silly enough, without deliberately using silliness as a form of entertainment to cover their inability to deal with the situation. Say what you have to say to the youngster, and then stop.

When you meet an adult with a child, it is probably best to address your first remarks to the adult. Then turn to the child, say a few words of greeting and, if you wish, ask about some activity of interest to him. Do not try to carry on a parallel conversation with both adult and child at the same time. But whatever you do, don't try to ignore the child. It is discourteous, and with most children it simply can't be done. A child will go through his entire repertoire of tricks to gain at least some little attention.

No matter what your relationship with the child, never forget that he is under the care of the parent or other guardian, who is responsible for his behavior and for his routine. It is a gross unkindness to subject a child to divided authority. "Never mind what your mother says. Here in my house you may do so and so." Never have words caused more ill will between adults, particularly between parents and grandparents. And never have they been more disturbing to the child, since he now no longer knows which voice to obey. It is easy to say, "Ask your mother if you may," and it pays dividends in parental good will. What seems to you an unreasonable prohibition may have been proven to them by bitter experience to be an essential safeguard.

Don't talk down to a child. Speak to him about things that interest him and in terms that he can comprehend. Particularly, in commenting upon his drawings or coloring, his efforts at carpentry, his attempts at writing, or the music that he has played or sung for you, focus his attention upon *what* has been done, not upon how well *he* has done it. An honest piece of work, at any level of accomplishment, deserves honest appreciation; comments upon the work leave the child free to participate in the conversation, instead of forcing him into bashful and self-conscious silence.

Do not embarrass a child by criticizing him for something beyond his control. "Why didn't you come to visit me as you promised?," when the visit or non-visit was not of the child's choosing, is an unkind question that can have no answer.

Even though the child seems to be absorbed in his play, don't think that you can talk about him, even in a foreign language, without his realizing that he is the subject. He probably will understand the tenor of the conversation. Even worse, he may not *quite* understanding your meaning, and will then fill in details from his own vivid imagination and fears. Half-understood ideas and misinterpreted terms have been a source of serious worry to many a child, particularly since even the most fortunate youngster usually has some phase of life in which he feels dangerously insecure.

When a child has been hurt, it is important to keep conversation on a matter-of-fact basis, sympathetic but casual. Because of his limited experience, the child evaluates his injury primarily by watching and copying the reactions of those about him; and hence by poorly chosen expressions of sympathy or by inviting him to recite and relive all the sad details of his trouble, you actually increase his pain. How often one hears, "Oh, dear! How did you bang up my little sweetheart like that? Tell me. How *did* you do it?" How seldom, "Well, you had a little bump, didn't you?" And rare, indeed, is the adult who has the good sense to drop the subject at this point and casually introduce some more absorbing topic.

Children can be fun, a pleasure to themselves and to all they meet. They can also be a source of embarrassment and annoyance, of humiliation and man's deepest grief. They want, earnestly, to learn to live in an adult world; they look up to all grownups, therefore, to teach them how to achieve this goal. It is the inescapable responsibility of every adult to do all that he can to help each child he meets in his effort to achieve maturity.

Forgotten Failures

HE STRUCK OUT 1330 times, a record in futility unapproached by any other player in the history of baseball. But that isn't what we remember about Babe Ruth. His 714 home runs completely obliterated the 1330 strike-outs.

Cy Young, perhaps the greatest pitcher of all time, accumulated 511 victories, a mark that never has been threatened. But what is generally forgotten is that Young actually lost almost as many games as he won.

One of the failingest men who ever lived was always trying experiments that were unsuccessful. Yet we never think of Thomas Edison as a failure.

At Fort Necessity, during the French and Indian War, a young American officer capitulated to the enemy. But George Washington is never thought of as the man who surrendered to the French.

People would feel a lot less sensitive about failure if they remembered it just doesn't matter, except as a guidepost for oneself. Success is a bright sun that obscures and makes ridiculously unimportant all the little shadowy flecks of failure.

— Harold Helfer in *The Kiwanis Magazine*

A plan to relieve you of the drudgery of an uncongenial job

How to Avoid Work

Condensed from
The American Magazine

William J. Reilly, Ph.D.
Career Consultant

s YOUR job work or fun? If it is work, you would probably be wise to get out of it before another month ends.
Work is doing something you don't enjoy doing. Your
life is too short and too valuable to fritter away on a job that
bores you, or forces you to be with people you don't like, or
calls for a knack you haven't got.

Yet all my studies indicate that a majority of Americans are
dissatisfied with their jobs and wish they were doing something
else. I see accountants who wish they were teachers or explorers,
and salesmen who wish they were cabinetmakers. I recently
talked with the son of a wealthy lawyer who was grimly studying law. He said, "Oh, I'll plow through these courses somehow." Deep in his heart he wanted to be a geologist.

A person in a job he dislikes reacts by being moody and
nervous. He becomes tired easily and is a victim of indigestion
and insomnia. As he continues to feel frustrated he becomes
rebellious, grows sour on the world.

Recently I counseled a young newspaperman who had been
advised to go into newspaper work because he had definite
writing abilities. He hated his work. Noncompetitive by nature,
he moved at a slow tempo. The newspaper pace distressed him.
He had always yearned to teach.

I persuaded him to take a teaching job in a boys' school and
he is now writing in his leisure hours. For the first time in his
life he feels whole and adequate.

Often it is not necessary to change to a completely new line
of activity. Some months ago I counseled the business manager
of a manufacturing firm who was approaching a nervous col-

lapse. Our diagnosis was that in his present business he was dealing with *things,* whereas his yearnings were to deal with *people.* My recommendation was that he stay in the field of business management but find a job where he could more directly serve people. A month later he wrote that he had become business manager of a hospital.

In many cases it may be impracticable to make an abrupt change of jobs. But it is always possible to test your desire out first by studying and experimenting in another field during your spare time. Then draw up a plan whereby you can shift the emphasis from one career to the other over a period of time. When Herbert Hoover decided he wanted to become an engineer, he took a job as a typist so that he could work somehow in an engineering firm.

The main thing is to stick to the plan. When you start making excuses for postponing action you are doomed to stay where you are. I've heard a thousand people make such excuses. It is always one of these:

"I don't have the money." Sometime ago I talked with a man nearly 50 who was hunched over a draftsman's board. He mentioned he had wanted to paint landscapes ever since he was in high shcool. "May I see some of your work?" I asked. "Oh, I've never painted," he replied. "I've never had the money to support myself while painting."

"I don't have the time." A gas-station attendant who wanted to be an accountant told me he had been forced to give up a correspondence course in accounting because he didn't have the time. But in the past week he had bowled, gone to the movies, played poker, and spent two hours at a bar.

"My family won't let me." Frequently wives try to restrain a husband from any "rash" change that would make undue demands on his time, involve low pay, or not add to the social prestige of the family. But most wives can be won over if the husbands are persistent and explain how much the proposed change means to them.

I know a man, 38, who became bored with his work as a factory foreman. He decided he wanted to be a country doctor, back in the Kansas village where he had spent his youth. Today he works as a garage mechanic at night and is studying medicine by day. This man is no longer bored. He's learning the feeling of achievement.

I have found that three factors are paramount in deciding your success in any job:

Your ability to do the job. Your capacity for getting along well with the people you work with. Your actual desire to do the job.

Of the three, ability is normally the least important and desire is overwhelmingly the most important in determining your success. One large corporation that began considering the actual desires of its salesmen, along with the other two factors, cut its turnover of salesman in half. And in a factory where two thirds of its line workers had been quitting or washing out every year, the turnover was likewise cut in half.

Thomas Edison worked out a simple plan for discovering the interests of new employes. He sent beginners around the laboratories and shops on tours of inspection. Each day they were to make reports, with suggestions and criticisms. One lad who had majored in chemistry in college had applied for a chemist's job. His reports, however, showed no constructive suggestions in that field, but many on production and layout. Obviously, these subjects were closer to his real interests, and he was assigned to production.

A few corporations expose new employes to a variety of jobs for the first few weeks and then ask them which they like best. I believe this is a shrewd investment; yet industry almost universally ignores the desire factor in hiring men.

Millions of people are held back by their failure at the human-relations level. If you are continually in conflict with associates your job is work of the worst sort. But when a person is careful about his human relations, almost any job is a pleasure. Lord Chesterfield revealed one clue for getting on congenially with others when he wrote his son: "Make other people like themselves a little better, my son, and I promise you they will like you very well."

Any job can also be made more interesting if you seek ways to improve upon what you are doing. Look for some phase of it that challenges your ingenuity.

However, the best way to achieve true happiness is to express yourself with all your skill and enthusiasm in a career that appeals to you more than any other. In such a career you feel a sense of purpose, a sense of achievement. It is not work. A doctor who has felt the pulse of life does not feel he is working when he must leave a party to deliver a baby.

Altogether too much emphasis has been placed on what we ought to do rather than what we want to do. Amelia Earhart once wrote: "I flew the Atlantic because I wanted to. If that be what they call 'a woman's reason,' make the most of it. It isn't, I think, a reason to be apologized for by man or woman.

"Whether you are flying the Atlantic or selling sausages or building a skyscraper or driving a truck, your greatest power comes from the fact that you want tremendously to do that very thing, and do it well."

Planning Parenthood

ONE enterprising mother solved the problem of getting her year-old infant to swallow a pill. She put first the pill, then the baby, on the playpen floor. True to the ways of small children, he promptly popped the pill into his mouth and gulped it down.

— Contributed by Mrs. J. M. Eshleman

A YOUNG WOMAN with three youngsters under six was trying to keep track of them and shop at the same time. When she picked out one of those divided plates with a built-in space for hot water to keep food warm for dawdling youngsters, the clerk asked: "Wouldn't you like two more — one for each of the children?"

"They get the food while it's still hot," she answered grimly. "This one is for me!"

— Contributed by Mrs. H. V. Davis

"SOME of us concocted a vacation plan last year that was so satisfactory we're repeating it this year," an acquaintance told my wife. "Four couples banded together and rented a country house for two months. Each couple spent their two-week vacation there, taking care of all 13 children."

"Good heavens!" exclaimed my wife. "I wouldn't call taking care of 13 children a 'vacation' — though it would be wonderful, of course, for the children."

"Oh, the two weeks were hell. The 'vacation' was the six weeks at home without the kids."

— Contributed by G. H. Hennegar

CULTIVATE THE MINOR ECSTASIES

Condensed from "The World in Tune"

Elizabeth Gray Vining   Author of "Windows for the Crown Prince"

ONLY A FEW people, and those few but infrequently, know great ecstasy, that state of being outside oneself and outside time, caught up in an overwhelming emotion. But there are minor ecstasies for all of us, however monotonous our days or cramped our lives. Something seen, something heard, something felt, flashes upon one with a bright freshness — and the heart, tired or sad or merely indifferent, stirs and lifts in answer.

I well remember the first minor ecstasy that I recognized and consciously put away in my mind, as a child hoards the birthday pearl to make a necklace. I was 15, and it was August at the seashore. One evening the western sky was filled with flame and molten gold, and gold and flame shone in all the moving facets of the water. The eastern sky was pearly; into it the moon rose, spilling pale silver over the gray-blue sea.

Even as I caught my breath at the lovely drama of the contrast, an airplane, a great silver bird more rare and wonderful then than now, came suddenly out of the heart of the sunset, sailed above the long, lonely beach, and flew deep into the moonlight. My young heart bounded against my ribs like a bird in a cage, and memory has held that scene for me in colors as bright and soft as those in which I first saw it. Ever since, that memory has been for me a yardstick; if what I see or hear makes me feel at all as that made me feel, then it is a minor ecstasy.

There have been countless others down the years: the fragrance of sun-warmed honeysuckle on stone walls; the flute passages in Beethoven's Fourth Symphony; the cold curve of the river in winter where it turns between purple wooded banks; shared laughter over nothing more than fundamental understanding; the whistle of a cardinal in the dark of a still February morning; the smell of wet wood and seaweed at a ferry wharf.

Once, when for long months sorrow had clamped tight my heart, it was a minor ecstasy that showed me that life might again hold joy for me. I woke in the morning to the sound, I thought, of rain on the porch roof, but when I opened my eyes I saw that it was not raindrops making that soft and playful patter but locust blossoms falling from the tree above. For a fleeting second my cramped and stiff heart knew again the happiness that is of the universe and not of itself and its possessions, and like Sara Teasdale, when in similar circumstances she heard the wood thrush through the dusk, "I caught life back against my breast, and kissed it, scars and all."

It is well to recognize and cherish such moments when they come; it is an added joy consciously to collect them, for a hoard of minor ecstasies brings more keen and lasting pleasure than all the autographs and little china jugs in the world. It costs but a notebook and the time it takes to jot down the few words that bring them vividly back to us when time has overlaid them in our minds with the dust of daily life.

Writing them down saves them for us. It reminds us in the blank periods that come to all that we have had these moments in the past and will have them again. "Things prized are enjoyed," wrote Thomas Traherne many years ago. Writing them down, treasuring them, not only makes our enjoyment keener, it makes us more aware of them, less likely to let them pass unnoticed through sloth or indifference. It serves to polish up the lens through which we see the world about us.

Now when bleak winds from a hidden future go howling past our naked ears, when the familiar treasures that have kept our safe lives snug seem to be dimming and receding, a collection of minor ecstasies can be a source of joy, secret, inviolable, inexhaustible.

Fragments of beauty and truth lie in every path. They need only the seeing eye and the receptive spirit to become the stuff of authentic minor ecstasies which can light the gray stretches of our lives like faint but unmistakable stars.

The Costly One-Third

ACCORDING to a new scientific study presented to the American Public Health Association, one-third of our adult population consists of unhappy, ineffective and upset persons who pose an "extremely high" burden of expense for the rest of society. For it is this third, the study reveals, that has most of the troubles — that fills divorce courts, jams hospitals and medical waiting rooms, overloads welfare agencies and burdens industry with a staggering cost in absenteeism and accidents.

Prepared by Drs. Lawrence E. Hinkle, Jr., and Norman Plummer from the New York Hospital-Cornell University Medical Center, the report is based on statistical study of the health records of 1297 female telephone operators and 1527 telephone craftsmen. Specific findings include these startling figures:

The average well woman had been disabled only 33 days in 28.8 years compared to the average ill woman's 1209 days' absence during 25.9 years. Also, the former had had less than one major illness compared to the average ill woman's ten, 6.1 minor illnesses to 62 and one accident to seven. Among the men, the average well employe had had only 19 days of sickness absence during 27 years compared to the average ill man's 581 days. The ill man had had 15 times as many minor illnesses, eight times as many major illnesses, twice as many accidents and four times as many surgical operations.

The presence of good or poor health during an adult life was found to correlate most closely with the individual's relation to his environment; health, happiness and satisfaction with the job were related, as were unhappiness, poor health and job dissatisfaction. Happy home life, too, was associated with lack of sickness.

Since this unhappy one-third is so costly to society, Drs. Hinkle and Plummer suggest it should be highly rewarding to make further medical study of the group to find out why they are disabled.
— Robert K. Plumb in New York *Times*

If You *Need* a Drink—
Don't Take It!

Condensed from Nation's Business   *Charles Stevenson*

AㅣcoHoLISM is a serious disease for the nation's 750,000 chronic alcoholics. It is a serious threat to 3,000,000 other excessive drinkers. But Yale University, which originated the movement for treating alcoholism in public clinics as a disease instead of a sin, has ascertained scientifically that the remaining 58,250,000 Americans who drink moderately can use alcohol with safety and sometimes even benefit.

Don't order a case of whisky on that! Instead, know the facts about alcohol as Yale has discovered them — then govern yourself accordingly, because men and women already on the highroad to alcoholism too often imagine they are moderate drinkers.

There was no shortage of willing martyrs to science at Yale. Both outsiders and staffers have lined up at weird cocktail parties to have whisky poured down their throats while the professors manipulate Rube Goldbergian devices to record reactions and learn that it isn't the amount of alcohol consumed that counts but the percentage showing afterward in the blood; that there are a lot of variables in its effect.

Absorption is slowed and the kick lightened by food in the stomach or cereals in the drink, as with beer. Inversely, carbonated mixtures are absorbed faster. The speed with which the liver burns alcohol depends on the individual and the drink (various distilled spirits show differences); thus the lasting power of the kick varies.

THIS article is largely based on findings of Yale's Laboratory of Applied Physiology, Section on Alcohol Studies.

Because a big man's body contains more blood than a small man's, it requires more liquor to put a significant concentration of alcohol in his veins. When the professors fed four ounces of whisky each to two men two hours after dinner, the 130-pounder showed a .04 percent alcoholic concentration in his blood while his 213-pound companion was only one half that far along.

Nevertheless, experiments have convinced the experts that, while everyone is sober with less than .05 percent of alcohol in his blood (two and a third ounces of whisky on the empty stomach of an average 150-pound man) and some may be tipsy at .1, everybody suffers some impairment at .15. The drinker becomes deeply intoxicated at .2 and .3, passes out at .4, when the alcohol completely depresses that part of his brain governing consciousness, and dies at .5 to .9 when it paralyzes the centers which control breathing. To achieve such a death means gulping quickly the equivalent of a quart or more of the strongest whisky at one brief sitting. Happily, unconsciousness would probably halt the attempt before it was successful.

It has been found that all functions take place at lower efficiency even after the smallest dose of alcohol. For instance, if you feel less tired after drinking, you simply are benumbed. Actually your muscular output drops. On two ounces of whisky, the average Yale subject's errors in reasoning jumped 20 percent; on a half-pint, 67 percent. No matter how you may insist liquor stimulates you, it does not.

Alcohol is related chemically to ether. It acts first by deadening the nerves of the brain to relieve physical and mental tension. If some people seem clearer-headed after a drink, this is only because they are so tense and self-conscious that, without a sedative, they are inhibited. A lawyer I know does better before the jury if he takes a drink. He could do still better were it possible to get rid of his inhibitions by other means.

Even small amounts of alcohol impair efficiency. Though one motorist can drive safely with enough liquor in him to put another atop a lamp post, the Yale experts caution every one to avoid the steering wheel for at least an hour after taking two ounces of whisky, two hours after four ounces, then to add an hour for each additional ounce.

However, the experts do not feel that well-motivated, moderate drinking is necessarily a bad habit. They contend that, in relaxing tension, it fulfills a psychological need. Moreover, there is no physiological or psychological ill effect from years of such drinking, whether it involves wine, beer, bonded whisky or fresh blends. Only admonition is: Whatever hard liquor you drink, dilute it.

There is nothing to the old belief that the more you drink the more you must drink to obtain the same degree of relaxation. Unlike the morphine addict, who at first might be killed by one grain and yet in time requires ten to feel like living, the drinker develops no tolerance for alcohol. He will need no more to relieve his tensions as time goes on, unless his tensions increase.

Dr. Howard W. Haggard, director of Yale's Laboratory of Applied Physiology, says moderate amounts of alcohol may aid digestion, although an excess will halt it. "For people past middle age it is one of the safest sedatives," he adds. "Many elderly people get much comfort from a small amount of alcohol; it relieves the aches, pains and chilliness of age, lessens the tensions and irritations and increases the appetite. It does not greatly affect normal blood pressure but it does prevent pressure from rising in anxiety and mental concentration."

However, any person who has reached the point where he wonders if he should discipline his drinking habits may be in the danger zone of excessive drinking. It is a confusing area. A man may fear he is an addict because his regular 5 p.m. drink has established such a habit pattern that he definitely *wants* a drink at that time. But habit does not necessarily imply addiction. Some genuinely heavy drinkers may be endangering their health, but are not yet addicts. On the other hand, a man may be a problem drinker though he limits himself to an ounce every other day.

What then is a problem drinker? What counts is motivation.

Let's look at an average sample of 100 alcoholics. About half of them are persons whose drinking is only a symptom of underlying mental disorder; alcohol cannot be blamed for their neurosis, for the fact that they are morons, for their epilepsy, dementia praecox or manic-depressive psychosis. But the other half are those who, starting as apparently well-integrated social drinkers, pamper their frustrations with alcohol until they can't face life except through a whisky haze.

If you rule out the mental misfits who really constitute other than an alcohol problem, it still does not suffice for an average drinker to insist it is impossible for him to become a problem drinker. Whether the incipient alcoholic's traits develop depends on the pressures to which he is subjected and on the social acceptance of heavy drinking by his circle.

Frustrations offer a fertile field for the alcoholic personality. One man may seek escape from the fact that he lacks energy to achieve his ambitions. Another with the same underlying characteristic will break out in drink only because he can't get a job. The reason for drinking may lie in childhood psychological experiences the drinker has forgotten.

There are tests which will help a man analyze his drinking habits. Can you enjoy a party only if there is liquor to release you? Do you long for the time of day when you can drink without hurting your job? Do you turn to alcohol each day to overcome anxiety, disgust, fatigue or frustration? Do you drink to offset difficulties with your wife, your boss, your children or employes? If the answer in any case is yes, says Dr. Abraham Myerson of Boston, one of the nation's leading psychiatrists, you are an alcohol dependent and in peril.

To put it in a nutshell, simply ask yourself: *"Do I need this drink?"* If the answer is yes, don't take it. The problem drinker is the person who drinks not because he enjoys it but because he feels he needs it. He is drinking to escape. He never craves alcohol specifically; but he is developing a genuine craving for anesthesia, which alcohol supplies.

It usually takes ten years to develop chronic alcoholism. Along with it may be liver trouble, or irritation of the throat and digestive system, resulting in alcoholic gastritis and improper assimilation of food. But most of the ills result from dietary deficiency, because alcohol is a food which in excessive amounts eliminates hunger. Moreover, it contains no vitamins, only calories — 200 to the ounce.

Though persons less than 30 years old rarely can be cured of alcoholism, upwards of 60 out of 100 can be helped in middle age. Among patients who are married and in skilled occupations, the Yale clinics achieve 81.5 percent successes at a cost of $60 to $100. Alcoholics Anonymous sometimes is regarded as having more success than any agency, although it does not suffice for all.

Nobody, though, ever was cured by nagging. Occasionally successful treatment involves psychological conditioning not of the drunken husband but of his nagging wife.

No remedy is successful unless it seeks out the underlying psychological reasons which prompt the drinking. In a surprising number of cases, the elimination of them will cure alcoholism. One woman's problem was traced to a mother-in-law allergy and cured by eliminating the latter (by fair means).

There is no recorded instance of an alcoholic without a personal problem which caused him to drink. However, alcohol in sufficient quantities supplies its own problem. If you habitually drink excessively, no matter for what reason, you finally will be drinking to escape the woe caused by your drinking.

The Heart of the Matter

WHEN Henry Norris Russell, the Princeton astronomer, concluded a lecture on the Milky Way, a woman asked him: "If our world is so little and the universe is so great, can we really believe that God pays any attention to us?"

"That, madam," replied Dr. Russell, "depends entirely on how big a God you believe in."

— Quoted by Bill Gold in Washington *Post*

A MAN came to the Rev. B. J. Howard, of Orange County, North Carolina, and told him of all the troubles he had had during the past year. He wound up with: "I tell you right now, preacher, it's enough to make a man lose his religion."

"Seems to me, Jim," Mr. Howard told him quietly, "it's enough to make a man *use* his religion."

— Carl Goerch in *The State*

We Didn't Get a Divorce

Condensed from Your Life
Anonymous

ONE evening about three years ago my husband turned to me and said quietly, "Mary, I want a divorce."

We were sitting in front of the fire in our house in the country, so perfect a picture of connubial bliss that for a moment I couldn't believe he had spoken the words I heard. If we had just had an ugly quarrel I might have understood it, or if I had "let myself go" mentally and physically, as some women do after ten years of marriage.

True, we had not been madly in love with each other since the early years of our marriage. But we had sensibly substituted fondness for infatuation, and tolerance for passion. We had many interests in common and had learned to live and let-live together with mutual respect. Why, then, did John want a divorce?

Because, he said, he wanted to marry someone else.

Bewildered, I stared at the flames. A slow, stubborn anger filled me as I thought of our two young sons sleeping peacefully upstairs.

"Well, you can't have a divorce," I said. "The boys' happiness is more important than yours. You can't desert them now."

His answer was the irrefutable argument that by refusing him a divorce I should be maintaining merely the empty shell of a home. The psychological effect on the children would be even more disastrous than that of losing their father.

Hurt pride bubbled through my anger and I was sorely tempted to take the first train to Reno. Then I thought of the women I had known who had set their husbands free for the Other Woman. I remembered the confused misery in their eyes that lingered long after they had girded their hurt with hard-boiled armor. My imagination leaped ahead to the bickering over alimony and the custody of the children. Gradually I swallowed my pride.

I went to the city next morning and asked the advice of two men whose opinions I value highly. One is a doctor, the other a lawyer. They were of one accord:

"The Other Woman is never sufficient reason for breaking up a home in which there are children. John will get over it in time and it would be a tragedy for everyone concerned if he gets over it too late."

"But," I asked, "how can I be sure that he will get over it?"

"Nine times out of ten," they explained, " 'the Other Woman' is an empty phrase. She is merely a symptom that John has reached the stage when he is wondering whether he has eaten his cake or still has it. Because you are his wife you're probably not as glamorous to him as another woman. The routine of married life is at the root of this; not you or the Other Woman. If he divorces you and marries her, the chances are that the same thing will happen all over again."

"That sounds sensible," I agreed. "But how can I make him understand this?"

"By a trial separation. Give him a month or two living away from you and the children in order to think it over. He will have, in effect, a divorce, but no drastic steps will have been taken."

Both lawyer and doctor answered the question in my eyes. "Don't worry, Mary. He'll want to come back even before the time is up."

But we did not separate right away. My husband wasn't earning enough money to support two establishments. In order to remove that obstacle we moved back to town and I got a job. But soon we discovered that almost every cent I earned went right out to maids and sitters and nursery schools.

This put the divorce project back in my husband's lap. If he wanted to have his cake and eat it, too, he would have to earn more money. Right at the outset he would have to save up enough to cover my trip to Reno, the salary of the housekeeper while I was gone, and the lawyers' fees.

We settled down to wait. Although our relationship during that time was outwardly friendly, my position as wife in name only was difficult. The door was temptingly open for me to take the boys away from their father emotionally. Often it would have been comforting to cry on my elder son's shoulder and tell him his father was going to leave us. And it would have been easy to smother the baby with the fondness and affection I would normally have diverted to my husband. John was working nights and week-ends now and saw very little of the children. In spite of my efforts not to turn them against him they sensed a division in their parents and naturally sided with me.

So gradually John was forced to face the fact that part of the price he would have to pay for a divorce would be the loss of his sons. If it was difficult for me, it must have been far more difficult for him.

I know now that our thoughts were running in the same groove. I relived our courtship and wedding. I went back to those days of hardship and happiness when we were barely earning enough to live. And my husband has since told me that he kept remembering how hard we had both worked until we had enough money in the bank so I could quit my job and have a baby.

Neither of us could ever forget the night our first son was born, nor the arrival of our second. We recalled the thrill of at last finding just the country place we had dreamed of; the first exciting months when we had started the baby chicks and the garden. Indelible too was the memory of the dreadful illness that had almost taken both boys from us.

Waiting gave John plenty of time to feel the tug of the strong threads that had woven into the pattern of our past. We had got through the difficult adjustment years with flying colors; had it all been for nothing? How easy was it going to be to start all over again with someone else?

Thus while we waited we were actually making progress toward a better relationship.

Both partners in almost every marriage have at some time

thought about divorce. Like many a wife, in moments of anger and disappointment I had wondered if my choice of a husband had been wise. For the sake of the children I had never allowed myself seriously to consider a break. Now I approached the subject from my own selfish point of view.

I did not want to face a future without a husband, and it would not be easy to get another one. I had thought of myself as an attractive, intelligent, independent woman. I promptly learned that I would not be independent until the boys were self-supporting, and the world, I found, was filled with attractive, intelligent, younger women without ties. In my business I met many attractive men and some who found me attractive, but those who had reached mental and emotional maturity were already married. I would not break up any other woman's home and the vision of the hide-and-seek existence of the gay divorcée of many affairs was distasteful.

I came to the conclusion that I had never before fully appreciated the value of a husband. For my own sake now I began to hope desperately that the divorce would never materialize.

When the time finally came for us to make the trial separation neither of us wanted to go through with it. But we did. And, as the lawyer and doctor had predicted, John wanted to come back after the first week.

Since his return he has been a better husband and a better father, and I have tried to be a better wife. He missed the boys intensely; consequently his patience with them has increased and he is more anxious to share in their guidance.

We are going back to the country next spring and I feel sure that we shall be there "for as long as we both shall live."

⬥⬥⬥○⬥⬥⬥○⬥⬥⬥○⬥⬥⬥

WE WERE discussing the philosophy of "Live each day as though it were your last."

"Well," said the sweetest old lady of the group, "that's a fine saying, but for 20 years I've been using a philosophy that's a little different. It's this: 'Treat all the people you meet each day as though it were *their* last day on earth.'"

— Contributed by Barbara Reid

Great men in all ages have turned to God for help; prayer
brings harmony to the life of the humblest

What Prayer Can Do

Condensed from Guideposts
Fulton Oursler
Author of "The Greatest Story Ever Told"

ONE SPRING MORNING when I was a small boy,
my mother dressed me up in my Sunday
best and warned me not to leave the front steps.
"We'll be walking over to see your aunt," she
promised.

I waited obediently until the baker's son from
the corner shop came along and called me a sissy. Then I sprang
from the steps and whammed him on the ear. He shoved me
into a mud puddle, splotching my white blouse with slime and
leaving my stocking with a bloody hole at the knee. Hope-
lessly I began to bawl.

But my grief was stilled at a sudden tinkle of bells. Down
the street came a peddler, pushing his jingling green cart —
"Hokey-pokey ice cream, one cent apiece." Forgetting my dis-
obedience, I ran into the house and begged my mother for a
penny. Never can I forget her answer:

"Look at yourself! You're in no condition to ask for anything."

Many a harum-scarum year went by before it dawned on me
that often, when we ask for help from God, we need to take
a look at ourselves; we may be in no condition to ask Him for
anything.

Believers admit no limits to what the power of prayer can
do, and even skeptics who study the results with an open mind
become impressed with the potency of faith. But if his prayers

are to be answered, a man has to meet his Maker half the way.

"The trouble is that most prayers are not honest to God," declares a psychologist, a man of no religious faith. "People have the ungracious audacity to ask for heavenly handouts although they are not on speaking terms with their next-door neighbor; they have forbidden relatives their house; they are spreaders of gossip and envious detractors of their best friends.

"To feel free of bitterness one must be rid of malice, resentment, envy, jealousy and greed, which are certain causes of mental illness and even physical disease. Simply by obeying the scriptural rule to be reconciled to our brother before prayer, we can wash away these breeding germs of neuroses and psychoses. Honest-to-God prayer is a kind of mental health insurance."

In his *Self-Improvement Handbook* Norman Vincent Peale gives two hints on how to forgive.

1. "Repeat the Lord's Prayer inserting your offender's name: 'Forgive me my trespasses as I forgive Henry Jones.'

2. "Speak to others in a kindly manner about the person against whom you harbor antagonism."

The more we can free our hearts of grudges and enmities, the closer we come to the supreme goal of inner peace. Then we begin to realize that prayer is infinitely more than an appeal for personal favors. It is itself the greatest of all gifts; an ever-richer experience, a continuous feeling of being in harmony with the constructive forces of the universe. It brings the wonders of "visiting with God" to the life of the humblest man of faith. And that sense of divine companionship will powerfully influence his thoughts and actions.

A young American Indian left his Huron tribe in northern Wisconsin to be educated in city schools. He became a lawyer and the green forests saw him no more, until in middle life he returned for a hunting and fishing vacation. Presently his woodsman guide noticed that at every sundown the Indian vanished for an hour. One day, beset with curiosity, the guide trailed him.

From behind the low spread of a hemlock tree, he watched the Indian build a fire in an open clearing; saw him balance a log across two stones on one side of the fire and place another such bench on the opposite side, then seat himself on one of the logs and stare into the blaze.

The guide started to walk toward the fire, when the Indian, seeing him, held up restraining hands. Without a word he arranged another log and invited the guide, by a gesture, to join in his vigil. For a half hour the two remained together in complete silence.

After they had returned to camp and eaten supper, the Indian explained the mystery:

"When I was a child my mother taught me to go off by myself at the end of each day and make a place for a visit of the Great Spirit. I was to think back over my actions and thoughts of the day. If there was anything of which I was ashamed, I must tell the Great Spirit I was sorry and ask for strength to avoid the same mistake again. Then I would sleep better that night. I had forgotten all about it, but here, among these tall trees where I played as a boy, I have found my lost faith. I have not known such peace since I was a child. And from now on I shall somehow manage to visit with the Great Spirit every day."

Ezio Pinza, who starred in *South Pacific,* has his own story about the pathway to peace. It is reported by Ed Sullivan in his famous syndicated column:

"On the night before *South Pacific* opened," said Pinza, "I told Mary Martin if she could not sleep because of nervousness to do what I'd found best — get up, dress and go to the nearest church. 'Just sit there in church,' I said, 'and soon all your nervousness will vanish, as if it had been smoothed away.' God has been so good to me and my career has been so crowded with great luck that I turn to Him all the time. Others may fail; God never. When I explained this to Mary she started to cry, and it was on this note that our friendship was founded."

Communion with the infinite is of solid value in our most practical affairs. I know of a manufacturer who likes to drive back and forth to work so that he can think about business problems without interruption.

"One morning," he relates, "I suddenly realized that problems were always coming up that I had not anticipated. How could I think about crises before they ever happened? Only by prayer. Right there I began to pray that I might meet wisely and well the problems of the day ahead. I arrived at my office feeling refreshed and confident, and I had one of my best days. I soon realized that I had hit upon a wonderful technique. Instead of praying to get pulled out of troubles, I was now conditioning myself in advance to make calm, rational and sound decisions on any problem that came up."

The divine promise "Ask and ye shall receive" does not guarantee that you will receive exactly what you ask for. Often we do not know what is good for us; the old Greeks had a proverb that when the gods were angry with a man they gave him what he wanted. Many of us have lived to be thankful that our prayers were denied. The wise person adds a proviso to every request: "Nevertheless, not my will but Thine be done."

There was Rosalie, the daughter of a poor Parisian, who showed early promise of becoming a great artist. But an artist needs more than promise. Rosalie wanted to draw from life and her father had no money to pay for a model. Very earnestly the girl prayed for enough francs to pay a model's hire, but no shower of money rained down on her back yard.

One day, as she was taking a walk, she had a sudden feeling that everything was going to be all right. Near a crowded market place she noticed a farmer's dray horse hitched for the day behind a vegetable stall. He would not object to being her model — not if Rosa did not mind drawing a horse! In the Metropolitan Museum of Art in New York City there now hangs a world-known canvas, *The Horse Fair*. It was painted by Rosa Bonheur, imperishably famed for her masterpieces of horses.

As horizons broaden, we learn to ask less for ourselves and to remember the needs of others, both friends *and* enemies — healing for the sick, comfort for the grieving, help for the jobless, mercy for all. "God make thee beautiful within," was Plato's prayer for those he loved.

When the late Laurette Taylor was starring in her last Broadway play, *The Glass Menagerie,* her friends knew that she was in poor health. They knew also that she had quarreled with her co-star, Eddie Dowling.

One midsummer matinee, in the course of a scene near a table at which Dowling was seated, Miss Taylor suddenly swayed and grabbed a chair for support. The company manager, fearing that she had been about to faint, rushed back to her dressing room as soon as the curtain fell.

"I'm all right," Laurette assured him. "It was just that something happened on stage that nearly knocked me off my pins. We were playing the part where Eddie is supposed to be trying to write something while I am scolding him. I happened to look over his shoulder and saw that he really was writing — and what he was writing was a prayer: '*Dear God — please make Laurette well and strong, and help us to be friends again.*'"

That prayer broke a black spell between the rival stars. Later I learned that for months at every performance Eddie Dowling had been writing prayers for friends and foes during that same scene. "It kept my mind sweet — which it badly needed," Eddie told me.

Even the old hostility of science is beginning to be tempered by a respect for the incomprehensible mysteries of faith. Only a few months ago, Dr. Robert A. Millikan, 82-year-old Nobel Prize winner, and head of the California Institute of Technology, told the country's leading physicists that a lifetime of scientific research has convinced him that there is a Divinity that is shaping the destiny of man. No scientist has delved more deeply into the mechanisms of matter than Millikan. It was he who first determined the charge and mass of the electron, the smallest particle in the universe. In his recent speech he said:

"Just how we fit into the plans of the Great Architect and how much He has assigned us to do, we do not know, but if we fail in our assignment it is pretty certain that part of the job will be left undone.

"But fit in we certainly do somehow, else we would not have a sense of our own responsibility. A purely materialistic philosophy is to me the height of unintelligence."

As by an infallible instinct, great men of all ages turn to God for help. They seem to by-pass intellectual doubt, finding a short cut to universal truth. No one has ever expressed it better than Abraham Lincoln: "I have had so many evidences of His direction, so many instances when I have been controlled by some other power than my own will, that I cannot doubt that this power comes from above. I frequently see my way clear to a decision when I am conscious that I have not sufficient facts upon which to found it. . . . I am satisfied that when the Almighty wants me to do, or not to do, a particular thing He finds a way of letting me know it. . . . I am a full believer that God knows what He wants men to do, that which pleases Him. It is never well with the man who heeds it not.

"I talk to God," Lincoln went on to say. "My mind seems relieved when I do, and a way is suggested. . . . I should be the veriest shallow and self-conceited blockhead, in my discharge of the duties that are put upon me in this place, if I should hope to get along without the wisdom that comes from God and not from man."

The hardest-headed skeptic can, through prayer, test this guidance for himself. Let him try it as Lincoln did. He may undertake the experiment as an unbeliever, but with an open mind, seeking to learn for himself what prayer can do. I predict for him a series of happy surprises.

Copyright 1950 by The Reader's Digest Association, Inc. (January 1951 issue)
Condensed from Guideposts, January 1951

▼▼▼▼▼▼▼▼▼▼▼▼

Some things will never change. The voice of forest water in the night, a woman's laughter in the dark, the clean, hard rattle of raked gravel, the cricketing stitch of midday in hot meadows, the delicate web of children's voices in bright air — these things will never change.

The glitter of sunlight on roughened water, the glory of the stars, the innocence of morning, the smell of the sea in harbors, the feathery blur and smoky buddings of young boughs — these things will always be the same.

All things belonging to the earth will never change — the leaf, the blade, the flower, the wind that cries and sleeps and wakes again, the trees whose stiff arms clash and tremble in the dark — these things will always be the same, for they come up from the earth that never changes.

— Thomas Wolfe's *You Can't Go Home Again* (Harper)

Why Do We Get So Tired?

Condensed from Today's Health   'Albert Q. Maisel

D o you seem to tire too easily? Do you often feel all in for
no clear reason? Do you sometimes wake up more tired
than when you went to bed?

If you are wearily nodding "Yes" to these questions, you are
far from alone. Most of us, at times, feel the same sort of
puzzling fatigue.

What causes that tired feeling? Most experts agree that
fatigue is a protective reaction against stress, a warning that
strains upon our bodies, our minds or our emotions are approaching a dangerous level.

Nature uses the same red lights whether our weariness is
caused by physical exertion, mental work or emotional frustration. Brain-fag, for example, may bring on the physical reactions — sweating, heart palpitations, shortness of breath —
that come with hard labor. Emotional frustration frequently
masquerades as fatigue. Mental performance falls off sharply
as physical exhaustion sets in.

How does hard work make us tired? It was long widely
believed that our muscles threw off some sort of "tiredness
toxin." Then scientists began studying the body's fuel supply.
They found surprisingly small reserves of oxygen and blood
sugar. As these become depleted, muscles starve and stall, the
way an auto engine falters when you cut down its air supply
or dilute its gas.

At rest, we require barely a cupful of oxygen a minute. But
as soon as we do any work, oxygen consumption skyrockets.
It may mount as high as six and a half *gallons* a minute. Yet

our lungs can step up the supply of new oxygen to barely one gallon a minute. We must "borrow" the rest of the oxygen we burn from the reserves stored in our red blood corpuscles. This totals only four to five gallons.

Our oxygen reserve enables us to spend our energies at an enormous rate — for a short time. When we run to catch a train or play a fast game of tennis, we may drain off nearly one third of this reserve. However, try as we may, it is almost impossible to drive ourselves to the point of utter exhaustion. All sorts of lifesaving discomforts force us to slow down. Muscles ache. We get a "stitch" around our heart. Lungs beg painfully for a chance to catch up with their work.

In moderate physical work, supply and demand of oxygen are more nearly in balance. But here another limiting factor comes into play. Our reserves of energy-giving blood sugar are small. Ordinary walking doubles the rate at which we burn up blood sugar. Heavy labor uses it up five to 15 times as fast.

Brain and nerves are particularly sensitive to lack of sugar and oxygen. Long before our blood is deeply drained of its reserves, they protect us by slowing down and cutting off the nerve impulses that spark muscle movements. Tiredness — the "normal" tiredness of physical exertion — sets in to keep us from destroying ourselves.

Why does mental work make us physically tired? The brain comprises only two percent of the body's weight. But even though it performs no mechanical work, it requires 14 percent of the total blood flow and consumes 23 percent of our entire oxygen intake. Its sugar consumption is also large.

We don't know exactly why the brain needs so much fuel. We do know that it converts the chemical energy of oxygen and sugar into electrical brain waves and nerve impulses. Having no oxygen or sugar reserves of its own, it must get a constant supply from the circulating blood. Cut that supply for a few minutes and the brain goes into coma. In barely eight minutes irreversible damage occurs and the brain cells die.

Since life and death hang so delicately in the balance, the brain must protect itself against even a slight decrease in oxygen or sugar. It flashes on the red lights of physical fatigue to slow down our other organs so that fuel can be shunted toward the endangered brain. Thus brain-fag and the physical feeling of tiredness go together.

How do emotions affect fatigue? Primitive man often had to mobilize all his strength to fight or flee from his enemies. His adrenal glands provided a device to tap energy reserves. Emotions like rage or fear sent a charge of adrenalin coursing through his blood to deepen his breathing and make his heart beat more rapidly. Blood was shunted toward the heart, the muscles and the brain, bringing them extra oxygen. Sugar was freed from the reserve in his liver. After the struggle was over and the adrenalin stopped flowing, he felt all in.

You and I have inherited this vital protective mechanism. It helps us to survive sharp, short-term crises. But unlike primitive man, we often face situations that cannot be solved by energetic action. We may dislike our work, but we fear the economic penalty of quitting. We may be constantly irritated by a nagging spouse or a noisy neighbor, but few of us express our anger physically. As long as conflicting emotions oppose each other, our energy-mobilizing machinery is jammed and we may suffer chronic fatigue.

Is chronic tiredness often a sign of physical disease? When we're sick, the fatigue mechanism discourages unnecessary exertion and channels all our energies into fighting the disease. Thus tiredness is a common symptom of most illnesses.

When persistent tiredness is the *only* obvious symptom, however, physicians have a hard time deciding whether they're dealing with a subtle physical disease or a neurotic, emotional tiredness. Recent research warns against too readily branding persistent tiredness as just a neurotic symptom. Without a thorough medical checkup, a serious physical cause may be overlooked.

Can frequent snacks ward off fatigue? Yes. At Yale, Physiology Professors Howard W. Haggard and Leon A. Greenberg studied workers who ate three meals a day. Their blood sugar and muscular efficiency rose to a peak one hour after each meal, then fell off rapidly. But when the workers switched to four and five smaller meals a day, both blood sugar and muscular efficiency stayed at a higher, more constant level. Fatigue was greatly reduced.

Can dieting cause persistent tiredness? Yes. Few people who diet are content to burn off fat slowly. Many eliminate all sugar, slash other carbohydrates and cut down to a mere 800 or 1000 calories a day instead of the normal 2400 to 3000. As a result, physical effort becomes intensely fatiguing and mental work suffers. The only way to avoid this is to plan a slower reducing regimen with the aid of a physician.

Can tiredness be caused by lack of exercise? Since we become tired after strenuous work or play, we blame exertion for our fatigue. But recent research indicates that our susceptibility to fatigue may often trace back to a lack of consistent exercise.

At Harvard, Professor Ross McFarland put athletes and sedentary students through identical exercises, then compared their pulse rates. The hearts of the athletes pumped more blood in fewer beats. In another Harvard study, Professor D. B. Dill found that people who exercised regularly required less oxygen to perform the same amount of work. Consistent exercise increased both the capacity and the efficiency of their lungs.

Other research has shown that sudden vigorous exercise taken by previously sedentary individuals may destroy from 12 to 30 percent of their red blood cells. This sharply lowers the ability of the blood to transport oxygen to the muscles and brain. That's why the man who sits at a desk all week may find himself peaked for days after a weekend of strenuous tennis or lawnmowing.

Why do we sometimes wake up tired? During sleep our energy-spending organs slow down much more than the processes that create energy reserves. Normally, in seven or eight hours, these reserves become replenished and we wake refreshed.

Let your blankets slip off in a cold room, however, and the body's work in fighting the cold will slow down the energy-restoring process. In a too-hot bedroom, lungs and heart have to work harder than usual to dissipate body heat.

Where deep-seated emotional conflicts are bringing on fatigue, sleep often fails to provide relief. The frustrations that haunted us at bedtime may remain quite as frustrating when morning rolls around.

Does coffee really prevent fatigue? Caffeine does stimulate the brain and facilitate muscle contraction. Coffee, tea or cola drinks can help us push exertion somewhat further before tiredness makes itself felt. But this is postponing fatigue rather than preventing it. When we finally *feel* our tiredness, we then need more rest to restore our more deeply drained reserves.

Are pep pills effective? Many people take amphetamine or closely related drugs to fight off fatigue. Even more than caffeine, they stimulate the brain and thus postpone the feeling of tiredness. But their undesirable effects are greater. They can be habit-forming. They depress the appetite. An overdose can bring on dizziness, headaches, insomnia, even death. Useful in the hands of a skilled physician, *they should never be taken except on a doctor's prescription.*

Does drinking relieve tiredness? Alcohol is a depressant rather than a stimulant. In small quantities it relieves tension and can temporarily suppress the feeling of fatigue.

Heavy drinkers, however, become more than normally susceptible to fatigue. Getting much of their calorie supply from alcohol, they lack other nutrients. Their blood sugar is usually low, their vitamin-starved nerves and muscles ache, their mood is depressed. They're half-tired before they exert themselves and fully fatigued when others are just getting into their stride.

Can smoking give you a lift? The nicotine in tobacco smoke increases the pulse rate and steps up blood flow. This may at first increase the brain's blood supply, bring it more blood sugar and thus relieve fatigue. But smoke also contains carbon monoxide which excludes oxygen from the red blood cells. The chain smoker who inhales soon accumulates enough carbon monoxide to counterbalance the lift he gets from nicotine.

Drugs, pick-me-ups and other devices that postpone fatigue may be useful, but only if used wisely, to get us through a short-term emergency. They can never replace rest and sleep, nature's method of curing fatigue.

Copyright 1954 by The Reader's Digest Association, Inc. (September 1954 issue)
Condensed from Today's Health, September 1954

❖❖❖❖❖❖❖❖

SUCCESS in dealing with other people is like making rhubarb pie —use all the sugar you can, and then double it.

— *Banking*

Your Mind
Can Keep You Young

Condensed from The American Magazine
George Lawton

THE FEAR of growing old can strike you at almost any age. As a consulting psychologist, specializing in the problems of the aged, I find that a goodly percentage of my clients are still in their 30's — men and women who are already worried by the specter of approaching age and want to learn how to head it off. What I tell them can be read with profit by anyone from 17 to 70 who's interested in remaining young.

But before I give you my formula perhaps we'd best define our terms. Age can't be measured by the number of your birthdays. In the first place, biological time isn't at all the same thing as clock time. As the years pile up, biological time slows down; the older you are, the more slowly you age. Physically, you don't change as much from 30 to 40 as you did from 25 to 30; from 55 to 75 as from 40 to 55.

Another reason why the calendar furnishes a false clue to age is that different parts of you grow old at different rates. Your eyes began to age at ten; your hearing around 20. By 30 your muscular strength, reaction time and reproductive powers have all passed their peak.

On the other hand, your mind is still young and growing at 50; your brain doesn't reach its zenith until ten years after that. And from 60 on, mental efficiency declines very slowly to the age of 80.

At 80 you can be just as productive mentally as you were at

30 — and you should know a lot more. Older people frequently suffer some loss of memory, but creative imagination is ageless. What's more, with age we develop insight and perspective. Our judgment and reasoning powers improve; so, thanks to a wealth of experience, does our strategy in tackling tough problems. In short, we acquire wisdom. That's why the old doctor, the veteran lawyer, the experienced craftsman, can usually hold his own against younger and more vigorous rivals.

Don't make the mistake of confusing emotional immaturity with true youthfulness. It takes a mature person to be really young. Men and women who refuse to grow up emotionally are usually the first ones to grow old; and the reason why, in later years, some people relapse into second childhood is that they never really emerged from their first. Masquerading as much younger than you are is a sure sign that you've not grown up emotionally.

My formula for staying young is simple: Concentrate on the part of you that's still young and growing — your brain. Keep your mind awake and you'll stay young all over. These are exciting times. Take an interest in the world around you. And make a point of learning at least one new thing every day.

Above all, don't "settle down." Psychologists are accustomed to seeing two contrasting personality types develop in the middle 30's. Some men and women, although keen about their families and jobs, are constantly broadening their other interests. They keep up with the newspapers and magazines; they busy themselves with creative hobbies, preferably ones that use their hands as well as brains.

Another man begins, at 35, to slump into a dull but comfortable routine. Day after day he does his job, comes home, has dinner, glances at the comic strips or sporting page, fiddles with the radio and goes to bed. His wife does the housework, looks after the children, listens to soap operas, reads an occasional love story and attends a bridge club.

People of the first type grow younger with increasing years. Men and women of the second group have already hit the skids; if they don't change they'll be old at 45.

Regardless of your age it's not too late to make your life more interesting. I know a housewife who, at 50, with no previous experience made herself into an outstanding industrial designer. I know a retired electrical engineer who has become a highly paid ceramic artist. One of my clients — a woman of 70 whose children thought she should retire to the shelf — conducts a successful cooking school for brides.

Get over the notion that you're ever too old to go back to school. I know a man who entered medical college at 70. He got his degree with honors and became an eminent physician. Another man went to law school at 71 and is now an active lawyer. And a 91-year-old California woman has just gone back to college for a refresher course in American history. I know a woman who learned to paint at 77, held a "one-man" show at 80, and today, at 86, is still going strong. It's never too late to add another skill to those you now possess.

Irrespective of years, staying young is easy for those who live in the future. You can do it if you care enough to try. Keep your mind awake and active; that's the only youth elixir guaranteed to work.

How to Enjoy the Happiest Day of Your Life

Joseph Fort Newton in Philadelphia Evening Bulletin

WE CAN DO anything for one day. So, just for today, let us be unafraid of life, unafraid of death which is the shadow of life; unafraid to be happy, to enjoy the beautiful, to believe the best.

Just for today let us live one day only, forgetting yesterday and tomorrow, and not trying to solve the whole problem of life at once. Lincoln said that a man is just as happy as he makes up his mind to be. Suppose we make up our mind to be happy just for today, to adjust ourselves to what is — our family, our business, our luck. To try to make the world over to suit us is a large order. If we cannot have what we like, maybe we can like what we have.

So, just for today, let us be agreeable, responsive, cheerful, charitable; be our best, dress our best, walk softly, praise people for what they do, not criticize them for what they cannot do. And if we find fault, let us forgive it and forget.

How to Get Along with People You Love

Condensed from The Kiwanis Magazine

Edward W. Ziegler

IT is one of the ironies of life that our intimates often provoke us more than our enemies.

I realized this with particular force when talking recently with a young man who had asked me to conduct the funeral of his father. What puzzled him was that his father and mother had never seemed to get along well together. He knew in his heart that the two loved each other and were loyal, yet his chief memory of father and mother was of their quarrels.

Our conversation set me thinking. Against bores and people we dislike we can adopt a defense in depth, and maneuver politely; but in the give and take of living at close quarters, we may frequently be angered or bewildered by some remark or attitude of a loved one, and against such intimate hurt there is no easy defense. Hence the relationships which might be the richest and deepest are too often scarred with superficial friction — by very reason of their closeness.

This is in part because we leave the most delicate personal adjustments to chance. We accept sporadic stresses as if they were inevitable, and meet them, as they rise, in makeshift fashion, perhaps with petty bickering or sulkiness. But surely a truly happy relationship should not be subjected to such recurrent crises. Getting along with people we can't get along without calls for deliberate planning to avert emotional emergencies and to cultivate harmony.

For this there are various simple yet neglected resources at our command. One is to note and act on the little things that bring pleasure to another person. Flowers are usually offered to celebrate some event; a surprise use of flowers, when there is no occasion at all, can have a very telling effect. Recently a woman told me how one evening when the family sat down to dinner there was a man-made bouquet as a centerpiece. Flowers meant nothing to her husband but he knew how much they meant to his wife. He had performed a very simple act — and therein lay its significance. Even as the woman told me the incident, I could see in her face some of the glow of her first pleasure.

Every day every one of us, through acts of gifted simplicity, could express the affection that we too often let atrophy until it is questioned. One calculated act of kindness will often change the mood of a house in an instant. Minor acts that are nicely timed set in motion an endless chain of reactions.

In a neighbor's home the other day an 11-year-old boy got up and cooked a waffle breakfast. The breakfast was a mess and from a practical standpoint the mother would much rather have done it herself. But even when I called in the afternoon the mood of the breakfast was still on the family. A well-prepared meal would have been enjoyed — a good deal more, no doubt — at the time. This one will be enjoyed for days.

A friend of mine was discouraged; he felt that he was getting nowhere fast. It would have been easy — and ineffective — for the wife to tell him to buck up or to chide him for feeling low. Instead she took the trouble to make a list of what he had achieved during the past year, touching not only accomplishments in his business but things he had done for her and the children as well. The list still serves to keep his spirits up and offers tangible evidence that his wife appreciates him and took the pains to tell him so in an intelligent way.

Largely families are held together by the things they jointly care about, dream about, plan for, and do with each other. Consider the excellent practice of reading aloud. It is an honorable custom, yet sadly overlooked in the clock-controlled rush of life today. We ought not overlook the spur it gives to fellowship; there is something of a ritual about it, a sense of renewing things in common. Especially is this true if we pause and discuss what we read, respecting each other's point of view and learning about each other through the reactions that are given.

Thus the value of such experiences exceeds our current enjoyment: they promote a sense of oneness and harmony that may remain as a buffer against later shocks of misunderstanding.

It is hard to keep from transferring unconsciously to our relations with those closest to us tensions that arise out of business or professional life. To report at home in resentful detail a quarrel with an office superior or associate is to take emotional advantage of those we love. This practice is the source of many seemingly unaccountable disputes, and should be guarded against at all costs.

The bride of a friend of mine used to correct his eating habits at the table. He would counter with remarks about pseudo-culture or affected mannerisms. Then the fight was on. One day he proposed that if either had a personal suggestion it be made in writing. The idea worked: either the little criticism was not worth writing about, or, if it was, it received favorable attention when one's pride was not publicly involved.

It is a good rule to face difficulties at the time they arise and not allow them to increase unacknowledged. How often in our relations we have trouble at the same point again and again because we don't fix matters right when they first go wrong! Some minor misunderstandings, of course, are just as well forgotten; but serious misunderstandings ought to be threshed out promptly, lest they grow and become rooted in our emotions.

To clear difficulties out of the way, there is no axe like a good principle. It is strange to hear some of us prate about principles in international life and forget all principles in dealing with those closest to us. We urge the rights of minorities and ignore the rights of our children. The right of privacy scrupulously respected on principle would go far toward ironing out many problems that create tensions in the home. We should at least accord our family the same courtesies we do our friends. If a friend is making a telephone call, we do not hang around; we do not open a friend's mail or go barging into his place without invitation or permission. Parents have no more right to throw away a child's "junk" than a child has to destroy a parent's "important clippings."

I once heard a strong and determined woman speak of "the

eternal right to slam a door." I know what she was talking about. Every one of us feels that he has certain citadels which should be held inviolate.

Besides the principle of respecting others' rights, the principle of tolerance (respecting other people's oddities) will settle many of our difficulties for us. Some of our severest tensions arise because we demand that our loved ones shall be perfect.

If you think your wife, husband, sons or daughters ought to be flawless, you are asking for trouble. If you expect those close to you to be never out of sorts, you are bound to be disillusioned. You ask too much of human nature. Many a crisis has been created between parent and child because the child did not conform to unreasonable expectations. To make no generous allowance for occasional failings and even outrageous blunders is to take friendship for a walk along the narrow edge of a precipice where one false step means disaster. Only a practiced habit of tolerance sprinkled with forgiveness will keep us from making impossible demands.

To keep relationships always harmonious requires wisdom and tact. For this, religion offers us a uniting and deepening power. The atmosphere of such devotions as grace at meals or prayers at bedtime is not encouraging to grudges or family rifts; rather, it inspires understanding, reconciliation, forbearance.

To preserve from petty misunderstandings peace of the home is surely worth some conscious effort. Differences will persist. But the miracle of human relations is that in spite of our differences we can get along. When we do, the result is a thing of beauty. What we must have is not just a scheme of trouble-shooting. We need rather a resolve to enrich in every way we can the relations which in our secret hearts we value most.

PAIN makes man think.
Thinking makes man wise.
Wisdom makes life endurable.

— From John Patrick's play, The Teahouse of the August Moon (Putnam)

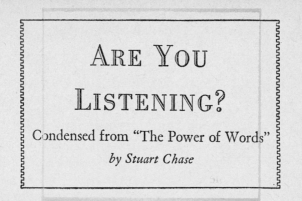

ARE YOU
LISTENING?

Condensed from "The Power of Words"

by Stuart Chase

Listening is the other half of talking. If people stop listening it is useless to talk — a point not always appreciated by talkers.

Listening isn't the simple thing it seems to be. It involves interpretation of both the literal meaning of the words and the intention of the speaker. If someone says, "Why, Jim, you old horse thief!" the words are technically an insult; but the tone of voice probably indicates affection.

Americans are not very good listeners. In general they talk more than they listen. Competition in our culture puts a premium on self-expression, even if the individual has nothing to express. What he lacks in knowledge he tries to make up for by talking fast or pounding the table. And many of us while ostensibly listening are inwardly preparing a statement to stun the company when we get the floor. Yet it really is not difficult to learn to listen — just unusual.

Listening is regarded as a passive thing, but it can be a very active process — something to challenge our intelligence. A stream of messages is coming in to be decoded: how close can we come to their real meaning? What is the speaker trying to say? . . . How does he know it? . . . What has he left out? . . . What are his motives?

Sometimes only about a quarter of an audience understands clearly what a speaker has said. To sharpen the ears of its members, the New York Adult Education Council has inaugurated "listening clinics." One member reads aloud while the others around the table concentrate on what he is saying. Later they summarize what they have heard and compare notes — often to find that the accounts differ widely. Gradually the listeners improve; often they find themselves transferring the skill to business and home affairs. As one member said:

"I became aware of a new attitude. I found myself trying to understand and interpret the remarks of my friends from *their* viewpoint, and not from my own as I had done previously."

Some years ago Major Charles T. Estes of the Federal Conciliation Service was called in to help settle a long-term dispute between a corporation and its unions. The Major proceeded to invent a technique for listening that has since had wide application in the labor field. He asked delegates from both union and management to read aloud the annual contract which was in dispute. Each man read a section in his turn; then all discussed it. If a dispute began to develop, the clause was put aside for later examination.

In two days the delegates really knew what was in the contract, and were competent to go back and tell their fellow managers or fellow workers what it contained. "We had conditioned them to communicate," said the Major. The contract was not rewritten but has continued in force with very few changes for ten years. Good listening has transformed bad labor relations into good ones.

Carl R. Rogers, University of Chicago psychologist, suggests a game to be played at a party. Suppose a general discussion — say on the French elections — becomes acrimonious. At this point Rogers asks the company to try an experiment: Before Jones, who is on the edge of his chair, can reply to the statement just made by Smith, he must summarize what Smith has said in such a way that Smith accepts it. Any attempt to slant or distort is instantly corrected by the original speaker. This means careful listening, during which emotion is likely to cool.

The result is that everyone in the circle, by listening and rephrasing, acquires a working knowledge of the other fellow's point of view, even if he does not agree with it. The players are quite likely to increase their knowledge of the subject — something that rarely happens in the usual slam-bang argument.

The experiment takes courage because in restating the other man's position one runs the risk of changing one's own.

F. J. Roethlisberger of the Harvard Business School, in a recent study of training courses for supervisors, describes a significant contrast in listening. An executive calls foreman Bill to his office to tell him about a change in Bill's department. A casting will be substituted for a hand-forged job, and the executive tells Bill how to do it.

"Oh yeah?" says Bill.

Let us follow two steps which the boss might take at this point. First, suppose he assumes that "Oh yeah" means Bill does not see how to do the new job, and it is up to the boss to tell Bill. This he proceeds to do clearly and logically. Nevertheless, Bill is obviously freezing up, and presently things begin to happen inside the boss. "Can it be," he asks himself, "that I have lost my power to speak clearly? No, Bill just doesn't understand plain English; he's really pretty dumb." The look which accompanies this unspoken idea makes Bill freeze up even harder. The interview ends on a note of total misunderstanding.

But, says Roethlisberger, suppose the boss sees from the "Oh yeah" that Bill is disturbed, and he tries to find out why. He says: "What's your idea about how the change-over ought to be made, Bill? You've been in the department a long time. Let's have it. I'm listening."

Things now begin to happen inside Bill. The boss is not laying it on the line, he's willing to listen. So ideas come out, slowly at first, then faster. Some are excellent ideas and the boss becomes really interested in Bill's approach — "Smarter man than I thought!" A spiral reaction is set up, as Bill begins to realize that he never appreciated the boss before. The interview ends on a note of close harmony.

In the first case, the boss did not listen to Bill, he *told* Bill; and though the telling was clear enough the goal moved farther away. In the second case, the boss listened until he had located what was worrying Bill; then they went along together.

So far, we have been talking about sympathetic listening in face-to-face situations, to make sure we grasp the speaker's full meaning. But critical listening, too, is needed in a world full of propaganda and high-pressure advertisers. Here are some techniques which help to develop critical listening to a speech or a conversation, a sales talk at your door or the testimony of a witness before a jury:

Look for motives behind the words. Is the speaker talking chiefly in accepted, appealing symbols — Home, Mother, the Founding Fathers, Our Glorious Heritage, and so on — avoiding the need for thought, or is he really trying to think? Speeches are often solidly larded with symbols, and the well-trained ear can identify them a long way off.

Is the speaker dealing in facts or inferences? With practice you can train your ear to find this distinction in political and economic talk, and to follow the shifts from one level to the next.

The listener should also consider his own attitude toward the speaker. Is he prejudiced for or against him? Is he being fair, objective, sympathetic?

The sum of careful listening is to work actively to discover how the speaker feels about events, what his needs and drives appear to be, what kind of person he is. The appraisal can only be rough, but it can be a decided help in dealing with him, in giving him a fair answer.

One other thing: I find that careful listening also helps me to keep quiet rather than sound off foolishly. The best listeners listen alertly, expecting to learn something and to help create new ideas.

Are you listening?

Anniversary Tale

A COUPLE on their Golden Wedding Anniversary were interviewed by a reporter.

"And tell me," he asked, pencil poised, "in all this time together did you ever consider divorce?"

"Oh, no, not divorce," the little old lady said, "but sometimes" — she paused and winked at her husband — "murder!"

— Helen Papashvily in *Good Housekeeping*

TAKE A DEEP BREATH

Condensed from Collier's

Helen Durham

Breathe to be healthy. Breathe to be handsome. Breathe to stand well, talk well, *be* well. On this point everyone agrees, cultist, faddist and physician.

"To breathe properly is to live properly," says the old Yogi philosopher. "Breath is the stuff of which voice is made," says the voice expert. The posture expert's first command is to fill your lungs. The honest beauty specialist admits that increased circulation brought about by good breathing will do more for your complexion than a lifetime of massage. As for the doctor, he will tell you that breathing is the first vital process of life. His business is to keep you breathing, from the time he thumps you on the back to get you going until he produces the oxygen to keep you from stopping. Most of us take in enough to sustain life but not enough to live it vigorously. We are like a car chugging along on only half its cylinders. If some of us actually filled our lungs with a great blast of air, we would have an oxygen jag, a lightheaded feeling — that is a physical fact. If you don't believe it try it sometime.

We are so accustomed to using only the tops of our lungs that we get the idea they end at the bust line. But they don't. On either side of the ribs they extend down to the waistline. Unless you constantly make use of this important lower-lung section in your breathing, you are a poor risk for the insurance company and flop in the beauty contest.

Vida Sutton, whose job is to train the tones of announcers of the National Broadcasting Company, says you never talk bet-

ter than you breathe. Without an ample column of air your
voice lacks color and richness. The voice of the shallow breather
is shallow, thin and squeaky. The person who breathes lazily
has a lazy, drawling voice.

Deep breathing is the actor's first aid against stage fright.
Even a seasoned star like Helen Hayes declares she could never
face a first-night audience without screwing up her courage by
a few deep breaths.

"It was Mary Garden," says Miss Hayes, "who first made me
aware of the importance of breath. I was introduced as 'little
Miss Hayes, the actress.' Miss Garden's response was to give me
a vigorous thump just above the belt. 'Actress?' she said. 'You
can't act, my child. You haven't the diaphragm of a baby.'

"For years I could play only ingénue rôles because I had only
a fluffy little flapper's breath. I could never have played Co-
quette without the power and poise I acquired from learning
how to breathe."

Many people stand badly because they breathe badly. When
chests are concave and torsos slump, the first point of attack is
the breath. Properly inflated lungs right the body just as proper
ballast rights the ship.

Now if you're curious as to whether or not you breathe correctly, unbuckle your belt and slip it up a few inches, half-way
between waistline and bust line. Exhale and pull your belt in as
tight as you can until you're empty as a pricked balloon. Now
take a whopper of a breath and see how many notches you can
expand. It is here that chest expansion should be measured,
instead of under the armpits as your old gym teacher believed.

Don't try to expand by swelling out in front. The old opera
singer with her ample breath pouch over her tummy is an illustration of what abdominal breathing alone will do for you.
Expansion should come not only in front but across the back
and sides. To see how much rear expansion you get, put your
hands at the small of your back, thumbs forward, middle fingers touching behind. Give yourself a tight squeeze, exhaling as
much as you can. Then inhale and see how far you can force
your hands apart. Your ribs are a flexible cage that protects your
lungs. As your lungs expand, the bony cage should expand all

around. One way to learn how to breathe deeply is to get the sensation of packing your breath well in against the back of your ribs.

"Ordinarily breathing should be unconscious," says Dr. Eugene Lyman Fisk, "but every day deep-breathing exercises should be employed. People who are shut in all day may partly compensate for the evils of indoor living by stepping out of doors and taking a dozen deep breaths whenever the opportunity presents itself."

Without the help of your diaphragm you can never breathe as you should. The diaphragm is the floor of the chest. It is a dome-shaped muscle, with the dome inverted. As we inhale, the dome drops downward, increasing the chest cavity for the air to rush in. As we exhale, the dome flattens upward, forcing the air out. Without the help of this important muscle you cannot make a sound. You cannot pant, sigh, cough, grunt or clear your throat. A man's diaphragm is placed lower than a woman's, which gives his chest more room; and his active habits of life have made this muscle stronger. Women, with a few exceptions, are shallow breathers, apt to neglect their diaphragms.

Happily, nature taught us how to use the diaphragm. Infants breathe correctly; so do sleeping persons. When we grow up or wake up we allow inhibitions to restrict free diaphragmatic action. A good way to reëducate your diaphragm, once it has gone wrong, is to lie flat on your back, discard the cares of the world and let the great muscle work naturally. If you do this until it becomes a habit you will breathe this way on your feet. The always spectacular Jeritza, whose operatic performances usually had a touch of the acrobatic in them, made it a point from time to time to sing a favorite aria lying on her back.

The only purpose of breathing is to get oxygen into our systems, for without oxygen we should quickly die. Every vital process in the body is dependent on oxygen for its performance. The more oxygen you have, the brighter will be your color, the more pep you will have; the smarter you'll be. If you're low in body, sunk in mind, awkward, ugly, rasping — even if you're a little bit crazy, "breathe" is the chorus of advice.

Copyright by The Reader's Digest Association, Inc. (August 1931 issue)
Condensed from Collier's, June 20, 1931

*Have you checked up on yourself lately? Maybe your idea of
how to get ahead is out of date*

WHY DIDN'T YOU

GET THAT PROMOTION?

Condensed from Collier's   Howard Whitman

THE WAY to get ahead in the world is changing. With psychological tests and "evaluation interviews," big companies are now determining not only how good a man is at his job but how good he is *as a person* — and what he can develop into. Fitting square pegs into square holes is no longer enough. The trick is to find out what kind of wood the peg is made of, what quality, how durable.

"We are looking beyond the old idea of promotion," says Dr. Walter D. Woodward, psychiatrist at the American Cyanamid Co. "We are looking toward a man's long-term progress. We want to develop men who can fit into future vacancies, take jobs which don't even exist yet."

This new approach is based not so much on how well a man or woman can do a particular job but on how mature and well integrated he or she is. After all, the mainsprings of personality supply the incentive, integrity, vigor and enthusiasm a person brings to his work.

A study by Chandler Hunt covering 80,000 clerical and office workers in 76 companies analyzes the reasons why people are not promoted. Lack of skill accounts for only 24 percent of the trouble. Personality failings — lack of initiative and ambition, carelessness, noncoöperation, laziness — account for 76 percent.

These personality failings can be observed in surface behavior. But today's personnel experts listen also for deeper rumblings. Let's say the management is considering Mr. A for promotion to foreman. To find out what kind of director of other men Mr. A will be the personnel expert asks a "revealing situation" question:

"Suppose one of your men has been late twice in the past ten days. Each time you spoke to him about it and received his assurance that he would be on time in the future. This morning he is late again, and an important job has been held up. What would you do about this man?"

"I'd fire him" or "I'd give him another chance" is the wrong answer. "I'd find out why he was late" is the right answer.

The man may have been late because his wife was suddenly taken to the hospital or for another emergency reason. To ask him about it shows an even, judicial temperament in a provoking situation. The man can be fired or forgiven after the facts are known.

Dozens of questions in today's personality tests have no right or wrong answers, but each answer adds another brush stroke to a person's portrait. Examples:

On meeting someone, do you wait for the other fellow to say hello first? (*hostility*)

Are you hurt if someone fails to return your call? (*inferiority feelings*)

Would you rather make a decision yourself or have someone help you make it? (*sense of adequacy, confidence*)

Would you speak up or let the incident pass if someone pushed ahead of you in line? (*aggressiveness, assertiveness*)

Is it hard for you to say no to a salesman? (*suggestibility*)

If a man says it is not hard for him to say no to a salesman he may not make a good salesman himself. Checking with control groups has shown that 90 percent of successful salesmen find it hard to say no to another salesman.

After the batteries of tests comes the evaluation interview — heart of the scientific approach to promotion. This is just talk, but extremely skilled talk.

In Cleveland, at Western Reserve University's Personnel Research Institute, I sat in at an interview held for the Solar Steel Corp. The interviewers were two psychologists, Dr. Erwin K. Taylor, director of the institute, and Theodore Kunin. The subject was a Solar Steel employe, Mr. X. Dr. Taylor had said to me in advance, "I intentionally will not introduce you. This is to be a 'stress interview,' and your unexplained presence will add to the stress." After half a dozen questions the stress was turned on. Dr. Taylor said, "Mr. X, I'll play the role of a customer, who for some reason has stopped doing business with your company. You have to win the business back."

Mr. X: I haven't had an order from you for some time. Is anything wrong?

Dr. Taylor: No, nothing's wrong.

Mr. X: Well — I mean, we took care of you when steel was short, didn't we?

Dr. Taylor: Do you think I'm under obligation to you?

Mr. X: I wouldn't say that. I just mean we took good care of you.

Dr. Taylor: You made a profit on every ton, didn't you?

Mr. X: All I mean is, I'd like to be fair about this thing.

Dr. Taylor: Oh, then you think I'm being unfair!

Mr. X: Oh, no. That's not what I meant. I just thought — well, steel might be short again sometime.

Dr. Taylor: Are you threatening me?

Poor Mr. X had considerable color in his cheeks by now, and just when I thought he'd blow his top Kunin came to the rescue by taking the interview up another path.

The interview lasted two hours and covered everything from life history and job history to hobbies and ambitions. There were no answers to many of the "stress" questions; they were framed expressly, as Dr. Taylor put it, "to get Mr. X in deep — and then get him in deeper."

The purpose of the stress test is to evaluate the man's resourcefulness, to see how much it takes to throw him off balance, to see what his quitting point is, to test his adroitness in handling people in impossible situations.

When the results of the tests and the interview have been collated recommendation is made for or against the man's promotion. Sure to be mentioned are the same traits of character which interested employers in grandpa's day — but evaluated scientifically.

Take the trait of thoughtfulness versus interest in overt activity. Psychologists find that the man who is a bit on the introvert side makes a better supervisor than the extrovert, because the extrovert "is so busy interacting with his environment that he is a poor observer of others and of himself. He is probably not subtle and may be lacking in tact. He dislikes reflection and planning."

The trait of aggressiveness has long figured in getting a man to the top of the ladder. A company chairman tells the board, "We want men who will tackle the job aggressively." Yet we condemn aggressiveness in such common remarks as "Don't push other people around" and "Don't try to get ahead by stepping on other people's toes." An aggressive person often finds himself disliked.

The personnel psychologist comes up with the answer to this apparent clash. Sheer aggressiveness he regards as a negative character trait. For most jobs it is undesirable. But "unobtrusive aggressiveness" — power, drive and alertness without offense or disregard for others — marks the socially mature gogetter.

Ola C. Cool, veteran management counselor and director of the Labor Relations Institute, said, "The men and women who know best how to get along with people — these are the ones who get the promotions." Cool told of a brilliant engineer, an MIT graduate, who was tops technically but missed out on promotion to a $25,000-a-year job. Cool explained, "This man was so good technically that he lost respect for the others around him, and he showed it. Result — he couldn't get good work out of his men."

The measure of leadership is no longer how well a man can drive workers but how well he can get them to follow him.

One industrial firm, before promoting a machine operator to supervisor, always makes him a machine fixer for three months. Why? "A machine fixer gets around. He has to deal with fellows all over the plant. He doesn't know it, but in three months we have a full-length portrait of his social adaptability."

The importance of human relations goes up the scale with the importance of the job. In most jobs the initial promotions, during the first two to five years, are based on skill. But when a man gets up to supervisory levels — when he stops handling tools and starts handling people — an almost total reversal of qualifications begins.

Know-how is 90 percent for a rank-and-file worker. For promotion to foreman know-how is 50 percent and human relations 50 percent. For promotion to executive know-how is 20 percent and human relations 80 percent.

In one company the personnel manager named a man for promotion to a job for which he had no previous training. When asked why, he said, "We can teach that man all the know-how he needs in six weeks — but it has taken him 32 years to become the person he is."

Welcome Stranger

THE MORNING after we moved to a new residence in a town near New York, my doorbell rang. A woman was standing on the step, a friendly smile on her face, and in her hand was a tray with a pot of coffee, cups and some buns. She introduced herself as Mrs. Mills, my neighbor across the street. As we chatted over our coffee, she told me about the town, the names of the neighbors and some details about them — where the men worked, what they did. She invited the youngsters to her house to play with her children that afternoon. When she left, I felt nice and warm inside, and I thought of her visit all day long as I unpacked.

She'd just returned the children to me about five o'clock when the telephone rang. The voice turned out to be Mrs. Hart, who lived three doors away. "Mrs. Mills told me you'd just moved in, so I know you're busy and scarcely will have time to eat. But I've a stew ready. Bring your whole family over whenever you're hungry."

The next day another neighbor called to chat and acquaint me with more of the town. She mentioned good grocers, butchers, cleaners and laundries, and said the first time I went downtown she'd go along and introduce me to the merchants. She left me a neatly written list of stores and doctors, dentists and baby sitters.

Later we learned the friendly spirit those neighbors showed wasn't just casual. Feeling that old-fashioned neighborliness had slipped too far away, they'd got together and decided to get it back. They planned to take turns performing the various neighborly services. Now that we are neighbors ourselves, we'll have our own turn to make some other family's move such a pleasant surprise.

— Roberta Fleming Roesch in *Today's Woman*

*The art of overcoming tension
is the key to happier living*

HOW TO RELAX

Condensed from "Relax and Live" Joseph A. Kennedy

MOST OF US, in practically all our everyday activities, are driving with the brake on. That brake is unconscious tension. We have worked and played in a tense condition for so long that we regard it as more or less normal. We do not notice the clenched jaw, the tight abdomen, the constricted muscles. Yet the resulting fatigue burns up our energy, impairs our skills and even dulls our appreciation of the world about us.

Tension is excess effort: trying too hard to do things that should be done automatically. It causes muscles to jam and contract. Make a conscious effort to speak correctly and you stutter or become tongue-tied. Let the accomplished pianist think about his fingers and he is likely to make a mistake.

Most of us put forth too much effort for the task at hand. Our muscles work better when we speak our orders quietly than when we shout at them. In order to see perfectly, for example, the eyes must make numerous minute movements, scanning the object under observation. This scanning is an automatic reflex; it is no more subject to your will than is your heartbeat. But when you stare — make a conscious effort

JOSEPH A. KENNEDY has taught his methods of relaxation to pilots at the Preflight School at Athens, Ga., where he was head of the Rehabilitation Department, and to overwrought business executives at the late Bill Brown's famous health center in Garrison, N. Y. He has assisted with physical education programs for the U. S. Naval Academy and other schools.

to see — the eyes become tense. They do not scan as they should and sight suffers.

Nor is the damage done by tension limited to the body. When muscles are tense, contracting without purpose, a feeling of confusion is relayed back to the brain. Why is it that a poised man whose ideas reel out effortlessly when he is in his own study suddenly finds his mind a blank when he is attending an important board meeting? Because tenseness, resulting from making too much effort, has jammed his psychomotor mechanisms.

Tension tends to become an unconscious habit; muscles tend to stay constricted. How, then, can you become conscious of unconscious tension? How can you relax?

First, by locating the tension in your muscles. For example, you are probably unaware of any tension in your forehead at this moment, but there is a good chance that some is there. In order to recognize it, consciously produce more tension: wrinkle your forehead into a frown and notice the feeling in the muscles. Practice sensing the tension that you thus consciously produce. Then, tomorrow, stop working for a moment and ask yourself, "Am I aware of any tension in my forehead?" You can probably detect the faint sensation already there. One student told me, "When I started to relax, I discovered layer after layer of tension of which I had been totally unaware."

Once you learn to recognize tension, you can learn to relax. The way to do this is first to produce *more* tension in your muscles. Don't *try* to relax! A muscle tends to relax itself. Consciously tense a particular muscle; then stop. The muscle relaxes and will continue to relax automatically if it is not interfered with.

The muscles of the brow and forehead need special attention, for they are closely associated with anxiety and confusion. With the brow relaxed it is practically impossible to feel worried. The next time you have a problem to solve, make it a point to keep your brow relaxed and see if the problem does not seem less difficult.

The jaw is one of the most expressive parts of the human body. We grit our teeth in rage, clench our jaws in determination. When your jaw is tensed, your brain, which is constantly receiving nerve messages from your muscles, reasons something like this: "We must be in difficulty, we must have a terrible job to do." You then become conscious of a feeling of pressure.

As soon as you relax your jaw muscles, however, your brain says, "Ah, we are out of difficulty now," and you get a feeling of confidence. So, every time you feel anxious or experience self-doubt, notice that you are contracting your jaws. Then stop.

The hands are the main executive instrument of the body. They are involved in almost everything we do or feel. We throw up our hands in hopelessness, shake our fist when we are angry. When hands are kept tense, the whole body is geared for action. Learn to relax your hands when you find yourself in a tight spot or when something irritates you. It will take the pressure off and give you a feeling that you are master of the situation.

If you were expecting a blow in the pit of the stomach, you would instinctively tense the abdominal muscles for defense. And if you habitually live on the defensive, your subconscious keeps your stomach muscles continually tensed. Thus, another vicious circle is set up. The brain receives defensive messages from the abdominal muscles and this keeps you feeling insecure. Learn to break the circle. When you feel anxious or worried, stop and relax your abdomen.

If you try to control your anxieties mentally, you will probably only make yourself more nervous. But you *can* control your key muscles.

Learn to relax your muscles quickly at midmorning, just before lunch and in midafternoon. Sit down and "jelly" yourself into the most comfortable position. Or lie on your back on a bed with your arms at your sides. Then check your key points for tension: brow, abdomen, jaw, hands, and so on. Tighten each, and then let go, allowing the muscle to relax by itself.

Breathing furnishes a valuable control for toning down the degree of excitement throughout the entire body. When we are emotionally tense, we say we have something on our chest. When a crisis is past, we say that we can breathe easier. But it works both ways. If we can learn to breathe easier in the first place, we won't get so tense.

It will help you to learn to breathe correctly if you recognize that the body has two separate breathing patterns. Nervous breathers breathe high in the chest by expanding and contracting the rib box. They also breathe too fast and too deeply. This particular breathing pattern was engineered for emergencies. It is the way you breathe when you are out of breath from running a race. Your chest heaves as you take in great gulps of air. Your muscles need oxygen fast, and this is the way to get it. Nervous people are so used to reacting with emergency behavior to simple, ordinary tasks that they use this emergency-breathing mechanism all the time.

Non-emergency breathing is belly breathing. It is done more from the diaphragm; most of the movement is in the lower chest wall and the upper abdomen. As the diaphragm smoothly contracts and lets go, a gentle massage is applied to the whole abdominal area. The abdominal muscles relax. It is virtually impossible to feel tense when you breathe habitually from your belly.

If you find yourself breathing nervously and fast, keep right on — but breathe that way because you *want* to. Take as many as 50 to 100 of these deliberate nervous breaths, thus bringing your breathing under the control of your will. This conscious control will in itself cause the feeling of nervousness to diminish. After a time you will find that it is an effort to keep breathing fast, and a relief to let yourself breathe more slowly.

One of the most malicious causes of tension is hurry. You can hurry while sitting down, apparently doing nothing, or while waiting for a bus. Many people feel hurried because they think there just isn't enough time. They would do well to heed Sir William Osler's advice to his students when he told them to think of how much time there is to use, rather than of how little.

Whenever you feel a sense of hurry, deliberately slow down. Everyone has his own best pace or tempo for doing things, and when we give in to hurry we allow external things and situations to set our pace for us. The great Finnish runner, Paavo Nurmi, always carried a watch with him in his races. He referred to it, not to the other runners. He ran his own race, keeping his own tempo, regardless of competition.

A basic cause of tension is putting too much emphasis on the ultimate goal, trying too hard to win. It is good to have a clear mental picture of your objective; but your attention should be concentrated on the specific job at hand.

And when that job is done, remember there will be something else to do tomorrow. So relax! Life is not a 100-yard dash, but more in the nature of a cross-country run. If we sprint all the time, we not only fail to win the race but we may not last long enough to reach the goal.

The Tie That Binds

WAITING for the pediatrician to give my husky three their tetanus shots, I was attracted by the shy smile of a tiny girl with a crutch beside her chair. "I'm going to walk pretty soon," she confided. "The doctor just promised me!"

The door of the inner office opened and her mother came out leading a little boy whose arm was shriveled.

I was shocked. "The mother of those two has a really hard row to hoe," I said to the doctor when they had gone.

"She's one of the happiest people I know," he replied. "Interesting thing. She had a sorry childhood — her father in a mental hospital, her mother obsessed by the fear that his illness would be transmitted to the daughter. She met her husband on a train as she was going to visit her dad. His mother was a patient there, too. Later, when they wanted to be married, they came to me. I told them what I knew — darned little — and they decided to go ahead but never to have children. However, they asked me to help them adopt a baby — 'Not a picture-book one, guaranteed perfect, but one with the cards stacked against it.'

"So I found Pete for them. A fine lad. When he was four, they found Meg. And they're going to have another child soon."

I stared at him. "You mean —?"

"As soon as Meg is walking, a kid who's been battling rheumatic fever all his life is joining them. They're raising the finest family in my whole practice."

— Contributed by Mrs. William Wallace

MARRIAGE

Condensed from The American Magazine

Booth Tarkington

"To be in love," said a cynical bachelor friend of mine, "is to be the victim of glamour. Glamour isn't only a false glow; it's an intoxication. And there you have the typical condition out of which youthful marriage is made: two dazed, immature and little more than childish minds, really unacquainted with each other, and blinded by temporary intoxication, enter into a kind of contract to which the most crazily reckless business man would not dream of binding himself. And all their relatives and best friends stand around beaming, and expecting only the good and beautiful to come out of an act of temporary insanity!"

Exactly to what degree my friend's "horror of marriage" is warranted, no one can say. We only know that, no matter how crazy the contract, most husbands and wives do "get along with each other somehow," not always happily, but "well enough," with more or less harmony, more or less conflict, and a great deal of the deepest devotion. What is surprising in an advanced civilization, is that they "get along" with only antiquated tradition to guide them. In this most difficult of human relationships, the wedded must still grope for individual salvation.

By a coincidence, my next visitor was a man who had just been divorced; and it was he who spoke of this groping. He and his wife had not even known *how* to grope for an individual salvation, he told me. "We were in love with each other, and thought life would be paradise because the marriage cere-

252

mony permitted us to live with each other. Unfortunately, we got over being in love; it lasted about three years, but kept growing paler all the time. I don't know what made it begin to pale, though it wasn't long until we began to have differences. We disagreed about friends. Then she wanted to join one of these foolish sects that spring up around queer 'prophets,' and we argued about it at first, and then wrangled. After that she went surreptitiously, and I found it out and told her I absolutely wouldn't stand for it; she'd got to give it up. She said I was unreasonable, and the only people she cared to please, when they asked unreasonable things, were people she loved; that I'd better do a little giving up myself and stop playing cards with some men I liked and she didn't. It was all as petty as that, you see. Finally it came to a showdown, and we realized that if the thing had been to do over, we would never have dreamed of marrying each other. It's been a hard experience — but how could we have done any better?"

Later, when I was able to think over the meaning of all he had said, it began to seem to me that his unfortunate experience had a significance fairly common in troubled marriages. Before marriage, he and the lady were happy. They were then in a condition defined as freedom. During marriage they were not happy. They were then not in a condition they thought of as freedom. Then they separated, in order to restore to themselves their previous condition of freedom, and, having restored it, they became happier.

I began to ask myself: is there a great essential element in the happiest marriages, and if there is, what is its nature? In other words, what, in such marriages, preserves "young love," or else substitutes for it a steady and unselfish devotion?

I remembered an odd, pleasant thing I had heard a man say about his wife. He is a middle aged countryman of no sophistication. "The only thing I'm sorry for is not marryin' her sooner. And I certainly would of, if I'd had any idea a woman could treat a man the way she's always treated me."

"How does she treat you, Sam?"

"How?" he said. "Why we been married full 17 years now, and she still treats me exactly the same as if I was a perfect stranger!"

What is this special kind of courtesy due to a *stranger*? Well, we meet him with a kindly manner that means a readiness to be of assistance to him; and we show him quietly that it will be a pleasure to help make himself comfortable. More, we are careful not to intrude upon him. We give him our best information, but we don't urge; far less do we say, "You shall," or "You shall not." All in all, we try to be useful to him, and in no way do we seek to interfere with his complete freedom of action and thought.

Thus, then, I found three suggestive instances: my old bachelor friend, with his "horror of marriage" as a bondage entered upon in delusion; my divorced friend, whose marriage was broken for the sake of a freedom he and his wife found impossible to obtain as long as they remained bound in wedlock; and finally this contradictory happy case of Sam and his wife, to whom marriage is not a bondage at all. The bachelor could therefore have felt no horror of such a marriage as Sam's, and my second visitor might have studied Sam and his wife with surprise and profit. They are happily devoted to each other because each respects the other's right to be an "independent human being." Remembering that sect his wife wished to join, the divorced man would perhaps be interested to learn that if Mrs. Sam should tell her husband that she had joined the "Holy Jumpers," Sam would say, "Didja?" and probably add, "Well, some say it's a good thing. Ole Man Kinney prophesies we're goin' to have a warm spring again."

The divorced man might be critical of Sam's position here; he might say, "What! Was I to let my wife make a fool of herself?" Here is a question of primary importance. How far may a wife or husband profitably interfere with the other, when the other is doing a silly or injurious thing?

Now, to interfere means to curtail freedom. Those whose freedom is curtailed do not like it; they have a powerful native instinct for liberty, and also an instinct for equality, both of which are set in revolt by the curtailment. Between sane individuals, the effort to impose the one's will upon the other, no matter how noble the motive, is, in its essence, an act of tyranny, and though it may in some instances produce the kind of harmony known between slave and master, this is not precisely the kind of harmony we find in what we call happy marriages.

To a stranger, about to become involved in error, we tactfully present information, avoiding any appearance of pressure or controversy. Between man and wife this seems all that can be safely done. There must be freedom for conclusions.

An elderly family physician, with whom I had been talking, expressed the opinion that treatment as a perfect stranger isn't always possible. "Last month the wife of one of my patients signed up for a $3000 automobile without consulting him. Another woman is actually made sick — she's sick in bed and seriously — because her husband insists on having his mother live with them. And in a third case a lovely girl married a man who seemed in every way attractive; but marriage brought out a brutality in him, as marriage sometimes does, that had been latent till then. How does your freedom work in these cases?"

"It doesn't," I said. "In the infinite variety of human-kind there is a proportion of fools, brutes, and freaks; and the unfortunate person who enters into bondage with these must suffer. It can't apply to them and I don't think you've understood what I'm trying to discover. I'm looking for the essential element in the happiest marriages, with the idea that if we found it somebody might be able to inject it into marriages not so happy. I didn't mean that *all* marriages could be happy, but I am inclining to the opinion that freedom must be an element in happy marriages; and that intelligent and well-meaning people can make their marriages happy by introducing it."

"How about a wife whose husband is infatuated with another woman, or a husband whose wife is in love with another man? Ought married people to consent to *that* freedom?"

"Freedom, it seems, would bring the greatest approach to happiness. If a husband constrains his wife, she will still care as much as before for the other man; the husband has therefore gained nothing of her *heart,* and her heart is surely the important thing. Of course I don't insist that, under these circumstances, the marriage would be a happy one, though it would have a better chance of becoming one, in time, than if the wife's freedom were curtailed by compulsion. I have not supposed that freedom of itself creates a perfect happiness. A man with a lively toothache is not happy, no matter how much liberty he has. All marriages having freedom may not be happy, but to have freedom is to have the greatest chance of happiness in marriage; a marriage cannot be happy, lacking it, except with the pallid happiness of master and complacent serf."

I saw that he remained somewhat skeptical; but at least I had convinced myself, and that is certainly something! My definite conclusion was of the simplest possible kind; that although the prisoner with shackles on his body may be happy if his spirit be free, there cannot be happiness in a *heart* held to bondage. Therefore freedom is the great essential element in a happy marriage. For without it, marriage is bondage.

Life with Father

No amount of coaxing could persuade our 16-month-old son to take his medicine in any shape, form or fashion. In utter disgust I gave up and left the room. When I came back, I stared in amazement, for there stood my son gleefully opening his mouth for it.

My husband had solved the problem by mixing the medicine with orange juice, putting it into a water pistol and shooting it into him! — Mrs. Hobby Stripling in Atlanta *Journal and Constitution Magazine*

Each time I put our two-year-old on the closed front porch to play, he objected violently when I locked his gate to make sure he stayed there. Then one day my husband put the youngster in his "playroom" and locked the gate, and for once he didn't scream, but played happily.

My husband's explanation was simple. "I just told him I was locking the gate," he said, "so that you couldn't get in and bother him." — Contributed by Lil Oswald Olsen

Joe Laurie, Jr., tells about a friend of his who made the mistake of leaving her baby daughter in her husband's care while she closeted herself in the library to pay bills. He buried himself behind his newspaper and forgot about the baby until he heard a series of thumps, followed by a horrendous wail. Clearly, baby had fallen down the stairs.

"Martha," called the father excitedly. "Come quick! Our little girl just took her first 24 steps!" — Bennett Cerf in *This Week*

It's More Fun to Be Fit

By
Gene Tunney   Commander, U.S.N.R.

PHYSICAL FLABBINESS has always seemed to me a criminal, even sacrilegious abuse of that wonderful instrument, the human body. Ever since boyhood I've made a religion of keeping in shape by regular, conscientious exercise. Adhering to a high ideal of stamina and endurance has paid me dividends not only in the prize ring but in the almost equally gruelling struggle of everyday life.

To enjoy the glow of good health, you must exercise. I don't recommend that you develop bulging biceps or go in for exhausting roadwork and bag-punching. But I do say that if you will regularly devote 15 minutes a day, preferably before breakfast, for 60 days to the simplest set of exercises that I've devised for conditioning men in the navy, I guarantee that you will enjoy the increased physical buoyancy and mental vigor that are so necessary in these times. Perform them faithfully and you can take puffy inches off your waistline, recondition unused muscles, feel better, work better and live longer.

The man who has allowed his body to deteriorate cuts a pitiful figure — chest collapsed, stomach protruding. His sagging diaphragm forces his visceral apparatus out of place, hindering digestive and eliminative processes. He tires easily and complains that he feels like the breaking up of a hard winter.

The first thing this human mealsack must learn is proper posture, the basis of all physical conditioning. "Head up, chin in, chest out, stomach in" — that's what we tell recruits in the navy. It's important for civilians, too, and not merely for the sake of appearance. Proper body-carriage conserves the energy that postural defects drain away.

The worst of these defects is the protruding paunch caused by abdominal muscles that have become flabby through disuse. There are broad bands of muscle like cinch-straps around our waistline, whose job is to hold the stomach, intestines and liver in place. When these muscles lose their firmness or "tone," they allow the intestines to sink down and become impaired in function. Indigestion, headache, constipation and chronic fatigue follow.

To toughen the abdominal muscles, I developed exercise No. 1. If you perform it 20 times every morning, gradually working up to 50, you'll

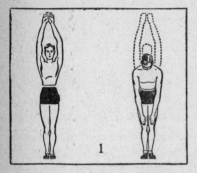

(A) Raise arms to front and above head, inhaling deeply. (B) Lower arms, keeping them stiff and straight, until hands touch knees, with head dropped until chin touches collarbone. Bend at diaphragm, not at waist. Draw stomach up as far as possible. As hands touch knees, exhale. Do 20 times.

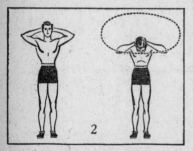

(A) Clasp hands behind head, heels 5 inches apart. (B) With diaphragm drawn up and shoulder muscles relaxed, swing upper body in circle, ending at original position. Exhale on way down, inhale on way up. Circle to left 10 times, then to right 10 times.

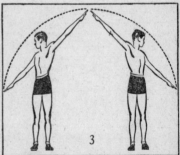

(A) Extend arms sidewise at shoulder level. Drop right hand 10 inches, raise left 10 inches. Draw stomach up; hold hips stationary. Swing right hand behind and down, the left going forward and up. Keep arms in straight line. Pivot from diaphragm, eyes and head following hand that goes back and down. Inhale as head comes up. (B) With stomach drawn up, exhale as head follows left hand around and down. Do 20 times to each side.

get rid of that paunch and the evils that accompany it. Remember that it's never too late to start rehabilitating broken-down muscles. The material is there, waiting for you to begin working on it.

Another deformity of posture is the flat, sunken chest, which occurs when we persistently neglect to use full lung capacity. We can get along on only 20 percent of our lung capacity, but that dragging sort of existence is a poor substitute for the vitality we enjoy when the twin bellows of our lungs are taking in great drafts of oxygen. As Dr. George Crile said, "Oxidization is the only source of animal energy. We *live* in proportion to the amount of oxygen we get into our lungs."

A concave chest means that your diaphragm is sagging. This elastic wall of muscle, the

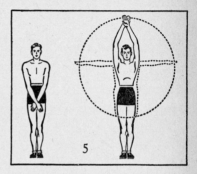

(A) Stand at attention; cross hands. (B) On count of 1, slowly raise arms in semicircle to front and overhead, rising on toes and inhaling steadily. Hands cross each other before reaching top position. On count 2, bring arms in semicircle slowly down to sides, holding breath until they reach original position. On count 3, exhale completely. Do 6 times vigorously.

(A) Stand with heels 15 inches apart. Inhale while rising on toes and reaching arms overhead. (B) Bring arms down stiff and straight between legs, exhaling and bending knees and touching floor with backs of hands as f r behind heels as possible, to stretch back, hips and abdominal muscles. Repeat 20 times.

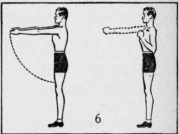

(A) Stand at attention; slowly raise arms straight to front, shoulder width apart. Inhale, filling lungs, and clench fists. (B) Move arms back and forward as vigorously as possible 6 times, holding breath. On 6th stroke, exhale and return to attention. Do this 6 times.

partition between your abdomen and chest, forms the major part of the bellows mechanism that we use in breathing. If the diaphragm sags, the bellows won't work properly; you can't breathe deeply and therefore don't get as much oxygen as you need. According to Dr. Herman N. Bundesen of Chicago, a sagging diaphragm may lead to a stroke of coronary thrombosis. He explains that an insufficient supply of oxygen slows down heart action; the blood flow becomes sluggish; a blood clot may form and clog the coronary artery of the heart, stoppering it like a cork.

Exercises Nos. 1, 2 and 3 will strengthen and put new resiliency into the diaphragm, and draw blood-purifying oxygen into every recess of the lungs. But the job isn't done when the exercise period is over. Keep your chest out and keep your stomach in, until it becomes a habit. At the end of a month you will have doubled your lung capacity, and thereby benefited every cell of your body.

Many people complain of a chronic weariness that sleep will not banish. Their trouble is that too little blood is being pumped through the body per minute; this sluggishness, permitting poisonous waste matter to accumulate in every cell, clogs the channels of energy.

Sinking into an overstuffed armchair is not the cure. You must speed up your circulation. The only way to do this is to exercise. A brisk 20-minute walk will send 25 to 30 quarts of blood coursing vigorously through your arteries every 60 seconds — blood that contains four times as much oxygen as it possesses when you loll in a chair.

While walking, inhale deeply for six paces, holding the breath, then exhale slowly. Do this 10 or 15 times during your walk. Like a cleansing torrent, the increased circulation and fresh oxygen will sweep away stagnant, toxic impurities — and take with them your tired feeling.

In youth, we get plenty of exercise through games and running around, but as middle life approaches, we settle down, literally and *figuratively*. Muscles that formerly were lean and resilient become slack and overlaid with fat. Fat is one of the chief enemies of the heart because it has to be plentifully supplied with blood and thus needlessly increases the pumping load that the heart must sustain. The less superfluous lard that you carry around with you, the easier job your heart has.

I never fully realized this until I saw ghastly proof of it in the surgical amphitheater. A grossly fat patient lay on the operating table; the surgeon, who had to slice through three layers of yellow fat to reach the patient's internal organs, pointed out to me the thousands of fat-embedded blood vessels that were putting extra strain on the man's heart. But what shocked me even more were the pillows of yellow suet surrounding his liver and digestive organs, crowding and hampering them in their functions. This shameful, useless burden, one carried to a degree by every overweight man and woman, is recognized as one of the principal factors in premature death.

Excessive fat can't exist in a body that gets proper exercise. Physical activity, by increasing your metabolism, "burns" it up. If you are accumulating pads of fat around hips and abdomen, or if your once-lean arm and leg muscles are becoming suety, you must decrease your intake of starches and fats, and take regular exercise. Not violent week-ends of golf and tennis or sporadic outbursts of squash, but a daily drill that becomes as much a part of your life as brushing your teeth. The six exercises shown here, if performed every morning on rising, will not only strengthen the diaphragm and lungs but will also take off a pound a week.

Exercise should be regarded as tribute to the heart. This marvelous organ — which is a tough bundle of muscles — thrives on a good workout, and no person free of organic heart trouble need fear that exercise will strain it. More hearts have failed from flabby degeneration than from overexercise. If you're in doubt about the advisability of exercising regularly, see your family doctor and have him check you over.

Yesterday the paunch, the stoop, and the glazy eye didn't matter so much. But these pitiful signs of flabbiness and decay do not fit into the picture of a nation grappling with mortal enemies. To be in poor shape in our present crisis is unforgivable.

You can buy substitutes for exercise in any drugstore — headache powders, antacids, laxatives, pick-me-ups — which promise to confer priceless blessings. But you need never buy them again. You will not need the false stimulation of benzedrine or the painkilling effects of aspirin; you can shake off your dependence on habit-forming laxatives and overcome the acid torments of heartburn if you spend 15 minutes every day in exercise.

Today exercise is needed not only by soldiers and sailors who are fitting themselves for combat. It is a voluntary effort that all civilized men and women should make toward physical perfection — a quickening, cleansing discipline that does for the body what prayer does for the spirit. Stimulated by it, our life-flame burns with a clearer ray; nothing seems hopeless or impossible, and we are charged with the joy of being wholly alive.

cocecococococococo

The Great Discovery

I was a born worrier. If through the years I have acquired any aptitude for "rolling with the punches," it is due to the advice of three friends. Clarence S. Funk, manager of a big Chicago company, was one. I was just 22. The little business that employed me suddenly went busted, and I was out of a job. Funk called and said: "You are a very fortunate young man."

"Fortunate!" I exclaimed. "I've lost two years of my life and $1600 in unpaid salary."

"Any man is fortunate," he continued, "who gets his disappointments *early* in life. He learns to start over again. He learns not to be afraid. The man to be pitied is the one who, at 45 or 50, after getting all the breaks, has disaster suddenly descend on him. He has no inner strength born of previous struggles. He has never learned how to make a fresh start, and he is too old to learn."

My second counselor, Robert Updegraff, the business consultant, wrote: "Never complain about your troubles; they are responsible for more than half of your income." How true. Millions of jobs involve no responsibility and present no troubles. But they are never more than modestly rewarding. Only the jobs with big problems command big pay.

My third friend was an Irishman named George Buckley. "How old are you?" he asked one day. "Forty," I answered.

"Then you have five years before you make the Great Discovery — that trouble is not spasmodic. Trouble is chronic. Trouble is not an interruption in the normal processes of life. Trouble *is* life."

Our children have too much to see and hear,
not enough to do

Teach Them to Open Doors

By T. E. Murphy

IF NATURE continues faithful to her trust we shall have, in
the future, saucer eyes, ears like loving cups and double-
spread bottoms — the better to see, hear and sit. Our
arms and legs will shrink to sausagelike appendages; the head
will atrophy to a tiny thread connecting the used senses of eyes
and ears. For we are fast becoming a nation of watchers and
listeners; we have too much to see and hear, not enough to do.

A process that began four decades ago is now reaching its
logical conclusion with the advent of television. We watch
other men fight, make love, play baseball or football, even
attend religious services. (Catholics have to be warned that
hearing Mass by television does not fulfill the requirements of
Catholic doctrine.) We listen avidly to a dreary procession of
stale jokes and songs about dream houses and far-away places.
Because of these diversions we are giving up a good part of our
heritage. We are robbing our children, too. The classics of
childhood — *Huck Finn, Tom Sawyer, Alice, Treasure Island,
The Wind in the Willows* — are unopened books, unexplored
lands. We have supplanted them with the Lone Ranger and
Gorgeous George.

Living is more than watching and listening. It is *doing*. I believe in the heresy that it's more fun to kiss a pretty girl myself than to watch some shadowy figment go through the motion on a screen. I would rather bat a ball to a bunch of kids than watch a Joe DiMaggio hit a homer. Evenings, I would rather paint a picture or bake a cherry pie than to sit on my calluses listening to timeworn allusions to Jack Benny's miserliness or Bob Hope's nose.

Oh, I don't dislike spectator sports. Some of my best friends are spectators. In the course of a year I'm likely to see a couple of fights, some baseball and college football. I like them all in small doses. I refuse to let them dominate my life.

A few years ago I walked into the office of a distinguished elderly lawyer and found him reading a book of verse by an obscure 19th-century poet. Behind him were volumes on astronomy, botany and geology. When I expressed surprise at the range of his reading, he said: "Life is a corridor with many doors. I am hurrying to open as many as I can before the ultimate one is opened."

I thought of that next day when I tried in vain to hire a carpenter to screen a porch. At the library I got a book telling how to do it, and for the first time in my life I built something with my own hands. It wasn't an expert job. But I learned the thrill of doing something I'd always thought beyond me. It was a small door I opened then, but it was the first of many.

An important thing to remember is that, no matter what strange new door we plan to open, there are experts to guide us — *for free*. Want to paint a picture? There are hundreds of books to tell you how — books in which the great masters have spread out their own hard-earned knowledge. Want to build a swimming pool or a kitchen table? Want to be a sculptor in your spare time? Want to learn French or Italian? You can learn if you have enough curiosity to open a door.

One of my favorite doors opens into the world of gardening. A lot of jokes have been told about the "book" farmer. I'm a book farmer and don't care who knows it.

A neighbor of mine who had planted the same strain of corn for 50 years was inclined to look down his nose at book farmers. One day I gave him a handful of hybrid seed.

A few weeks later I stopped by. "It's the only corn that's any danged good," said my friend. Then, in reluctant capitulation, "I'd like to learn some more about them seeds."

Some people are timid about trying new things. I know one chap who'd been taking photographs for 20 years. One day, after a big local event, I asked him how his pictures came out. He looked surprised. "I won't have them back for a couple of days."

"Do you mean you don't develop and print your own pictures?"

He shook his head. "I'm afraid that's a little too technical for me."

I led him to the nearest drugstore. "Look at the label on this developer can," I said. "You can read, can't you? The manufacturer has been writing all these things for you."

He took the plunge and is now an excellent all-round photographer.

A woman I know was discouraged by the high prices of clothing during the war years. A complete novice at sewing, she found all the information she needed in manuals and pattern guides. Today, though dresses are cheaper, she continues to make her own. "Now I'm *doing* something while I listen to the radio," she explains.

I believe that doing things for yourself is the vital component for a sound personality and an exciting life. In the past two years I have done 50 or more oil paintings, most of them bad. I have written a little poetry and read a great deal more. I have baked everything from a loaf of bread to a mince pie. I have studied Spanish and geology. And because I have four children I have also fished, skated, played baseball, made snowmen, played badminton. Meanwhile I have held down a full-time newspaper job.

I believe fervently in the idea that the hallmark distinguishing man from beast is his creative instinct. It is one of the anomalies of our civilization that the most intensive efforts to satisfy man's creative needs are made in mental hospitals.

Creative expression is not confined to "making" something. I know one middle-aged woman with a grown family who refurnished her cellar as a club for teen-agers. In a few years a hundred young boys and girls had come under her warm and pleasurable influence. Another middle-aged childless couple acted as foster parents to state wards. They kept none of the board money but put it aside for the education of these home-less waifs. They've raised dozens of children and had fun doing it.

An industrialist friend of mine started out as a song writer and then went into a factory. He has made a lot of machinery and some money. But only when he organized a neighborhood singing club did he fulfill his ambitions. "Sometimes," he says proudly, "they even sing some of the songs I wrote."

These are doors to new worlds. They are tiny declarations of independence against being made into the faceless mass man who sits, listens and watches.

A philosopher once observed that man lives in a prison cell lined with mirrors. Today that prison cell is lined with loud-speakers and screens. All very fine, to a degree. But for a really full life we've got to burst out of the cell — and our children with us. For them the danger of growing into a race of super-robots is greater because the conditioning has begun earlier.

Teach them, by example, to open doors. Show them the value of a wide range of interests in contrast with the narrowly grooved life, the difference between apathetic acceptance of things as they are and inquiry. The result? It is the difference between man the intelligent, creative creature and man the vil-lage videot.

+++++++++++++

The Human Robot

AT A RECENT meeting of air scientists and pilots, the scientists made it clear that they would like to replace the pilot in the air-craft with instruments and servo-mechanisms. Scott Crossfield, a U. S. test pilot who has flown the Douglas Skyrocket at 1327 m.p.h., rejoined by asking:

"Where can you find another non-linear servo-mechanism weighing only 150 pounds and having great adaptability that can be produced so cheaply by completely unskilled labor?"

— New York *Times*, quoted in *Business Week*

Why I Am
For the Churches

By Roger William Riis

THERE was a time when I scoffed at the churches. Then one day during the last war, on a sudden whim, I attended a service — for the first time in 22 years. And what did the church offer me? A simple, reverent service, featured by a sermon on "Peter, the Rock," on the permanence and the beauty of the church.

I found that I was acutely interested in hearing about anything that had permanence, beauty and unselfish endeavor. It fell on my spirit like water on a desert, and I went out stirred and grateful.

A week later I took my curiosity to another church, and heard the minister — in a singularly lovely building — talk simply and beautifully on "The Ascending Life." Without a trace of sanctimonious heroics, he conversed informally about the insistent demand of life to rise, to grow, to improve itself. It was adult, it was spiritual; and to me it was helpful.

Since then I have made it a point to attend and study churches — all kinds. And I state with assurance that the critics of churches today don't know what they are talking about. True, a minority of churches offer a dull form of salvation, some in ugly buildings, some with painful music, some with humdrum ministers. But you don't have to go to those churches, nor need you condemn all churches because some fail.

It is obvious that the assailants of churches do not go to church. They don't know what the churches are doing these days. They don't know that the average minister is a more interesting, better-informed man than most of the critics.

I am for the churches because they have something for me, and something for civilization. Dr. Ernest Fremont Tittle, the late great minister of First Methodist Church of Evanston, Ill., said: "Let God be thanked there is on earth an institution that has a high opinion of man, declaring that he is in some sense a son of God, who has within himself divine possibilities; an institution that transcends race, nation and class; an institution which is loyally undertaking to embody the spirit of Christ, and in His name to relieve human suffering, promote human welfare and carry on a ministry of reconciliation among men."

I find myself unable any longer to answer that kind of platform with "I'd rather go into the woods and worship alone. Many of the clergy are dull, concerned over trivial taboos. Sunday is my day for loafing."

Countless times I have found in church something which lifted my spirit. That, I now believe, was what I unconsciously sought. The churches' varied social activities mean little or nothing to me. But others find social outlets in church work. So much the better; they get what they seek, and so do I.

New York's beautiful Church of the Ascension has great wooden doors which open outward, but they are carved on the inside because they are never closed. Every year, 30,000 persons slip in for quiet meditation. They get what they seek.

The remote hamlet of Jonesville, Va., has been holding an annual four-day prayer meeting for more than a century. The day I was there 2000 people were in attendance. Men, women, children, earnest and devout. Revival stuff? No. Simple, direct Christianity. Love-thy-neighbor stuff. Good stuff. These people get what they seek.

The Dominican Sisters at Corpus Christi Church in New York conducted a "project" in tolerance in their church school. Not an attack on intolerance, but a positive, laboratory experiment in tolerance. This demonstration by Catholic, Jewish and Protestant children raised a wild flurry of hope in my heart; if human beings can do this sort of thing, we'll get this world fixed right yet!

When you go to church you should actively seek something.

You must not go like an empty bucket, waiting passively to be filled. When you go to a movie you take at least a hopeful, sympathetic attitude. That's the least you should bring to a church. In many and many a church in every part of the country every Sunday you can see congregations of 1000 and 1500 people, obviously getting whatever values they seek. Church attendance, by the way, is bigger than skeptics think, and growing. Go see for yourself.

Why is one church a power in its community, while others are not?

The personality of the clergyman is the most important reason. Churches are human institutions, clergymen are human beings and they are not all great spiritual leaders. But when they are — and they are often — they make your relations with God an astonishingly practical, useful, alluring thing.

The clergyman himself is the real factor in a church, much more important than architecture or music or furnishings. Most sermons are surprisingly good, and useful. It has been said that no one can deliver a vital address as often as a cleric must. But why miss the many vital addresses he does deliver? It is said that sermons are remote from world affairs. Yet half those I have heard interpreted world affairs from the Christian viewpoint. A third of them were concerned exclusively with Gospel teachings.

Successful churches are those whose clergymen set forth uncompromising Christianity, sticking closest to Christ's very difficult but challenging teaching. That is the great asset of the church. The more vigorously a church proclaims it, the more people respect and follow that church.

What I like most about going to church is that it turns one's attention, willy-nilly, to higher things for at least a little while each week. Man does *not* live by bread alone; he requires cultivation of his spirit. Even when I have wandered into a church where the minister was dull, the music bad, the interior ugly, I have been compelled by my very presence there to think about things loftier than my daily affairs. Even if you differ with what a minister says, you have to listen to him and organize your opposing reasons, and that's good for you. I know it is good for me.

In a world haunted by violence, churches do their very best to represent the spirit. I am warmly grateful for that. Significantly, the two nations which in my lifetime have been officially anti-church are the nations of Nazism and Communism. In nations where the spirit of man is free, churches flourish as men turn toward God.

It may be that the democratic way will not finally overcome the tyrannical way until and unless the democracies somehow crusade under the banner of the church. How can we defeat the destructive dynamics of Communism unless we employ the constructive dynamics of the spirit?

William Penn said, "Men must be governed by God or they will be ruled by tyrants." The world for a quarter century has been his witness.

"To love God," said a beloved minister, "is to believe, despite every appearance to the contrary, that slavery, war and crippling poverty can be banished from the earth, and that conditions favorable to the highest development of the human spirit can be created."

That is extraordinarily practical Christianity. In fact, I cannot distinguish it from the democratic ideal in action. Believing that, I can no longer say that I would rather do my worshiping alone, that Sunday is my day for loafing.

It is an exciting spiritual adventure, this going to church. Try it. Pay no attention to denomination while you investigate. Just out of the curiosity you owe your spiritual health, explore a little. You will almost certainly find, in every community, one church that will give you what *you* want, even though you cannot put that want into words.

Whether or not we realize it, each of us has a personal spiritual quest. It is the most important thing we should be about, and it is only ourselves we cheat if we ignore it. In this, of all ages, it is time we pushed that quest. I have found the churches a good place to pursue it. If they offered nothing but that, they should now be upheld by all men of intelligence and good will.

What Makes a Husband
Easy to Live With?

Condensed from Woman's Home Companion

The Testimony of Twelve Wives

My Soul Is My Own

M y husband — and he's a Scotchman too — is easy to live with because he's generous. He likes detective stories; I enjoy Russian literature. He likes golf; I like the movies. He likes fishing; I like dancing. What do we both like? Each other! Never in the nine years of our married life has he attempted to impose a detective story or a golf club on me. Never has he tried to choose my friends, my clothes, my amusements. Never has he pawed over the grocery bill — liberal in everything from his ideas to his checking account.

He drops cigarette ashes in all the vases, brings guests home without forewarning and forgets our wedding anniversary, but every fault is erased by his liberality of spirit. Easy to live with because my soul and mind are my own: he may explore them but he never attempts complete ownership!

Freedom from Curiosity

I have been married nearly 40 years and my husband has many qualities that make him easy to live with. But the outstanding one is his freedom from curiosity. I have a very generous allowance but am never questioned as to how I spend it or whether or not I am saving any of it. I can be out late, have unexpected callers, without tiresome explanations. It isn't that he isn't interested but he trusts me to take care of my affairs as he does his, without questions. This may seem a trifle but to me it means peace and happiness.

A Peaceful Husband

My husband is easy to live with because he is not fault-find-ing. In the five years of our married life I do not recall a single meal made unpleasant by disagreeable comments upon the food nor a single night's rest interrupted by useless arguments and recriminations. I am ready and willing to admit that my hus-band is not perfect, but who wants a perfect husband anyway? As for me, I say, "Thank God for a peaceful husband."

Occasional Absence

One thing that helps to make a husband easy to live with is an occasional absence from him. It doesn't need to be for any great distance nor for any great length of time. Married couples often take too much for granted. If Jack is on a trip for a few days Mary is soon spending time each day appreciating him. And when he comes home again doesn't Mary's cooking taste good, doesn't the house look extra clean and pretty? Isn't Mary her-self sweet? And as for Mary, she think's that Jack is just *won-derful!*

He Covers His Tracks

I have chosen "picking up after himself" as the best among my husband's many easy-to-live-with qualities. If there's anything that makes a tired mother desperate it's to try to teach her children to hang up their hats, put their shoes in the closet and their soiled clothes in the hamper, in the face of the living example of a husband and father who casts off clothing and all responsibility for it in the general direction of the nearest chair. Any woman will seethe with resentment if she has to follow in the tracks of a man picking up the collars, newspapers, shoes and shirts he sheds. From my heart I thank my mother-in-law, who taught her son to "cover his tracks" in the house.

Pleasure in Simple Things

A sense of humor makes a husband easy to live with. I don't mean the kind that will make a man ridicule his wife before guests but a real appreciation of the humorous aspect of simple everyday things and the faculty of getting a lot of pleasure out of simple things.

Billy-Goat Appetites

Husbands with billy-goat appetites are easiest to live with! Most wives find that menus have a way of becoming tasteless through many repetitions — but to have to plan for a husband to whom onions are anathema and who "doesn't care for potatoes or starchy dishes" or cabbage or carrots or — on indefinitely — the menu-planning becomes a nightmare indeed.

Words of Praise

My husband never forgets that besides being a wife I am also a Feminine Person and as such love to hear that my dress was the prettiest there, that my nose never shines except in the privacy of my boudoir and that no lemon meringue pie in the world can equal my lemon meringue pie. Such honeyed words, not to say downright blarney, make my husband a mighty easy man to live with.

When to Be Quiet

I so very much appreciate my husband's quiet way when I am struggling to make a train, or to get to some certain place on time. He may look at his watch and ask "Do you think you can make the 2:15 bus?" And I make it, unruffled and unflurried. Whereas should he hustle me and become impatient I lose my equilibrium and probably the bus as well.

And then again I'm thankful for his quiet help in getting the last-minute things ready for the picnic and his quiet manner of taking the responsibility of fixing windows and shades, and seeing that wraps and luggage are all together and doors locked when we are leaving home for a vacation.

I think an understanding husband and the one who knows the times when it helps most to be quiet is an easy man to live with.

Martin the Approachable

Martin, my husband, has a close friend, John, married to

Kate. Kate said to me the other day, "I wish you'd ask Martin how John feels about us all going camping together."

Ask Martin? Why not ask John direct? I did not put this question to Kate. I was afraid of probing a tender spot. But in my heart I sang paeans of praise of Martin the approachable, the responsive.

Here I had been blissfully ignorant of a remarkable quality that makes life with Martin as comfortable as an old shoe. Anything from dollars to doughnuts I can broach. No reticence, no explosion: just response, fair and frank. We can disagree with zest but somehow no debris from the past encounter clutters up the future approach.

He Argues with Me

Bless my husband—he argues with me! Now no girl, unless raised in a family where all female opinions were ignored completely or indulgently over-ridden, could appreciate the joy of having a husband who considers one's opinions worthy of refutation. Dick will listen attentively to my reasons why the mountains are the only sensible place to spend the summer vacation, and then ever so courteously he begins to pick my logic apart, to show me, with infinite patience, meticulous care and flattering seriousness, where I'm wrong. My, but it's easy to live with a man who takes the trouble to argue matters out with one!

Something to Say

Well, a gift of gab helps a lot. What a difference it makes to a wife who often has been in the house all day occupied with a round of seemingly petty and certainly irritating duties to have her husband come home with something to say — interesting news or trifling gossip, thoughts, impressions, anything at all but that stony wall of silence that makes one want to scream, "Talk, talk, for heaven's sake talk."

We often hear of the wife who talks too much but don't forget to be sorry for the wife of the husband who talks too little.

The job-seeker with an idea and the
initiative to put it into practice sets himself apart from 99 percent of applicants

Ideas Get the Job

Condensed from Forbes
James D. Woolf
Former vice-president of J. Walter Thompson Co.

UNLESS an employer has a definite job to offer an applicant,
he is likely to turn him away with the response, "I'm
sorry, but we don't need anyone right now."

If this happens to you, don't forget that the employer may be
mistaken. For often there is a job just waiting for somebody
with imagination to come along and create it.

This is a lesson I learned as a boy. Anxious to earn extra
money, I asked all three drugstores in my town for a job — any
kind of job. There were no openings. But a week later I found
that one of these stores had taken on a new boy. Screwing up
my courage, I asked the owner why.

"Well, I'll tell you, son," he said. "I didn't *think* I had a
job open when you asked for one. But then Freddie came in
with an idea. He owns a bicycle, and he suggested that I start
a delivery service, meaning himself. That's a new notion for
this town. It's going to make a hit."

Well, I had a bicycle, too, but Freddie had something I didn't
have — an idea.

A friend of mine, for many years the successful sports editor
of a big Pennsylvania daily, also *thought* himself into his first
job. He wanted to be a newspaperman, but the only paper in
his small town turned him down. So he started to study the
paper for weak spots. Presently he settled on its almost total
lack of sporting news and its meager coverage of farm happen-
ings.

Seven days later the young fellow went back with two ideas

—and a fistful of copy to back them up. It had been a busy sports week: two high school ball games, an amusing horse-shoe pitching contest, and horse races at the county fair. He handed the editor a brisk account of these events as the pattern for a sports column. Then he suggested another column, "Farm Doings," a collection of items he had picked up from farmers. He was hired on the spot.

Recently a lad in Iowa, back from war work in California, got his start by *making* it. A good mechanic, he tackled the owner of a garage. No job! But the youngster didn't give up: he had an idea. He offered to help around the place without pay. The owner said he didn't mind.

The garage had only one repair truck; hence many calls from stranded motorists were turned down. The unpaid helper fixed up a broken-down motorcycle with a side-car and loaded it with tools for emergency repair jobs. The owner, pleased, gave this returned war worker a well-paying job.

Simple ideas? Maybe so. But consider this fact: During more than 30 years as an advertising agency executive I have inter-viewed at least 5000 job hunters—and not more than 50 of them came up with even the simplest idea that applied to problems we were talking about.

When scouting for ideas, make a habit of observing *critically* jobs that are being poorly done. The indifference of others may spell opportunity for you. Take, for instance, the case of a man who started life carrying newspapers in Paterson, N. J. He noticed that boys who distributed handbills for stores threw them around so carelessly that most of them were wasted.

"How much more profitable it would be," the lad thought, "if each circular were handed to the housewife at the door." He took this idea to the owner of a new store about to open in Paterson, and got the job of distributing his announcements.

The youngster spent four days distributing fliers that another boy would have handled in one day. But on the morning of the opening, there was such a rush of business that the store nearly had to close its doors. The newsboy was hired. Four months later, at the age of 16 (believe it or not!) he was asked to man-age another store in the chain. That newsboy, T. J. Grassey, became president of Great Eastern Stores—63 of them.

Make it a habit also to keep on the outlook for unusual ideas that others are already using successfully. Your idea needs to be original only in its application to your prospective employer's business. Watch the advertising in your local newspapers for new angles in store service. Study, too, the classified sections of the big telephone books. You will find many ads of specialized businesses with a novel twist, and you may have some talent or experience that fits right into one of these slots.

Every field of human activity is covered by America's 1700 trade journals, whose business is to report new ideas and developments. They're full of better ways of doing things. Employers and managers are often so busy they cannot search their trade magazines for ideas. The job-seeker who shows he has the energy to root them out, and the initiative to put them into practice, is sure to get an interested hearing.

The rapid growth of new developments — television and other electronic devices, air conditioning, civilian aviation, food freezing, and many others — will furnish a fertile field for imagination and initiative. Today's job-seeker will find about him on every side fresh problems to be solved, and better solutions of old problems to be thought out. The ever-changing needs of postwar America are calling to him — and it's up to him to hear and heed that call.

Master Touches

A FAMOUS headmaster of a school said that if he saw a boy in despair over his work he always gave him a higher mark than he deserved. The following week the boy always made a higher mark himself.

— Joseph Fort Newton, *Living Up to Life* (Harper)

A TEACHER who regularly makes a practice of hunting up the most unattractive child and whispering in her ear, "You're getting prettier every day," says it always works; almost at once the child begins to blossom into something close to beauty.

— Marcelene Cox in *Ladies' Home Journal*

Peace of Mind

A condensation from the book by

Dr. Joshua Loth Liebman

O NCE, as a young man, I undertook to draw up a catalogue of the acknowledged "goods" of life. I set down my inventory of earthly desirables: *health, love, talent, power, riches* and *fame*. Then I proudly showed it to a wise elder.

"An excellent list," said my old friend, "and set down in not unreasonable order. But it appears that you have omitted the one important ingredient lacking which your list becomes an intolerable burden."

He crossed out my entire schedule. Then he wrote down three syllables: *peace of mind*.

"This is the gift that God reserves for His special protégés," he said. "Talent and health He gives to many. Wealth is commonplace, fame not rare. But peace of mind He bestows charily.

"This is no private opinion of mine," he explained. "I am merely paraphrasing from the Psalmists, Marcus Aurelius, Lao-tse. 'God, Lord of the universe,' say these wise ones, 'heap worldly gifts at the feet of foolish men. Give me the gift of the Untroubled Mind.'"

I found that difficult to accept; but now, after a quarter of a century of personal experience and professional observation, I have come to understand that peace of mind is the true goal of the considered life. I know now that the sum of all other possessions does not necessarily add up to peace of mind; on the other hand, I have seen this inner tranquillity flourish without the material supports of property or even the buttress of physical health. Peace of mind can transform a cottage into a spacious manor hall; the want of it can make a regal residence an imprisoning shell.

Analyze the prayers of mankind of all creeds, in every age — and their petitions come down to the common denominators of daily bread and inward peace. Such pleas for spiritual serenity must not be identified with ivory-tower escapism from the hurly-burly of life. Rather, they seek an inner equilibrium which enables us to overcome life's buffetings.

Peace of mind cannot be won by any brief or superficial effort. Association with noble works — literary, musical, artistic — helps to promote inward peace, but these alone cannot wholly satisfy the dimensions of the soul. Certainly we shall not find peace in the furious pursuit of wealth which slips like quicksilver through our grasping fingers. And finally, not even in the sublime sharings of human love — that emotion which most powerfully conveys the illusion of perfect happiness — is peace of mind reliably to be found.

Where then shall we look for it? The key to the problem is to be found in Matthew Arnold's lines:

> *We would have inward peace*
> *But will not look within . . .*

But will not look within! Here, in a single phrase, our wilfullness is bared.

IT is a striking irony that, while religious teaching emphasizes man's obligations to others, it says little about his obligation to himself. One of the great discoveries of modern psychology is that our attitudes toward ourselves are even more complicated than our attitudes toward others. The great commandment of religion, "Thou shalt love thy neighbor as thyself," might now be better interpreted to mean, "Thou shalt love thyself properly, and *then* thou wilt love thy neighbor."

A prominent social worker received a letter from a society woman who wanted to join in his crusade to help the poor of New York. She spoke at some length of her imperfections and ended by saying that perhaps her zeal for *his* cause would make up for her shortcomings. He wrote a brief reply: "Dear Madam, your truly magnificent shortcomings are too great. Nothing could prevent you from visiting them on victims of your humility. I advise that you love yourself more before you squander any love on others."

Some will argue that this is a dangerous doctrine. "Human beings love themselves too much already," they will say. "The true goal of life is the rejection of self in the service of others." There are errors in this estimate of human nature. Is it *true* that we are spontaneously good to ourselves? The evidence points in quite the opposite direction. We often treat ourselves more rigidly, more vengefully, than we do others. Suicide and more subtle forms of self-degradation such as alcoholism, drug addiction and promiscuity are extreme proofs of this. But all the streets of the world are teeming with everyday men and women who mutilate themselves spiritually by self-criticism; who go through life committing partial suicide — destroying their own talents, energies, creative qualities.

Such actions constitute a crime not only against ourselves but against society. He who does not have proper regard for his own capacities can have no respect for others. By loving oneself I do not mean coddling oneself, or indulging in self-glorification. I do, however, insist on the necessity of a proper self-regard as a prerequisite of the good and the moral life.

THERE ARE myriad ways in which we show contempt for ourselves rather than self-respect. Our feelings of inferiority, for instance: how often we attribute to our neighbors superior powers; we exaggerate their abilities, and sink into orgies of self-criticism. The fallacy here is that we see in others only the surface of assurance and poise. If we could look deeper and realize all men and women bear within themselves the scars of many a lost battle, we would judge our own failures less harshly.

To one who goes through life hypnotized by thoughts of inferiority, I would say: "In actuality, you are quite strong and wise and successful. You have done rather well in making a tolerable human existence out of the raw materials at your disposal. There are those who love and honor you for what you really are. Take off your dark-colored glasses, assume your place as an equal in the adult world, and realize that your strength is adequate to meet the problems of that world."

Another road to proper self-regard is the acceptance of our imperfections as well as our perfections. Most men have two pictures of their two selves in separate rooms. In one room is hung the portrait of their virtues, done in bright, splashing colors. In the other room hangs the canvas of self-condemnation, painted equally as unrealistically in dark and morbid shades.

Instead of keeping these two pictures separate, we must look at them together and gradually blend them into one. We must begin to know and accept ourselves for what we are — a combination of strengths and weaknesses. It is enough if we learn to respect ourselves with all our shortcomings and achievements; to know that true love of self neither exaggerates its powers nor minimizes its worth.

The great thing is that as long as we live we have the privilege of growing. We can learn new skills, engage in new kinds of work, devote ourselves to new causes, make new friends. Accepting, then, the truth that we are capable in some directions and limited in others, that genius is rare, that mediocrity is the portion of most of us, let us remember also that we can and must *change* ourselves. Until the day of our death we can grow, we can tap hidden resources in our make-up.

EVERY person who wishes to attain peace of mind must learn the art of renouncing many things in order to possess other things more fully. As young children, our wishes were sovereign; we had only to wail and the adult world hastened to fulfill our every desire. We knew, at that stage of development, very little about the postponement of satisfaction or the necessity of renunciation. But as we grow older we learn that every stage of human development calls upon us to weigh differing goods and to sacrifice some for the sake of others.

The philosopher Santayana pointed out that the great difficulty in life does not so much arise in the choice between good and evil as in the choice between good and good. In early life, however, we do not realize that one desire can be quite inconsistent with another. The young boy may vacillate between a dozen different plans for the future, but the mature man will have to renounce many careers in order to fulfill one. The same truth exists in the realm of emotions. It is fitting for the adolescent to transfer his love interest from one object of affection to another, but it is tragic when the grown man still plays the role of the adolescent. The man trying to wear youth's carefree clothing, the woman costuming her emotions in doll's dresses — these are pathetic figures. They have not yet learned that human growth means the closing of many doors before one great door can be opened — the door of mature love and of adult achievement.

THE FIRST fundamental truth about our individual lives is the indispensability of love to every human being. By "love" I mean relatedness to some treasured person or group, the feeling of belonging to a larger whole, of being of value to others.

Our interdependence with others is the most encompassing fact of human reality: our personalities are made by our contacts with others. A boy may catch the contagion of courage from his father, or receive the misery of fear from his mother. In a spiritual sense, we digest our heroes and heroines and make their way of life part of our own emotional substance. Thus every saint and every sinner affects those whom he will never see, because his words and his deeds stamp themselves upon the soft clay of human nature everywhere. There is, therefore, a duty which falls upon all of us — to become free, loving, warm, coöperative, affirmative personalities. If we understand this relatedness with others we shall get on noticeably better with our family, friends, business associates — and ourselves.

Next to bread, it is simple kindness that all mortals most hunger for. In times of catastrophe and disaster it finds a natural expression, good to contemplate in men's actions. But too often it is lacking in our daily lives. Many of us are dictatorial or bad-tempered toward others — employes, salespersons, domestic help. "I call no man charitable," said Thoreau, "who forgets that his barber, cook and hostler are made of the same human clay as himself." When we fail to be kind to all men, we destroy our own peace of mind. The jeweled pivot on which our lives must turn is the realization that every person we meet during the day is a dignified, essential human soul.

In the exchange of simple affection lies the true secret of marriage — which at its best is mutual encouragement. When we are accepted, approved, *needed* by those who know all about us and like us anyway, we have the first inkling of the peace that transcends understanding.

To love one's neighbors is to achieve an inner tolerance for the uniqueness of others, to resist the temptation to private imperialism. Among our renunciations we must renounce undue possessiveness in relation to friends, children — yes, even our loves. The world is full of private imperialists — the father who forces his artistic son into his business, or the mother who rivets her daughter to her service by chains of pity, subtly refusing the daughter a life of her own.

When we insist that others conform to our ideas of what is proper, good, acceptable, we show that we ourselves are not certain of the rightness of our inner pattern. He who is sure of himself is deeply willing to let others be themselves. He who is unstable in his own character must reassure himself by trying to compress others into his mold. We display true love when we cease to demand that our loved one become a revised edition of ourselves.

EVERY normal person experiences countless fears and worries. But it is possible to master these enemies of serenity.

It is true in a sense that man is blessed by his capacity to know fear. Fear is often the stimulus to growth, the goad to invention. Moreover, fear experienced in the presence of real danger is desirable. But are not most of our fears groundless? Scrutinize that large body of fears coming under the heading of "personal anxiety." Sometimes we are afraid about our health; we worry about our hearts, our lungs, our blood pressure, our insomnia. We begin to feel our pulse to find evidence of disease in every innocent or meaningless symptom. Or we become concerned about our personalities. We feel insecure, bemoan our failures, and imagine that others scorn or disapprove of us.

We must realize, of course, that our fears may disguise themselves. Some deep self-distrust may appear as an unreasoning fear of high places, of closed rooms. Again, our fears cunningly cloak themselves in the garments of physical pain. The new science of psychosomatic medicine has demonstrated that a whole gamut of illnesses, from the common cold to crippling arthritis, can often be traced to mental rather than physical troubles. It is so much easier to be sick than courageous! The ill health enjoyed by many chronic invalids is no more than an elaborate disguise for deep-seated fears.

Many such feelings of insecurity are hangovers from childhood when we really *were* inadequate and inferior, and knew that there was a vast difference between our weakness and the strength of the adult world. This difference disappears as we grow, but our childhood is a blackmailer that makes us pay over and over again for failures or mistakes that long ago have been outgrown.

Are we obsessed perhaps with a fear of death or the thought of punishment in an afterlife? Let us come to see that such fear is a projection from some early experience when we were punished by a parent, locked in a room, left alone. Are we continually haunted by the disapproval of others, frightened of social rejection? Let us look at these anxieties in the light of maturity, see that our neighbors are no less fallible than ourselves, and realize further that in the adult world we should not expect to be coddled as we were in childhood.

A source of hope lies also in the fact that our moods are temporary. This is a hard lesson to learn. When we are tired, every pinprick becomes the stab of a knife. But it is natural and normal to have depressed moods, and we should always remember that we will come out into the light again. We human beings are very tough organisms, able to withstand many shocks, to shed many tears, to live through many tragedies without breaking. Let us learn not to take the depression of the day or month as the permanent state of our life.

IT IS natural to experience fear concerning our economic and social future. Countless people are frightened of unemployment or the collapse of their careers. These fears are very real. But firmly attached to them are highly neurotic residues. Americans particularly are engaged in a marathon race in which the runners are extremely anxious about those panting at their heels and envious of those ahead. This relentless race for economic success is the source of many breakdowns and premature deaths.

A yearning for achievement is an admirable attribute of human nature. Where, then, do we go wrong? We err in the excessive energy that we devote not to real accomplishment but to neurotic combat. A man may have a home, possessions, a charming family, and yet find all these things ashy to his taste because he has been outstripped by some other runners in the race for material things. It is not that he does not possess enough for his own wants but that others possess more. It is the *more* that haunts him and makes him minimize his real achievements.

The time has come to say: "I am no longer going to be interested in how much power or wealth another man possesses so long as I can attain sufficient for the dignity and security of my family and myself. I am going to set my goals for myself rather than borrow them from others. I refuse any longer to destroy my peace of mind by striving only for money; I will also judge myself in the scale of goodness and culture."

WE HAVE learned that unexpressed emotions ultimately have their vengeance in the form of mental and physical illness. This truth illuminates for us the problem of achieving peace of mind in the face of bereavement and grief.

Dr. Erich Lindemann, in clinical work at the Massachusetts General Hospital with hundreds of grief patients, has uncovered the basic fact that to repress real feelings of grief may lead to morbid reactions later. Dr. Lindemann's patients included some who developed severe illness or depressions years after the loss of a loved one. Amazing cures of the mental and physical ills resulted when patients were persuaded to express the pain and sorrow that should normally have found outlet before.

How absurd is that notion which has gained currency in modern society that men and women must repress emotional outbursts. It is not those outbursts but the avoidance of them which scars the fabric of the soul.

The first law, then, which should be followed in the time of the loss of a loved one is: *give way to as much grief as you actually feel*. Do not be ashamed of your emotions; released now, they will be the instrument of your later healing.

The discoveries of psychiatry — of how essential it is to express rather than to repress grief, to talk about one's loss with friends and companions, to move step by step from inactivity to activity again — remind us that the ancient teachers of Judaism had an intuitive wisdom about human nature which our more sophisticated age has forgotten. The Bible records how open and unashamed was the expression of sorrow on the part of Abraham and Jacob and David. Our ancestors publicly wept, wore sackcloth, tore their garments, and fasted. It is unfortunate that in our time the expression of honest emotion has become taboo. Let us understand that the unrepressed experience of pain somehow has a curative function and that any evasive detour around normal sorrow will bring us later to a tragic abyss.

Armed with such knowledge, if we are courageous and resolute we can live as our lost loved ones would wish us to live — not empty, morose, self-centered and self-pitying but as brave and undismayed servants of the greater life.

It is not often that we are brave enough to come face to face with the thought of our own mortality. Yet man is not free in life unless he is also free from the fear of death.

As far as our own deaths are concerned, we should remember what science teaches about the process of dying. We needlessly frighten ourselves with anticipated horrors which never come to pass. As the famous physician, Sir William Osler, put it, "In my wide clinical experience, most human beings die really without pain or fear. There is as much oblivion about the last hours as about the first."

Montaigne said a wonderfully wise thing about this: "When I have been in perfect health, I have been much more afraid of sickness than when I have really felt the sickness. . . . Death is not to be feared. It is a friend."

No, death is not the enemy of life but its friend, for it is the knowledge that our years are limited which makes them so precious. Plato was right when he declared that infinite life on this earth would not be desirable, for a never-ending existence would be without heights or depths, without challenge or achievement. It is profoundly true that the joy of our striving and the zest of our aspirations would vanish if earthly immortality were our lot.

At the same time, we dare not ignore the hunger in the human heart for some kind of existence beyond this narrow span of life. There is an almost universal feeling that God could not shut the door completely upon our slowly developed talents — that there must be realms where we can use the powers achieved here. And one should not lightly dismiss the thoughts of the philosophers who insist that there is nothing inherently impossible about life in undreamed dimensions; that just as infrared rays are invisible to our eyes, so a creative, growing universe might well have hidden unsuspected continents beyond the perception of our senses.

Moreover, we should always remember that there are other forms of immortality besides personal survival. Man displays perhaps his most remarkable and his most unselfish genius when he turns from the thought of individual immortality and finds inspiration in the immortality of the human race. The more we concentrate upon the immortality of mankind, strangely enough, the richer becomes our own individual life. As we link ourselves to the heroes and sages and martyrs, the poets and thinkers of every race, we come to share the wisest thoughts, the noblest ideals, the imperishable music of the centuries. Poor, indeed, is the man who lives only in his own time. Rich is the man who participates in the riches of the past and the promises of the future.

BOTH science and religion teach us, at last, that the obstacles to serenity are not external. They lie within ourselves.

If we acquire the art of proper self-love; if, aided by religion, we free ourselves from shadow fears, and learn honestly to face grief and to transcend it; if we flee from immaturity and boldly shoulder adult responsibility; if we appraise and accept ourselves as we really are, how then can we fail to create a good life for ourselves? For then inward peace will be ours.